E. M. JUNG-INGLESSIS

The Holy Year in Rome

Past and Present

LIBRERIA EDITRICE VATICANA
00120 CITTÀ DEL VATICANO

Original title:

Das Heilige Jahr in Rom - Geschichte und Gegenwart.
Translated by E. Francisco Julius.

The illustrations contained in this book are published
by kind permission of Athesiadruck in Bozen.

Cover:

John Paul II is passing the Holy Door for the opening ceremony of the
Holy Year 1975.

© Copyright 1997 - Libreria Editrice Vaticana - 00120 Città del Vaticano
Tel. (06) 698.85003 - Fax (06) 698.84716

ISBN 88-209-2400-5

CONTENTS

In Christianity, time has a fundamental importance. Within the dimension of time the world was created; within it the history of salvation unfolds, finding its culmination in the "fullness of time" of the Incarnation, and its goal in the glorious return of the Son of God at the end of time. In Jesus Christ, the Word made flesh, time becomes a dimension of God, who is eternal. With the coming of Christ there begin "the last days" (cf. Heb 1:2), the last hour (cf. 1 Jn 2:18), and the time of the Church which will last until the Parousia.

In view of this, the two thousand years which have passed since the Birth of Christ (prescinding from the question of its precise chronology) represent an extraordinarily great Jubilee, not only for Christians but indirectly for the whole of humanity, given the prominent role played by the Christian community during these two millennia. It is significant that the calculation of the passing years begins almost everywhere with the year of Christ's coming into the world, which is the center of the unparalleled effect of the Birth of Jesus of Nazareth on the history of mankind.

The term "Jubilee" speaks of joy; not just an inner joy but a jubilation which is manifested outwardly, for the coming of God is also an outward, visible, audible and tangible event, as Saint John makes clear (cf. 1 Jn 1:1). It is thus appropriate that every sign of joy at this coming should have its own outward expression. This will demonstrate that the Church rejoices in salvation. She invites everyone to rejoice, and she tries to create conditions to ensure that the power of salvation may be shared by all. Hence the Year 2000 will be celebrated as the Great Jubilee.

JOHN PAUL II, Apostolic Letter *Tertio Millennio Adveniente* (nos. 10, 15, 16)

I

Pilgrimages in the Early Christian Era

P ilgrimage is part of Christian existence. Beginning with Abraham we wander along the path of faith which should lead us to the heavenly Jerusalem, "the city of the living God" (Heb 12:22). In Holy Scripture the comparison between life and pilgrimage is often made. In answering Pharoah's query: "How many years have you lived?", Jacob replies: "My life of wandering has lasted one hundred and thirty years" (Gn 47.8-9). The Psalmist prays: "Yahweh, hear my prayer, listen to my cry for help, do not stay deaf to my crying, I am your guest and only for a time, a nomad like all my ancestors" (Ps 9:13). The apostles Peter and Paul are also often found to state that they are simply "strangers and nomads" (2 Co 5:6-8; Heb 11:13; Ps 2:11), as indeed are we all as we search for the heavenly fatherland. It is for this reason that the Christians of the first centuries are depicted in the mosaics of their basilicas as the people of God on pilgrimage, ever nearing the heavenly Jerusalem. So too, the pilgrimages to Jerusalem, Rome, Lourdes, Fatima or Santiago de Compostela are a visible expression of this inner spirituality. The Holy Years figure then as milestones along this pilgrims' route upon which the centuries move towards God, their eternal goal.

This tradition is age old, as we find with the ancient Jews who used to journey to the temple of Jerusalem each

1. The Empress *St. Helen*. She is holding the cross as her attribute, as it was she who was said to have found the True Cross of Christ. Marble Statue by Andrea Bolgi, 1639. In St. Peter's.

year for the feasts of the Passover, Pentecost and Tabernacles, singing psalms along the way (Ps 120-134). As we read in the Gospel of Luke (2:41-49), both Mary and Joseph made the journey at Passover with the young Jesus to the Temple of Jerusalem, where they lost him only to find him again after three days. This Jewish custom was taken over by Christians. They wanted to see the places where Christ had lived, worked and suffered. Then as now, they combined a religious goal with a cultural one.

From the *History of the Church* written by the bishop Eusebius of Caesarea (between 300-320), we learn of third century Christian communities already undertaking pilgrimages to Jerusalem with their bishops. This was to become a common practice once religious freedom was granted in 313. St. Helen, the Empress-Mother, set the example and went to the Holy Land in c. 326 in order to search for the relics belonging to the life of Christ (fig. 1). She discovered, as it was believed, the true Cross, the nails of the Crucifixion, Christ's robe, the table of the Last Supper, the Holy Steps and whatever else legend has added with the passage of the time. The greater part of the relics were sent to Rome and enshrined in the church of the Holy Cross and in the Lateran, while the robe found its way to Trier.

In the wake of Helen's example, a Father of the Church, St. Jerome, is most worthy of mention. In 385 he left the noisy capital, Rome, and sought the solitude of Bethlehem. Joined by his spiritual companion, Paula, and her daughter, Eustochium, they founded a monastery and a pilgrims' shelter close to the pilgrims' route.[1]

In the *Peregrinatio Etheriae*, a travel diary kept by a Spanish noblewoman, this virgin consecrated to God described for her sisters, who had remained at home, what she saw on her pilgrimage made around the year 400. At Easter she was in Jerusalem, from where she proceeded to Edessa and the sepulchre of the apostle Thomas, then to Abraham's tomb at Charris and to the foot of Mount Nebo where Moses had died, and so went on to see many other holy places of both the Old and New Testaments. She described what today would be called "the liturgy of the Word" which was held in these places and consisted of prayer, readings from Holy Scripture and the singing of hymns.[2]

Not only were the holy sites of the Old and New Testaments venerated, but also the *memoriae* of the confessors and martyrs. These were shrines which in most cases had the form of an altar or a small monument built above a tomb, either upon the site of their martyrdom or upon their place of dwelling. Later these would also be built where their relics were found. A monument of this kind

9

was called, in Latin, an *aedicula* (small building or temple), or, in Greek, a *tropaion,* which means a victory monument, since the site of martyrdom or burial is the place of the triumph of life over death, of faith over unbelief.

Tropaia of this kind stood over the graves of both Peter and Paul, and the presbyter Gaius, who lived in Rome at the time of Pope Zephyrinus (199-217), boasts about these in a Greek dialogue with his opponent Proclos: "If you leave the city heading for the Vatican or for Ostia you will find the *tropaia* of those who founded this Church".[3] We now know what a *tropaion* looked like since that of the apostle Peter was brought to light in excavations directly under the high altar of St. Peter's (fig. 2). The *tropaion* built over St. Paul's grave was most probably very similar.

The veneration of the apostle Peter was, from the very beginning, closely linked to that of St. Paul. Together they were revered as the founders of the Roman Church, as the presbyter Gaius has just informed us. Together, they were invoked in prayer, as we can read in the graffiti found on the walls at the catacombs of St. Sebastian, and shared a common feast day, the June 29. This is confirmed by St. Ambrose of Milan (339-397) in his hymn in honor of the two apostles.[4] He describes the multitudes of pilgrims who filled the three ancient roads of the city: one led to the sepulchre of St. Peter in the Vatican, another, the Ostian Way, led to the sepulchre of St. Paul and the third led to the catacombs of St. Sebastian on the Appian Way. These were then the three major pilgrimage destinations.

St. Paulinus, bishop of Nola (352-431), complained about the crowds and the interminable religious functions. He came to Rome every year for the feastday of Peter and Paul "out of devotion to the apostles and martyrs", but lamented: "With so much to see, one doesn't manage to see anything". Thus Prudentius (348-405), who came from Spain, upon seeing the procession to the sepulchre of the apostles, exclaims: "Tell me friend, what is going on? All of Rome is on the go".[5] He became the first poet of the cult of the martyrs.

2. Reconstruction of the rediscovered *tropaion* (or *aedicula*) which was the first small monument built towards the end of the 2nd century. It stands against a red plaster wall and opens down to St. Peter's grave.

Therefore, it was not only the Romans who venerated the *memoriae* of their martyrs, but Christians who came from all over. The first pilgrim to come to Rome whose name we know was Bishop Abcrkios of Hierapolis in Phrygia in Asia Minor. He was in Rome between 180 and 200. Today his tombstone can be found in the *Museo Pio Cristiano* (nr. 19 & 20) in the Vatican. His epitaph, written in hexameters in that mystical language so loved by the early Christians, reads: "A disciple am I of a pure shepherd... who sent me to Rome, to see a realm and a queen in golden robes and golden shoes. There I saw a folk that possessed a golden seal...".[6] Evidently the pure shepherd is Christ and the queen in golden robes and shoes is supposedly the Church of Rome.

St. Irenaeus, a Greek Father of the Church and bishop of Lyons (c. 200), called Rome "the mother of all citizens

11

of the New Testament".[7] Soon after him Origen of Alexandria (c. 212) came to Rome: "... in order to see the very ancient (!) Church of the Romans".[8] Then Maximus, bishop of Turin and a Father of the Church (c. 400), said in his homelies: "Christ illumined the East through his Passion. In order that the West should be no more less so, he illumined it with the blood of his apostles. Where once the princes of the pagans were to be found are now the princes of the Church".[9]

Pope Damasus (366-384) composed inscriptions in verse and had them inscribed on marble plaques which he had placed in different places of worship in Rome. This was done with the aim of explaining their significance and origin. He also had stairways and crypts built in order to facilitate easier access for the pilgrims to the places of the martyrs' tombs. At Porto, the port of Ostia, which was at that time the pilgrims' main point of arrival, there was erected a great *xenodochium*, a shelter for poor and infirm pilgrims. Another six were built in the city. The one most commonly frequented lay near the Vatican and was founded by St. Gregory the Great around 600.

It can clearly be seen, therefore, that from the very beginning the veneration of the holy shrines in Rome was for Christians a very natural and spontaneous thing to do. *O Roma felix* was and is still sung today on the feastday of Peter and Paul, for the city is blessed "by the glorious blood of two princes", and has not only one patron saint but the whole "*Corona Sanctorum Martyrum*".

II

Bishops, Emperors
and Postulants in Rome

When Romulus Augutulus, the last of the Roman emperors, was deposed in 476, the empire, already weakened by the barbarian invasions, began to fall apart. The ancient consular roads fell into a state of abandon and, consequently, the means of transportion deteriorated. The journey to Jerusalem became increasingly more arduous and even more so after the city fell to the Arabs in 638. It was for this reason that the pilgrims' attention turned to Rome, to the "second Jerusalem". For the first time written travel guides appear: *Notitia regionum urbis Romae*; *Notitia ecclesiarum urbis Romae*; *De locis sanctis Martyrum qui sunt foris civitatis Romae*; and later the *Mirabilia urbis Romae*, the medieval guides written for the pilgrim to Rome describing "the wonders of the capital city of Rome".

In the 7th century the nature of pilgrimages began to change. No longer did one go on a pilgrimage in order to visit and venerate holy places, but rather, one went to do penance. Church penance in the early centuries was very severe and could go as far as to ostracize a church member and exclude him from religious rites. Gradually, however, pilgrimages and alms-giving took the place of such punishment. The books of penance of those times imposed pilgrimages in reparation for particularly serious sins. In this regard, the Irish and Anglo-Saxon peoples stood out for their strong religious zeal and severity. Taking inspiration from Abraham in the Old Testament, they left the

13

land of their fathers and went into self-imposed exile, holding vigils and fasting in mystical asceticism. These penitential pilgrimages were also aimed at converting heathens. It was thanks to this threefold purpose of making pilgrimages: to do penance, to evangelize and even to desire martyrdom, that St. Boniface, an English nobleman (675-754), became the apostle of the Germans. Boniface set the precedent of episcopal visits to Rome. He went to Rome three times, first in 718, then in 722 and again in 733. There he took the name of the Roman martyr Boniface (his real name was Wynfrith), was consecrated a bishop and charged with preaching in the name of Peter, prince of the apostles, and baptizing in the Latin Rite. A special pledge of faith bound him to the Pope, and he asked the pontiff's counsel and decision upon all matters. "The knot was tightened that henceforth would link the German Church to the Pope and Rome".[10] This resulted in veneration towards St. Peter, especially on the part of the Franks and Anglo-Saxons, since Peter had been the first disciple of Christ, was prince of the apostles and keeper of the keys, the guardian of the gates of heaven and their heavenly patron.

With the passage of time St. Boniface's example was imitated and a tradition was established that required the bishops to come to Rome at regular intervals *ad limina*, i.e. to the threshold of the tombs of the apostles, later taken as meaning to the steps of the papal throne. Today all bishops of the Roman Catholic Church are required to appear before the Pope once every five years. These visits *ad limina* have played a very important role in strengthening the link with Rome. Pope Paschal II (1099-1118) decreed that every archbishop was to come to Rome in person to receive the *pallium* (a small white woolen stole). Then, as now, the pallium was kept near the "body of St. Peter", i.e. above the tomb of the apostle, in the so-called "Pallium niche" underneath the papal altar, until the moment when it was laid upon the shoulders of the newly created metropolitan archbishops. The pallium symbolizes the bond that ties the local churches to Rome and the metropolitans to the pope.

14

3. The Church of *Santo Spirito in Sassia* with its Romanesque bell tower and Early Baroque façade dates back to King Ine of Wessex who founded a home for Anglo-Saxon pilgrims on this site in 726. Hence the designation "in Sassia".

For the Anglo-Saxon pilgrims who came to Rome, King Ine of Wessex, who had given up his throne and had himself become a pilgrim, in 726 built a pilgrims' hospice near St. Peter's (fig. 3). Today, this church is still called *Santo Spirito in Sassia*. Ansa, consort of the Longobard king Desiderius, founded a home for the Longobards, the *Schola Langobardorum* which stood to the right of St. Peter's, while the Frisians were located to the left of St. Peter's Square in their *Schola Frisorum* which today survives as the *Church of Saints Michael and Magnus*.

15

4. The *Campo Santo Teutonico* as seen from the roof of St. Peter's. Founded shortly before 800, this former schola and hospice for Franks is today a German college for priests and stands adjacent to the cemetery for pilgrims and local residents who come from the German speaking countries.

Pilgrimages to Rome now became popular with the Gauls and the Franks. The latter founded a hostel, the *Schola Francorum*, for their clergy and pilgrims. Next to this house a cemetery grew up for those pilgrims whose untimely death was often the result of the exhausting journey. Thus, they were laid to rest near the tomb of St. Peter, the goal of their pilgrimage. This cemetery, still in use today, is called the *Campo Santo Teutonico* (fig. 4). It is laid out upon part of the former site of Nero's circus, where, as Tacitus recounts, the first Christians were martyred in autumn of the year 64.[11] On one of the walls which enclose the cemetery is a large image in ceramic tiles which shows Peter surrounded by a group of Chris-

16

tians as he awaits martyrdom in the circus (fig. 5). Suddenly, he has a vision: he sees the dome of St. Peter's rise above the clouds, and indeed the dome was built right next to this spot some 1500 years later.

The pilgrims' home has become the *Collegio Teutonico in Campo Santo* for German priests. Upon the facade of this edifice a large image of Charlemagne stands out. It bears the proud declaration: "Charlemagne founded me", and the Hapsburg double-headed eagle rising up from the roof signifies that all the peoples from the lands of the former Holy Roman Empire of the German Nation have the right to stay there.

* * *

After pilgrims, penitents, bishops and kings, the emperors, too, now began to make the journey to Rome, the precedent having been set by Charlemagne. He came to

5. A modern ceramic tile mural on the interior wall of the Campo Santo Teutonico depicts the Apostle Peter praying in Nero's circus awaiting his marterdom. Suddenly he has a vision of the dome of St. Peter's rising above the clouds.

Rome for the first time at Easter in 774 "*orandi gratia*", praying for grace, as reported by the chronicles of this unusual event. He arrived in Rome on the April 2. The news of his arrival filled Pope Hadrian I with "*magno stupore et extasi*".[12] The Romans went to meet him singing and cheering, bearing palms, olive branches, crosses and icons. He dismounted his steed and entered the Eternal City not as a conqueror, but as a pilgrim, not in armour, but in the guise of a Roman senator. Pope and clergy awaited him at the entrance to St. Peter's. The king kissed each one of the steps that led up to the basilica and when he arrived at the summit pope and king embraced, joined hands and walked into St. Peter's as the choir sang *Benedictus qui venit in nomine Domini*. They knelt before the tomb of St. Peter and vowed fidelity and mutual protection. The parchment copy of their pact was placed on the *confessio*, the tomb of St. Peter, as a pledge of this new bond by which Rome now definitively freed herself from all allegiance to Byzantium and allied herself to the Frankish rulers.

Charlemagne returned to Rome, if only for brief stays, in the years 781, 786, 787, and finally in 799. On Christmas day 800 (not Christmas Eve!), which by the old calendar was New Year's Day, the king and his entourage attended morning mass. After the Gloria, the pope, Leo III, quite suddenly placed a golden crown upon Charlemagne's head while the Romans let out a triple cheer: "To Charles, the most pious, crowned *augustus* by God, to the great and peace-bringing emperor, life and victory!"[13] The coronation, as recounted in the *Vita Leonis* of the *Liber Pontificalis*, was the result of "an inspiration from God and St. Peter". Yet, most likely, the Pope and the Romans had previously agreed upon the time to act as well as upon the wording of the proclamation.

As a result of his coronation, Charlemagne's political standing was increased morally and religiously, while at the same time the popes, too, added to their authority. From this point onwards, the German kings would have to come to Rome in order to be proclaimed and crowned

6. Mosaic from the *triclinium* or banqueting hall in the Lateran executed at the command of Leo III immediately after the imperial coronation of 800. The Pope himself kneels on the righthand side next to Charlegmagne who is holding the banner of the Holy Roman Empire given to him by St. Peter, while on the left Constantine receives the same from Christ.

Imperator Romanorum, emperor of the Romans, not as German emperor. This meant that only the pope, with the acclamation of the Roman people, could crown the emperor.

Charlemagne's coronation is represented in the great mosaic still to be seen upon the side wall of the building of the *Scala Santa*. This originally decorated the *triclinium* or dining hall of the papal palace at the Lateran. Leo III commissioned the mosaic shortly after the event. Both he and the emperor are depicted with square halos which signify that they were both living at the time of the mosaic's execution and yet were already considered as saints by virtue of their office (fig. 6). In this mosaic St. Peter is seen giving Charlemagne the *vexillum*, or standard, of the Roman empire, while on the left Constantine is depicted receiving the standard from Christ. This is to show that Charlemagne is the heir to Constantine's legacy, he is the second founder of the "Holy Roman Empire". The

7. The ancient *Cathedra Petri*, originally the throne of Charles the Bald and brought by him to Rome for his imperial coronation in 875. Later it was used as an episcopal chair in St. Peter's until it was enclosed in a bronze case and set up in the apse of the basilica (see fig. 105).

Sacrum Imperium founded by Constantine shall live anew in him. But although Rome would remain its point of origin and spiritual heart, the center of power now shifted to the land of the Franks.

Another imperial coronation is brought to mind by the old *Cathedra Petri* (fig. 7). This wooden throne, inlaid with gold and ivory, was thought to have been used by the Apostle Peter himself, whereas in actual fact it was a work of the Carolingian school at Metz and had been brought to Rome by Charles the Bald for his coronation in 875 and then given to the pope. For centuries it served as a papal throne, until Bernini, in 1666, created a protective shell in gilt bronze and elevated it gloriously in the apse of St. Peter's. A reproduction of the original chair is in the Treasury of St. Peter's and there, on the back of the chair, we can see a likeness of Charles the Bald (who is not bald at all!) with a great mustache and crown.

Some emperors found not just the crown in Rome but death as well. Otto II died there in 983 and was laid to

8. The *Isola Tiberina*, the Tiber Island, with the church of *San Bartolomeo*. Built in the year 1001 by the emperor Otto III, it stands on the site of an ancient temple dedicated to Aesculapius. Engraving by Willem van Nieulandt, 1600.

rest in the atrium of St. Peter's and later in an ancient sarcophagus in the underground church. His son Otto III, who dreamt of making Rome the imperial capital once more, ruled from the Aventine. He, likewise, died quite young in 1002 on *Monte Soratte*, the holy mountain of the Romans, but was buried in Aachen. An ever present reminder of Otto III is the church on the Tiber Island which was built by him on the site of a pagan temple of Aesculapius and dedicated to St. Bartholomew (fig. 8). Otto is to be seen depicted on a circular marble fountain in front of the altar as the donor of the church, together with Christ

21

the Savior, the apostle Bartholomew and St. Adalbert the martyr. The piece is most likely a work of the sculptor Pietro Vassalletto (1154-86).

In total, 27 of the 30 imperial coronations took place in Rome. Charlemagne was crowned in 800, Lothar I in 823, Louis II in 850, Charles the Bald in 875, Charles III in 881, Wido in 891, Arnulf in 896, Louis III in 901, Berengar in 915, Otto I in 962, Otto II in 967, Otto III in 996, Henry II in 1014, Conrad II in 1027, Henry III in 1046, Henry IV in 1084, Henry V in 1111, Lothar of Saxony in 1133, Frederick I in 1155, Henry VI in 1191, Otto IV in 1209, Frederick II in 1220, Henry VII in 1312, Louis the Bavarian in 1328, Charles IV in 1355, Sigismund in 1433 and Frederick III in 1452.

This was the last imperial coronation in Rome. However, the Hapsburg Frederick III did not appear, as his predecessors had done, with military escort and knights in shining armor. He was accompanied, instead, by the humanists and representatives of the different German cities and classes. This was more a historical-cultural event than a religious or political act. A year later Constantinople was to fall to the Turks thereby putting an end to the Byzantine Empire which had been at the same time the model, counterpart and bulwark of the Christian Empire of the West.

In 1508, Maximilian I proclaimed himself, with papal consent, "Elected Roman Emperor", elected but not crowned. Charles V was the last emperor to be crowned by a pope, who in this case was Clement VII. The coronation, which took place in 1530, was held at Bologna, the emperor not having time to come all the way to Rome. Certainly, Rome would not have provided the ideal setting for an imperial coronation after the terrible destruction recked by imperial landsknechts during the *Sack of Rome* in 1527. Thus, after 700 years, Rome lost its role as the seat of coronations and the emperors would no longer be crowned by the popes. In 1806 Francis II abdicated the title of emperor of "The Holy Roman Empire of the German Nation". This happened after Napoleon, who considered himself the new Charlemagne, had seized the imperial crown out of the Pope's hands in order to crown himself in Notre Dame in Paris. With this the rite of coronation lost its religious significance and any link with Rome.

* * *

At the approach of the second millenium, a new kind of pilgrim began to appear who came neither out of devotion to the martyrs, as the earlier pilgrims did, nor out of atonement, as the Anglo-Saxons had done. This new kind of pilgrim came rather to obtain either dispensations or privileges from the Roman Curia; to make appeals in legal disputes or to obtain benefices and prebends. The Roman Curia was in the process of developing its various offices and courts of justice: the Roman Chancery, the Apostolic Chamber, the Apostolic Signature, the Datary, the Penitentiary and the Sacred Roman Rota. Centralization of the Roman Church was growing and this inevitably brought about the necessity to appeal to Rome in the final instance.

In addition, the various religious communities that sprang up in the Middle Ages needed papal approval. Therefore, even *St Francis of Assisi*, to name the most famous example, came to Rome. The well-known scene painted by Giotto in the upper church of St. Francis in Assisi shows Francis kneeling before Pope Innocent III with his first eleven companions (fig. 9). The saint is in the act of asking for approval of his new religious way of life, living free in nature, in absolute poverty and in the pure spirit of the Gospel. Francis' audience took place in the year 1210 in the Lateran Palace, the papal residence at the time. On the night before, the Pope had a dream that the church of the Lateran was falling down, but a little monk appeared bracing it upon his shoulder and saved the church from collapse. When, on the following day, Francis came and knelt before the Pope, the pontiff immediately recognized him and gave oral approval to Francis' petition. This submission to papal authority from the very outset of

9. *St. Francis* kneeling before Innocent III in petition for the approval of his new rule. Fresco by Giotto painted shortly before 1300 in the upper church of *San Francesco* in Assisi.

the movement was to prevent it from later falling into heresy, as other contemporary pauperistic movements did, and led to an awakening of new and vital energy within the Church. Saint Francis became the veritable savior, not only of the Lateran, as in the Pope's dream, but of the Church at large.

* * *

In the 11th century *Santiago de Compostela* in Northern Spain began to rival Rome as a pilgrimage destination. It was venerated as the site of the tomb of St. James the Greater, the brother of St. John. Soon good roads were to lead there, along whith pilgrim-homes which were made available free of charge. They were called "hostels of God" and helped to ease the rigors of the journey. Since 1175, when St. James' Day falls on a Sunday, a special indulgence can be gained and a "Holy Year" is celebrated (the term, however, was applied at a later date in imitation of Rome). The term *pellegrinus*, at that time, indicated a pilgrim going to Santiago, while a pilgrim going to Rome was called a *romeo* in Italian (to distinguish him from a native of Rome, a *romano*), and a pilgrimage to Rome was called a *romeria*. Pilgrims going to Jerusalem were called *palmieri*, as they wore a miniature palm as a sign of identification. Pilgrims to Santiago wore a scallop shell upon their hat or clothing. The symbol of the *romei* became, as we shall see, Veronica's veil. Ultimately, that which distinguished the *romei* from the pilgrims going to other holy places was their belief in the oneness and universality of the Church which they held to be embodied and guaranteed by St. Peter and his successors.

III

The First Jubilee Year 1300

The Crusades brought about a new impulse for pilgrimages to the Holy Land and new attention was given to the East as there had been at the dawn of the Christian era. In order to encourage participation, Pope Urban II proclaimed in 1095 that by joining a crusade a full plenary indulgence would be granted. For the second crusade in 1147, St. Bernard of Clairvaux preached: "*annus remissionis, annus vere jubilaeus*", the year of the remission of sins is a true jubilee year or jubilee.[14] Here the word "*jubilee*" or "jubilee year" appears for the first time, with an obvious alllusion to the Jewish jubilee year, and was associated with hope of liberation and pardon.

Every seven years, the Jews of the Old Testament had celebrated a sabbatical year; a year of repose. The number seven had a symbolic significance for them since God had rested on the seventh day of the Creation, the Sabbath. During a sabbatical year one had to release one's brethren from all debts or pledges (see *Deuteronomy* 15:1-11), and when seven times seven years had passed, that is forty-nine, the fiftieth was a very special year of repose. In the twenty-fifth chapter of the third book of Moses, *Leviticus*, verses 9-13,23,39-43, it is written:

> "And on the tenth day of the seventh month you
> will sound the trumpet-call; on the Day of Expia-
> tion you will sound the trumpet throughout the

land. You will declare this fiftieth year to be sacred and proclaim the liberation of all the country's inhabitants. You will keep this as a jubilee: each of you will return to his ancestral property, each to his own clan. This fiftieth year will be a jubilee year for you; in it you will not sow, you will not harvest the grain that has come up on its own or in it gather grapes from your untrimmed vine. The jubilee will be holy thing for you; during it you will eat whatever the fields produce. In this year of jubilee, each of you will return to his ancestral property" (9-13).

"Land will not be sold absolutely, for the land belongs to me, and you are only strangers and guests of mine" (23).

"If your brother becomes impoverished while with you and sells himself to you, you will not make him do the work of a slave; you will treat him like an employee or guest, and he will work for you until the jubilee year. He will then leave you, both he and his children, and return to his clan and regain possession of his ancestral property. For they are my servants whom I have brought out of Egypt, and they may not be bought and sold as slaves. You will not oppress your brother-Israelites harshly but will fear your God" (39-43).

The term "jubilee" derives from the sounding of the *yobhel*, or ram's horn, that was blown in order to announce the begining of a jubilee year. The Hebrew word *yobhel* has taken on a number of meanings: horn, jubilation, liberation and the sound of the horn itself. In the *Vulgate*, the Latin Bible, the term was translated by association into *jubilaeum, annus jubilaeus*, as the jubilee was meant to be a year of true jubilation. The jubilee year began with the feast of Yom Kippur, the Day of Atonement. This was the only day of the year that the high priest entered the temple's inner sanctum to ask God's forgiveness for the sins of the entire community. Therefore, repentance, atonement and reconciliation already constituted the premise of the Holy Year in its Old Testament origins. This Mosaic precept was of great importance to Jewish social fabric which was based upon kinship and real property. Not only did man and beasts have to rest, but the tending of livestock, fields and vineyards was suspended and property had to return to its original owner or his heirs since no man is ultimately owner and master but simply a vassal of the Lord. Also all Jewish slaves had to be freed, given the fact that no Jew could ever be considered a slave since God had liberated the Jews from their bondage in Egypt and made them His servants.

Strangely enough, the Old Testament does not make any other mention of the jubilee, and, apart from laying down instructions for its observance, leaves no real proof that it was in fact observed. There is just a brief allusion made to it in the New Testament: Luke narrates (4:16-21) how Jesus read from Holy Scripture in the synagogue of Nazareth: "Unrolling the scroll, he found the place (Isaiah 61:1-2) where it is written: 'The spirit of the Lord is on me, for he has anointed me... He has sent me... to proclaim a year of favor from the Lord'. Then he began to speak to them: 'This text is being fulfilled today even while you are listening' ".

The year of favor which Isaiah mentions is a true jubilee year, because it is the year of the birth of Our Lord, "the year of salvation", as Christians used to call it. For them it no longer signified a year of liberation from prison and slavery but rather from guilt and punishment. The release from debt was transformed into the remission of guilt, and reconciliation amongst the Jews became reconciliation with God, and this would of course lead to reconciliation with one's fellow-man. For both the Jews of old and for the Christians, it meant a year of liberation and reconciliation, of joy and jubilation, a jubilee that would recur regularly.

This parallel was drawn by the general of the Dominican order *Humbert of Romans* when he preached a crusade, as Bernard of Clairvaux had done before. In instructions to his brother monks (1267), he compares the indulgence for the crusades to the jubilee of the Israelites, defining it as the *jubilaeus cristianorum*: "Now we have not only the jubilee of the Jews but the jubilee of the Christians, which is far superior. In the Judaic jubilee year worldly debts were cancelled, but in the Christian one the guilt of sin is pardoned. Whereas before property returned to the original owner here we acquire heavenly goods. Before the Jewish slaves were freed; now, the devil's slaves return to blessed freedom as children of God".[15]

Such comparisons were common in the preaching of the time and were part of the thinking of the Middle Ages which loved to draw parallels between the Old and New Testaments. The Old Testament was seen as the prefiguration and preparation of the New Testament (as illustrated in the fresco cycles on the sidewalls of the Sistine Chapel).

The term *jubilaeus* became synonymous with "indulgence", and "indulgence year" with "jubilee year". In the thirteenth century, the remission of temporal punishment for sins was given not only to those who went on crusades, but to anyone who took up arms against heretics (the Albigensians or Waldensians). At first the intent was the liberation of the Holy Land, but later it came to mean liberation from false teachings.

Partial indulgences were also granted to benefactors who built churches, hospitals, roads and bridges. This served as a great stimulus for social and charitable works. Lastly, special indulgences were granted to those pilgrims who journeyed to particular churches. St. Francis, for example, in 1216, had asked for the Portiuncula chapel the so-called Indulgence of the Portiuncula, which was granted every 2nd of August. Pope Celestine V confered a special indulgence upon the church of Collemaggio in his native L'Aquila. To end, Nicholas IV declared that on certain days of the year one could obtain an indulgence of seven years and seven times forty days if one visited St. Peter's in Rome. With this we are already very close to the first Holy Year.

* * *

In the thirteenth century the Middle Ages reached its apogee. The West had achieved a political, social and religious identity. The cities and universities, commerce and trade all flourished; the gothic cathedrals soared up to the heavens; a summary of all philosophical and theological knowledge had been set down by Thomas Aquinas in his great "Summa". The reform movements of the Franciscans and Dominicans attracted great numbers of followers; the spirituals, the hermits and the itinerant preachers all dreamt of everlasting peace, a millenial realm, an era of the Holy Spirit, just as Joachim da Fiore had predicted. A great desire for reconciliation with God and all men filled the hearts of everyone. The Christians of the Middle Ages had a greater sense of guilt and sin than modern man. For this reason, their yearning for expiation and pardon and their willingness to make sacrifices and do penance were much greater than they are today.

Their way of thinking was markedly juridical and made a subtle distinction in civil law as well as in religious life between *culpa* and *poena*, between the guilt of sins, removed by the sacrament of confession, and the punishment due to sins, which remained despite repentance and confession. These could be reduced only through good works and acts of penance; only a plenary indulgence could remove them entirely. When Jerusalem was definitively lost in 1244 and the crusades became impossible, the hope of obtaining a plenary indulgence vanished. It was then that the Christians turned their eyes in hope towards Rome, the religious center of the time.

Representative of this longing for salvation is the folk legend of Tannhäuser, who would have lived in Bavaria in the thirteenth century. In his desperate attempt to rescue his soul from the temptations of the Venusberg, he makes a pilgrimage to Rome to throw himself at the pope's feet. "With such an ardent heart, as no penitent ever knew, I searched for the road to Rome", sings Tannhäuser in Wagner's opera of the same name.

The apocalyptic expectations which had already filled men's minds as the year 1000 had approached were reawakened towards the end of every century. Fear and hope accompanied the arrival of the new. Around the year 1300, particular unrest was felt. A great event was awaited, an extraordinary grace. The idea was in the air, and a rumor circulated saying that at the begining of the new century truly special indulgences might be gained in St Peter's. It was the 1st of January, the eighth day of Christmas and Feast of the Circumcision. In Rome one breathed an almost mystical air, so much so that Cardinal Jacopo Stefaneschi, an eminent cardinal of the Roman Curia, exclaims in his famous chronicle of the first Holy Year, *De centesimo seu Jubileo anno liber*: "It's a wonderful thing! The secret of this great pardon remained hidden for the whole of the first day of January. But in the evening, as the sun was setting and the silence of the night began to fall, little by little this mystery began to reveal itself to the Romans. They began coming in droves towards St. Peter's basilica and pressed against the altar, blocking each other, making it difficult to get near at all. It seemed as if, when this day had passed, this blessing would disappear or at least the greater part of it. We do not know if they came on account of a sermon about the hundredth year, or jubilee, which most likely had been given that morning in the basilica, or out of their own free will, or because they had been attracted by some heavenly sign, which is more likely... After this beginning, faith and pilgrimages increased steadily amongst the citizenry and amongst the foreigners".[16]

31

In the same vein, Gugliemo Ventura writes: "In the year 1300 countless numbers of men and women came rapidly to Rome from all parts of Christendom, from all social classes, from East and West, and begged of Boniface, supreme pontiff: 'Give us your blessing before our days end' ".[17] A true folk-movement was at work here. No one had beckoned them on, no one had promised them anything.

The pope at that time was *Boniface VIII* (1294-1303), of the noble Caetani family of Anagni. He was a masterful lawyer and a strong statesman, the exact opposite of his predecessor, Celestine V. The latter had certainly been a pious monk and hermit, but understood nothing of the government of the Church and had soon abdicated. Dante placed him in his *Inferno* because of this abdication but reserved the same treatment for Boniface whom he accused of simony and reproached for his antagonistic stance towards the emperor, although the poet never put into question the pope's authority as such. In Boniface VIII the papacy reached its theocratic zenith: "I am Caesar, I am Emperor!", he was reported to have affirmed. No pope before or since had ever, or would ever, proclaim papal authority in the way he did. In his famous bull *Unam Sanctam* of 1302, he pushed to its literal extreme the dictum of Cyprian of Carthage: "*extra ecclesiam nulla salus*"[18] (there is no salvation outside the Church). The following year the Pope would suffer the greatest humiliaton: he was arrested and slapped by the followers of the French king. Whether the "slap" was a real one or just metaphoric is yet to be established, but the fact remains that the Pope did not recover from this blow and died soon afterwards.

Boniface was still at the height of his powers when he witnessed the great swarms of pilgrims stream into Rome. He did not know what really to do with them. It was not he who had called them. He held counsel with his cardinals and ordered the papal archives to be searched for some precedent, but none was to be found. A Christian jubilee year had as yet never taken place, even if some pilgrims stepped forward maintaining that their forbears had come to Rome exactly one century earlier and had obtained a great pardon. Still others were of the belief that the custom went as far back as the time of Sylvester II, that is, the year 1000. In the end, it seems the pope himself came to believe this, since the bull which with he instituted the first Holy Year begins with precisely these words: *"Antiquorum habet fida relatio..."*. "The true or trustworthy account of ancient date states that all those who set foot in the venerable basilica of the prince of the apostles shall receive great forgiveness and indulgences...".[19]

After two months of hesitation and consultation, Boniface VIII decided to harness this popular religious movement, "so as not to extinguish the spirit", as Stefaneschi puts it. By giving it his blessing, the Pope set this spontaneous movement on an ecclesiastical footing. The Jubilee was therefore neither his idea nor a stratagem of ecclesiastical politics, as some critics still insist. Just as Innocent III had welcomed the Franciscan movement for the revitalization of the Church, so too Boniface VIII was able to recognize the "spirit of the times". This was to his great merit. Unintentionally and unknowingly, he profoundly influenced not only the religious development, but also the social, political and cultural life of the Western World. The Holy Years were to bring about not only a religious revival but also understanding and brotherhood amongst men. It was a peace movement, since during the Holy Years war and hostilities were banned. It put into effect social equality since all pilgrims, rich and poor, noble and peasant, were all treated alike. The same pilgrim garb hid the differences of social status. Women, too, participated in the Holy Year, which was not at all common at the time. The Holy Years also provided an educative stimulus by broadening the pilgrims' cultural horizon. They stimulated new building, new literature and new works of art, as will be seen in the course of our history.

10. *Boniface VIII* announcing the first Holy Year on 22nd of February 1300. The pope, dressed in pontifical vestments and crowned with the tiara, is standing upon a pulpit draped with fine cloth. While he gives his blessing, a deacon reads the papal bull.

Giotto, the great painter of the early Renaissance, has preserved in fresco the scene of Boniface VIII proclaiming the first Holy Year (fig. 10). This painting was once to be seen in the benediction loggia of the Lateran but is now on a pier in the church interior. In it we see the Pope with cope and tiara giving his blessing from a loggia as a deacon reads the bull of indiction from a parchment. It is not known if this scene really took place in the Lateran as this fresco and a miniature copy in the Ambrosian Library in Milan seem to indicate. Stefaneschi makes no mention of it; on the contrary, he tells us that the Pope held a solemn function in St. Peter's. He was escorted by a number of cardinals (among whom the cardinal and general of the Franciscan order, Matthew of Acquasparta), ascended to the silk-draped ambo and gave a very moving sermon to the great throng. Then he laid the bull upon the altar of

Peter's tomb as a "gift" to the prince of the apostles, but also to emphasize his power and authority as successor of St. Peter. He gave the order that the text be incised upon a marble plaque which was later placed high up, to the left of the Holy Door in the portico of St. Peter's. The original papal bull is to be found in the Chapter archives of St. Peter's (fig. 11).

The papal bull *Antiquorum habet fida relatio* was drawn up on the February 16th in the papal residence which at that time, as has been said, was the Lateran palace. Later on Boniface VIII had it postdated to the 22nd, the feast of the *Cathedra Petri*, changing the site as well: "*apud sanctum Petrum*", as we can read at the bottom of bull and is reported by Cardinal Stefaneschi, the chronicler of the first Holy Year. This story is very much in keeping with the Pope's character, and conforms to his general church policy. Appar-

11. The papal bull *Antiquorum habet fida relatio* with which the first Jubilee Year was announced by Boniface VIII on 22 February 1300. The original is kept in the archives of St. Peter's.

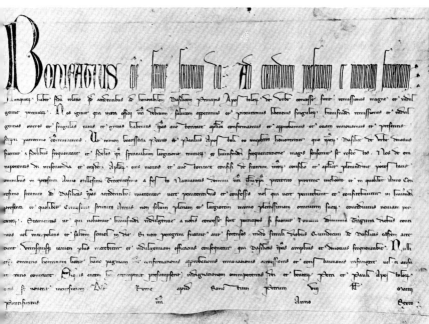

ently he wanted to emphasize the importance of St. Peter's chair and its occupant. The text reads:

> For this reason, in order that the blessed apostles Peter and Paul shall be more honored, and their basilicas more reverently visited by the faithful, and by this, these same faithful shall feel more strengthened by the dispensing of spiritual gifts of mercy, We, trusting in the mercy of God almighty and the merit and authority of the self-same apostles, with the counsel of our brethren and in the plenitude of the apostolic power, to all those who in the present year one thousand and three hundred, just recently begun with the feast of the nativity of our Lord Jesus Christ, and in whatever other subsequent hundredth year shall accede to the aforementioned basilicas with reverence and truly contrite and confessed, not only do we concede full and complete, but extraordinary pardon of their sins".[20]

Neither the expression "jubilee" nor "jubilee year" are contained in the text. No reference to the custom of the Old Testament is made (in contrast with the circular letter of the scriptor Sylvester). There is no mention at all of a plenary indulgence, but the wording: "full, complete and extraordinary pardon of their sins", which had to be contritely confessed, means, according to the language of the period, not only the complete remission of guilt from sin but also of punishment due to sin.

The first condition, of course, in order to obtain a plenary indulgence was the proper spiritual attitude, followed by contrition and confession. In addition, a devout visit to the sepulchres of the apostles was required. For the Roman citizens a series of thirty visits over a period of thirty different days was required; for foreigners only half the number of visits was prescribed. Obviously, it was not enough simply to cross the threshold fifteen times. These

12. The circular letter written by the scriptor Sylvester in which he presents the Jubilee Year. At the end, in the lower lefthand corner, is the doggerel verse to be memorized: *Annus centenus – Romae semper es jubilenus*. A copy is in the Vatican Archives.

visits had to be made on fifteen different, if not consecutive, days.

The very same day the *scriptor domini papae*, Sylvester, addressed a circular letter to all "present and future Christian believers", in order to explain the importance of the new *indulgentia* (a copy is preserved in the Vatican archives. Fig. 12).[21] He also added a triplet of easily memorizable doggerel at the end of the text:

> *Annus centenus - Romae semper est jubilenus,*
> *Crimina laxantur - cui poenitet ista donantur,*
> *Hoc declaravit - Bonifacius et roboravit.*

> Once in a century - is Rome's jubilee festivity,
> Crimes are forgiven - to the contritely shriven,
> This hath been promulgated - Boniface hath it corroborated.

Armed with these verses, which were easily imprinted upon the memory, the itinerant preachers went from place to place to recite them in pulpits and in piazzas. We find the verses inscribed upon a marble plaque over the right entrance of the cathedral at Siena. The news of this great event in Rome and of the "great pardon" to be obtained that year spread with great speed. Undescribable jubilation reigned throughout Christendom. Cardinal Stefaneschi tells us in his chronicles that the news of the jubilee spread throughout Italy, Germany and Hungary "with lightning speed and that such numbers moved towards Rome like an army or a swarm of bees".[22]

Giovanni Villani, who also was am eyewitness the jubilee of 1300, describes the same thing in his *Nuova Cron-*

ica: "A great number of Christians who lived at that time, women as well as men, undertook this pilgrimage coming from different lands, both near and far. It was the most wondrous thing that I had ever seen... All husbands, wives and children, locking up their homes, together they went there, filled with devotion for the said indulgence".[23]

The reason for the Holy Year was at first a Christocentric one: the commemoration of Christ's nativity, "*a reverenza della natività di Cristo*" as Giovanni Villani wrote. This does not appear explictly in the papal bull; however, another contemporary, Cardinal Giovanni Monaco, explains in his commentary on the bull: "*A nativitas domini nostri Jesu Christi, in qua verus jubilaeus incepit*", "at the birth of our Lord Jesus Christ, with which every true Jubilee begins".[24] This spirit is in keeping with Franciscan piety, which at that time inspired all Christians by emphasising the humanity of Christ. Boniface VIII was in addition motivated by a personal or rather papal reason: to strengthen the prestige and the influence of the Holy See. This was not a calculated gesture, at least not initially. The claim made by Ventura,[25] that both night and day clerics stood near St. Peter's altar and litcrally collected alms by "raking them in", is surely exagerated.

Villani also says that "the treasures of the Church increased greatly during the Jubilee Year", and that "many Romans became rich through trade".[26] We know in fact, precisely how much money was collected in St. Peter's and St. Paul's. Stefaneschi provides us with the figure of 51,000 gold florins for both churches. He adds though that most of this came from money of small coinage from the most distant countries. From this we can deduce that the greater part of the donors were poor people and came from far away. The money was used for the maintainance of the two basilicas, and in part put towards the acquisition of estates (e.g. Castel Giubileo near Rome). The Pope was an excellent administrator. It was he who conceived of buying food provisions and stocking them up, instituting price controls and suppressing duties. Villani assures us: "Everyone was provided with food and was happy, horses as well as people. All this went off without noise or quarreling, and with great patience. I can attest to this as I was there and have witnessed it".[27]

When certain chroniclers, such as Guglielmo Ventura, cite "two million pilgrims", this is not to be taken as factual as some writers still do. In the first place, Rome in this period had a population of only 50,000. It would have been impossible, therefore, for the city to receive two million people in one year, especially when one considers that each one of them had to stay for at least fifteen days in order to gain the indulgences. Secondly, the statistic would have been almost impossible to measure. Giovanni Villani is probably closer to the truth when he writes: "During the whole year, in addition to the resident population there were 200,000 pilgrims coming and going from Rome".[28] In any event, the fact remains that never before had such a multitude of pilgrims been seen. They came from everywhere, by land, by sea, on foot, on horseback or in coaches. The old saying: "All roads lead to Rome", had never been truer since the fall of the ancient Roman empire.

The whole city underwent a period of renovation and embellishment. *Santa Maria Sopra Minerva* was built, and repairs were made in the church of the *Ara Coeli*. It was the period in which the Roman basilicas (the Lateran, St. Mary Major, Santa Maria in Trastevere, etc.) were embelished with magnificent gold leaf mosaics which would fill the pilgrims with awe. Also in this time Arnolfo di Cambio created the nativity scene at S. Mary Major, the two ciboriums or marble canopies in the churches of St. Paul's and St. Cecily's, as well as the tomb of Boniface VIII in the Vatican "grottoes" (fig. 13). Giotto, who has already been mentioned, painted the altar piece for St. Peter's, now in the Vatican Painting Gallery (fig. 14). He also designed the famous mosaic *la Navicella,* "the small boat", i.e. the small boat of the apostles on the Sea of Galilee, now under the portico of St. Peter's (see fig. 97). Both works were commissioned and donated by Cardinal Jacopo Gaetano Stefaneschi (1270-1373) who appears in both as donor.

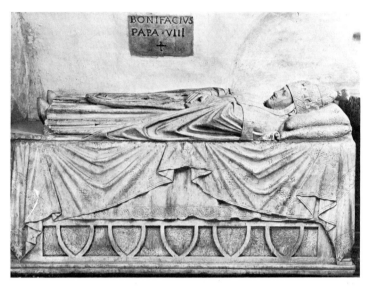

13. The tomb of Boniface VIII (died 1303) in the lower church of St. Peter's. Possibly the work of Arnolfo di Cambio.

Stefaneschi was an important figure both in the Roman aristocracy and in the Roman Curia, as well as a friend and patron of artists. He was also the author, as we already know, of the chronicle of the first "Jubilee Year". This was the original term for "the year of the great pardon", as it was commonly known. Only later, in 1400, as we shall see, did the term "Holy Year" come into use.

The Jubilee Year provided stimulus not just for artists but for poets as well. Dante was certainly the most noteworthy of all. In his *Vita Nuova* he asks some pilgrims, "Oh wanderers, why do you go so absorbed in thought?" Perhaps he too belonged to the devout and pensive pilgrims of that year. The impression made upon him was such as to induce him to begin writing his masterpiece, *The Divine Comedy*, during Holy Week in the year 1300. In an ingenious vision, Dante journeys through Hell and Purgatory until he reaches the heavenly Paradise. From

14. Altar painting by Giotto (shortly after 1300) commissioned by Cardinal Stefaneschi, who is seen kneeling as the donor in the lower lefthand corner. Originally conceived for the papal altar in the old St. Peter's, it is today housed in the Vatican Pinacoteca.

there he views all three as one real and undivided entity, exactly as it would have been conceived by the true believers of that time. It was precisely the Holy Year which served to strengthen this experience of the unity of Christianity, since people came from all nations and all walks of life to assemble in Rome in faith and prayer for the living as well as for deceased believers.

The Florentine chroniclers, Giovanni Villani and Dino Compagni, as well as the anonymous author of the first romance of Spanish literature, *El libro del Caballero Cifar,* were all in Rome for the Jubilee. Just as Dante had done, they too made the Holy Year the starting point for their narratives. The Jubilee of 1300 was for them as well as for many other contemporaries such a decisive moment that they believed they were at the begining of a new era.

IV

The Jubilee of Saint Bridget 1350

Pope Boniface decreed in his bull *Antiquorum habet fida relatio* that a Jubilee Year would be celebrated every hundred years. Yet fifty years later another Holy Year took place, and this time without the presence of the Pope.

After the tragic end of the pontificate of the powerful Boniface VIII (1294-1303) and the short reign of Benedict XI (1303-1304), a French cardinal, archbishop of Bordeaux and friend of King Philip the Fair, was elected Pope with the name of Clement V (1305-14). The new Pope did not feel safe in Rome and prefered to put himself under the protection of the French king, transfering his residence to Avignon, a fief of the popes. It was in this way that in 1305 the "Babylonian captivity of the popes" began, so called in reference to the captivity of the ancient Jews in Babylon (586-538 B.C.), and lasted for seventy years. Six more French popes came to the throne, all promising to bring the papacy back to Rome. No one, however, was able to achieve this, as the city was in a state of total chaos. Rome had been left to itself with no one to administer law and order. The noble families and their feuds left the citizenry abject, an earthquake struck bringing down the decrepit buildings, and, as if this had not been enough, the plague was threatening the city. When it had passed by without many victims, the Romans wished to give thanks

15. The church of *Santa Maria in Aracoeli* with its great marble stairway from which Cola di Rienzo addressed the crowd. On the right is the stairway designed by Michelangelo which leads up to the Capitol Hill. Between the two stairways is a statue of Cola di Rienzo near the spot where he was killed in 1454.

by building the steep staircase of 124 white marble steps leading up to the church of *Santa Maria in Aracoeli* ("the altar of heaven", fig. 15) on the Capitol hill. From the heights of these steps Cola di Rienzo (1313-54), known to many through Richard Wagner's opera, *Rienzi*) addressed the Roman populace, exciting them with his talk of the ancient magnificence and of the renewal of Rome and the Church. In 1343 he was in Avignon to persuade the Pope to return to Rome, and by his vivid description of Rome's undoing, he was able to elicit a promise that the pontiff would return. This did not happen due to the political

45

complications of the time, especially the ongoing conflict between England and France. A truce, at least, was obtained between the two warring countries for the period of the Holy Year. The Roman delegation, under the artifice of not wanting to exclude any generation from the blessings of a Holy Year, asked that the intervals be reduced to fifty instead of one hundred years. In so doing they were reviving the idea of the Old Testament, but the true reason behind this plea was to win new fame and prosperity that a jubilee always brought with it. The Pope eventually granted the request out of "compassion".

Cola's self-confidence was nourished by these successes. He saw himself as a leader of the third age that had been promised by the Spirituals, which he would initiate with the opening of the jubilee. He began preparing the city for the Holy Year. Then in 1347 from the summit of the steps of the *Ara Coeli* he had himself proclaimed tribune of the people; but he quickly aroused the emnity of the nobles and the mistrust of the Pope. When the Pope threatened to cancel the Holy Year unless Cola was overthrown, Cola was imprisoned in Castel Sant'Angelo and later exiled from Rome. After a stay with some mountain hermits, he became even more convinced of his mission. He showed up secretly in Rome in 1350 and in June he was received by Emperor Charles IV in Prague. From there he journeyed to see the pope in Avignon and returned to Rome in the suite of the papal legate. He entered the city triumphantly and was nominated senator. He raised an army, but his arrogance and cruelty soon made him unpopular, so that he was murdered here, near "his" steps, in 1354. When Cola was rediscovered in the last century by the nationalistic movement and celebrated as a precursor of modern Italy, a monument by Girolamo Masini (1887) was erected near the spot where he was killed. From it Cola still harangues the crowd with his arm outstretched in the gesture typical of Roman orators.

As has been stated, the Pope never came to Rome; not even for the Holy Year. He sent his legates instead. One of them, Annobaldo da Ceccano, was disrespectfuly nicknamed "the monkey" by St. Bridget because he was ugly and vain. He became quite unpopular when he decreed that, while the Romans still had to visit the basilicas on thirty different days, the pilgrims from outside Rome needed only fifteen days, while for those who came from beyond the Alps, the prerequisite could be reduced to as low as ten, five or even one day, depending upon the length of their journey. The longer the pilgrimage, the shorter the stay required. These measures were taken in order to avoid a dearth of food and shelter. But in so doing he had gone against the business interests of the Romans and in their fury there was even an attempt made upon his life. At this point the legate left the city, placing it under interdict and this in the midst of the Holy Year!

Once again people came from all parts of the Christian West. Young and old, men and women, single pilgrims and entire families set out in order to receive the graces of the Holy Year. They came via the Alps, across the sea, along the Tiber; some dragged iron chains and huge wooden crosses, or walked barefoot and flagellated themselves. They were mostly dressed in the same manner, with a long robe of sackcloth of a murky nondescript gray-brown color. A wide-brimmed hat served at once as umbrella and parasol. When it was not worn it hung by a cord upon the back. Often a scallop shell was affixed to the hat (this habit came from Santiago de Compostela as earlier stated) or a palm leaf if they had come from Jerusalem. On their return from Rome, the pilgrims often wore a miniature reproduction of Veronica's veil upon their hats. A long walking staff was always part of their garb, and if it rained they made use of the pelerine (the word comes from *pellegrinus*, i.e. pilgrim), a wax impregnated cape. Their only bag was a shoulder sack, their only utensils were a hollow gourd used as a flask and a shell which served as a bowl.

47

What drove them on and motivated them was the hope of obtaining the great remission of sins, guilt and punishment. Therefore no sacrifice nor danger was too great. They endured hunger and thirst, hot and cold weather, they were attacked and robbed. It was common to draw up one's will before starting out, as it was never sure if one would return safe and sound. When someone did die along the way, he was neither mourned or sorrowed over. No, he was envied instead, as it was believed that one who died while on a pilgrimage went straight to heaven and was spared purgatory. Though the road was filled with danger, it was still the surest path to heaven.

The pilgrims motto was: *Nulla mihi patria nisi Christus nec nome aliud quam Christianus*, "I have no other fatherland but Christ, and no other name but Christian". This is attributed to St. Pellegrinus, a fifth century bishop and martyr from Gaul, who was especially venerated by the Frankish pilgrims.

The main flow of pilgrims came in spring and in late autumn. This was due to liturgical feast days and also to meteorological and agricultural considerations. It was impossible to hike over the Alps in the winter. In the summer, those who could, avoided the heat. At this time, it took fifty days to travel from Paris to Rome, twenty from Brenner to Rome (by coach). The route went via Bologna, Florence, Siena, Bolsena and Viterbo and there were twenty-four posts along the way where both wayfarer and horses could rest. The majority of pilgrims, however, journeyed on foot. Those who came from the north (and most of them did) finally reached Monte Mario, which at that time was called *Mons gaudii*, "the mount of joy", since from its heights one could finally see the panorama of the Eternal City. The cry of joy, after all the trials and dangers that had been faced, would be easy to imagine. Many fell upon their knees and kissed the ground (fig. 16) and began singing a hymn which is still sung today by Holy Year pilgrims. Its first verse goes:

16. Pilgrims on *Monte Mario*, formerly known as *Mons gaudii*. Some are so overcome by emotion as they look down on the City, that they kiss the ground. Print from a painting by Sir Charles Eastlake (c. 1815-1830).

O Roma nobilis, orbis et domina
Cunctarum urbium excellentissima
Roseo martyrum sanguine rubea
Albis et virginum liliis candida
Salutem dicimus tibi per omnia
Te benedicimus, salve per saecula.

O noble Rome, mistress of the world,
Of all its cities, the most eminent,
Made brilliant by the red blood of martyrs,
Spotless white by virginal white lilies,
We sing your praises and bless you,
Hail to thee for eternity.

This stanza is in praise of Rome, the second is dedicated to St. Peter and the third and last to St. Paul.

17. The *Ponte Milvio*. The historic *ponte molle* where emperor Constantine defeated Maxentius in 312, signalling the triumph of Christianity over paganism. Later, all pilgrims coming to Rome from the north would have to pass over this bridge in order to enter the city. G. Vanvitelli: *Vedute*, about 1700, in the Capitol Museum.

From Monte Mario, the pilgrims headed directly towards St. Peter's by the *Via Trionfale* or the *Via dei Pellegrini*, or else went first into the city by crossing the Milvian Bridge (fig. 17), the historic *Ponte Molle*. It was near this bridge that in 312, on October 28, the Emperor Constantine defeated his rival, Maxentius. This was a crucial event as it led to the triumph of Christianity over paganism. This bridge still exists and has seen, in this order, pilgrims, emperors, artists and tourists pass over it. Distinguished visitors were received here and escorted into the city with song and banners unfurled. They were accompanied to the *Porta Flaminia* (later *Porta del Popolo*), the city gate for those arriving from the north.

For the common folk, however, this is where the first disappointments began. All the accomodations were overcrowded. The poet Buccio di Ranallo, with his biting wit, describes the pilgrim's predicament.[29] The inn owners stood before their doors with the most angelic faces and politely urged the pilgrims to stay with them, promising them the best rooms they had. When upon returning in the evening, exhausted and wanting only to sleep, the *romeo* would find his bed already taken by several other pilgrims. At this point it was necessary to make the best of it otherwise he would be thrown out into the street and have absolutely no roof over his head at all. In addition, the prices of daily essentials were constantly on the increase while the black market flourished. Refuse was heaped up along the streets and to this was added the stench of horse manure and the noise of the wooden wagon-wheels as they rattled over the uneven paving-stones. Rome was already the noisy and chaotic city it still is today.

* * *

St. Bridget of Sweden (1303-73) was surely the most famous pilgrim of this Holy Year. She belonged to an old and noble family. At the age of thirteen she had been given in marriage to a wealthy man, to whom she bore eight children. She journeyed throughout Europe, first to Santiago de Compostela, then to Rome and eventually to the Holy Land.

In a woodcut of the 15th century we see her in pilgrim attire, with a long staff and large hat and shoulder sack (fig. 18). At her feet a crown marks her noble rank. Rome, her destination, is indicated by the city's coat of arms with the four familiar letters, S.P.Q.R., which stand for *Senatus Popolusque Romanus*, "Senate and People of Rome". These letters still figure today on all municipal buildings and institutions.

18. *St. Bridget of Sweden* dressed in pilgrim's garb with staff and hat and with a crown at her feet. The coat of arms of the city of Rome indicates her destination. Early 15th century woodcut.

Along with St. James the apostle, St. Bridget is revered as patron saint of pilgrims. Besides being an energetic woman and strict mother, she was also a profound mystic. Her *Revelationes* made a deep impression upon the men of the Middle Ages. In one of these revelations she explains how God ordered her: "Go to Rome where the streets are paved with gold, and the roof tiles are made out of the blood of the martyrs and whence the road to salvation is shorter; there you shall wait until you have spoken to the pope and the king".[30]

Bridget followed this voice. But when she arrived in Rome for the Holy Year of 1350, she was greatly disillusioned and, deeply disturbed, she exclaimed to her father-confessor: "Master Peter, is this the Rome Christ promised me?" Instead of streets paved of gold there was dust and refuse, and instead of tiles red with the blood of martyrs she only saw broken-down roofs and delapidated houses. However, the promise that Rome was the quickest road to salvation held true, at least in Bridget's case. She took up residence on the present-day Piazza Farnese, where today a convent of the Brigittines, the order she founded, still exists (fig. 19). The church was built later, but the rooms where she lived are still intact and even the wooden board is there upon which she is said to have died in 1373. Part of the building is now used as a pilgrims' guesthouse, especially conceived for Scandinavian pilgrims and for Protestants in particular.

Bridget spent 23 years in Rome in prayer and contemplation, taking care of the poor and infirm and occupied with the recording of her revelations. In the basilica of St. Paul outside the Walls there is a very impressive 14th century wooden crucifix which is reputed to have spoken to

19. *Piazza Farnese*. On the left, Palazzo Farnese. Opposite is the church of *Santa Brigida* and the house where St. Bridget died in 1373.

20. Crucifix said to have spoken to St. Bridget. Early 14th century polycrome wooden sculpture in St. Paul's outside the Walls.

her (fig. 20). In the chapel of the Blessed Sacrament, where the crucifix is now kept, we find in a niche a statue of St. Bridget who on her knees is either listening or speaking to the crucifix. The statue was made around the year 1600, probably by Stefano Maderno. In St. Sebastian's church a painting by Antonio Carracci (1583-1618) depicts the saint praying in the catacombs. She also learned Latin in order to write to the Pope and exhort him to return to Rome. Bridget was nicknamed "the widow of Rome". There was a double meaning in this; she had been widowed in the meantime and she also wept widow's tears over the abandoned city. She painted the darkest picture of Rome and reviled the inhabitants with harsh abuse for their indifference, laziness and superstitiousness. Like a prophet out of the Old Testament, she promised divine retribution if the Romans did not reform: "I have to speak to Rome like the prophet to Jerusalem. Once justice reigned in this city, its leaders were princes of peace, but they have become assassins. The city is inhabited by toads and vipers, and the fish in my net are afraid of their venom and dare not lift up their heads... Oh, Rome, if you but knew the punishment that is to come for your guilt you would weep!"[31]

Not surprisingly, Bridget soon became much disliked by the Romans; they would have happily seen her burnt as a witch, yet later she was canonized by them. Such changes of heart were not rare. Her daughter Karin (or Catherine) followed her to Rome; she would be proclaimed a saint as well. It was said that she was particularly beautiful and much sought after, but, so as not to suffer temptation, she burned her face with acid. Today it is hard for us to understand such extreme religious fervor; however, it was certainly typical of the rigorism of that period.

King Louis of Hungary also came to Rome for the jubilee, and on this occasion founded a Hungarian pilgrim home next to the German one on the south side of St. Peter's. It was demolished in the 18th century when the great sacristy was built.

* * *

Every Holy Year has had its poets. If Dante was there for the first one, no less than *Petrarch* was present for the second. Raphael has pictured them both in his fresco of Parnassus, the paradise of the artists, together with the nine muses (fig. 21). The laurel crowns identify them as poets. Dante stands above with Homer and Virgil, while Petrarch is seated under a laurel tree.

Francesco Petrarch (1304-74) was born in Arezzo, but lived for a long time in Avignon at the papal court. Just like Cola di Rienzo, he dreamt of the former glories of ancient Rome and entreated the Pope to return to Rome. In

21. *Parnassus*, the artists' heaven. Petrarch is seen on the left sitting under a laurel tree, while Dante stands next to him wearing a pink robe. Fresco by Raphael, 1511, in the Stanze di Raffaello, Vatican.

1341 he was crowned poet-laureate on the Capitol hill, the greatest honor attainable. In him was the first awakening of the Italian Renaissance. He was constantly torn between sacred and profane love, but when his adored Laura died, he traveled to Rome as a pilgrim for the Holy Year. In a letter written to Guglielmo di Pastrengo he describes the stream of pilgrims: [32]

> *Cammina l'Ibero insieme col Cimbro,*
> *Con il Britanno, col Greco, con lo Svevo*
> *dalla fulva chioma.*

> The Spaniard wanders together with the Celt,
> With the Briton, with the Greek, with the Swabian
> of the tawny hair.

By the Swabian the Germans are meant. They came in especially great numbers during the Holy Years. In a famous sonnet (No. XVI), Petrarch mentions an elderly man:

> The little old white-haired man prepares to leave,
> The sweet place that has watched him grow old,
> And from that family filled with fear,
> Who sees their dear father leave,
> Then dragging his ancient limbs hither,
> To follow the object of his yearning,
> And comes to Rome,
> To gaze at the likeness of Him,
> Who he hopes to see again in heaven

The last reference is to the image of Christ left upon the veil of Veronica which was venerated in St. Peter's.

It's interesting to read how Petrarch described the beauties of Rome to his friend Philippe de Vltry: "Thus you finally arrive in Rome, mistress and head of all things. The pilgrim will visit the apostles' tombs and will tread the earth that is reddened from the martyrs' blood; he will see the face of the Lord which is preserved in the woman's veil (Veronica's) as well as inside the church, mother of all churches (the Lateran). He will enter *Sancta Sanctorum*, a small spot filled with heavenly graces. He will visit the Vatican and the cemetery of Calixtus (the catacombs) filled with the bones of the blessed; he will see the manger of the Savior (St. Mary Major); he will contemplate the severed head of St. John the Baptist (St. Sylvester in Capite) and St. Lawrence's gridiron. He will meditate upon the place where St. Peter was crucified (in the Vatican) and where St. Paul's blood was shed and three springs issued forth (Le Tre Fontane) and the site, where after the miraculous summer snowfall, the foundations were laid of a beautiful temple (St. Mary Major)".[33] All of these sights are still to be seen today and we will visit them with the same devotion that Petrarch showed in 1350.

V

The Four Patriarchal Basilicas

At this point we should get to know the four patriarchal basilicas of Rome. As has already been said, in the beginning only two basilicas were prescribed for the pilgrims desirous of obtaining the Jubilee indulgence: St. Peter's and St. Paul's. Let us try to imagine what they looked like at that time.

The sole means of access from the city proper to St. Peter's was via the Sant'Angelo bridge. This ancient marble bridge had been built by the emperor Hadrian (117-138) (fig. 22). It was not yet embellished with the angels

22. *Castel Sant'Angelo* and the gate to the Vatican on the left. The Ponte Sant'Angelo is depicted as yet without angels, while in the background there is the dome of the Pantheon. Engraving by A. Salamanca (1500-1562).

23. *The Tiber, Ponte Sant'Angelo, Castel Sant'Angelo* and *St. Peter's* in 1700. G. Vanvitelli (1655-1736): *Vedute*, Capitol Museum.

added by Bernini in the Baroque era (1668-79). Now each angel holds a different symbol of Christ's Passion so as to create a reverential air for the pilgrim as he approaches St. Peter's (fig. 23).

Such was the congestion that pressed upon this bridge, that as early as the first Holy Year, it was necessary to regulate the flow by dividing it into two lanes: one for coming and the other for going. Dante provides us with a first hand account *in The Divine Comedy* (*Inf.* XVIII, 28-33):

> Romans, in their own fashion quite ably,
> In Jubilee Year, in crossing o'er the Tiber
> Have the pilgrims pass it over so orderly,
> So that on one side no one ever,
> Sees more than the castle and heads to St. Peter's,
> While hither to the mount they tread'pon the other.

24. In the Middle Ages the Vatican was a fortified city with high walls and towers. Woodcut from the *Buch der Chroniken und Geschichten* by Hartmann Schedel, Nürnberg 1493.

The Sant'Angelo bridge leads to Hadrian's mausoleum. Today this magnificent round structure is called Castel Sant'Angelo, as it is surmounted by a statue of St. Michael the Archangel which serves to remind us of a miracle that is said to have taken place here in the year 590. In that year the plague had been raging in Rome and Pope Gregory the Great led a procession in order to invoke divine intervention. While about to cross the bridge, an angel appeared at the top of the mausoleum and was seen to insert his sword in its scabbard symbolizing the cessation of the plague. In recognition, the Pope is said to have erected a statue of the angel just as he had seen him in his vision, i.e., resheathing his sword in a gesture of peace and salvation. Later replacements were made of marble and eventually in bronze. After this event the mausoleum was renamed "Castel Sant'Angelo".

To the left of the castle, the Vatican rose, fortress-like, with its many guard towers and its high walls. The city map of Hartmann Schedel of Nuremberg, in his *Book of Chronicles and Stories* (1493), can give us an idea of what the Vatican looked like to the pious pilgrim (fig. 24). Pope Boniface VIII had enlarged the gate in the Leonine walls at the point near Castel Sant'Angelo and also is said to have built an archway that connects it to St. Peter's Square. The square at the time had no real shape nor decoration. The view of the basilica was blocked by the papal *loggia* and St. Peters' forecourt which was reached by a series of stairs and gates. The pilgrim's expectations would grow with each step until he arrived in a beautiful courtyard called the "the garden of Paradise" (fig. 25). The courtyard was surrounded by a colonnade and in the middle there was a famous antique gilt bronze fountain in the shape of an enormous pine cone. Here, the tired pilgrims made their ablutions and prepared themselve both physically and spiritually before they entered the House of the Lord. The façade of the basilica was decorated with gold mosaics, while the five interior naves were lined with nearly a hundred white marble columns. There were shimmer-

25. The forecourt of Old St. Peter's with the fountain for ablutions in the center and the mosaic façade of the church. Drawing based on a description of the ancient basilica of St. Peter in the Vatican by Giacomo Grimaldi prior to 1620. Cod. Barb. Lat. 2732, fig. 63.

26. Reconstruction of the large monument erected by Constantine over the tropaion and original grave of St. Peter, including the red wall and the wall g. Lined with marble and surrounded by columns, it stood in front of the apse of the old church.

27. The Constantinian Donation shown in the setting of Old St. Peter's as it appeared before its demolition. Fresco by Giulio Romano and Francesco Penna, 1524-28. In the Hall of Constantine, Stanze di Raffaello, Vatican.

ing mosaics and countless oil lamps giving off their mystical light and at the same time, incensing the air.

As we have already seen, towards the end of the second century a small monument called an *aedicula* (see fig. 2) had been built over Peter's earthern grave. Now Constantine in circa 320 erected a large rectangular monument (memorial) above this last and had the remains of the apostle re-enshrined in it. This monument, faced with white marble and porphyry, surrounded by a bronze railing and surmounted by twisted marble columns, stood by itself before the apse in the background (fig. 26). Later still, the level of the presbytery floor would be raised and the monument would have an altar built over it so that the pope could say mass directly on top of the tomb of St. Peter. With his relics thus sealed up in the monument, no one even thought of searching for them let alone exhuming them once more, lest they disturb the repose of the prince of apostles. For the faithful it was enough to lower kerchiefs, hanging lamps or incensers through the holes in the tomb coverstone and later through a protective grill.

64

The original Constantinian basilica (built between 320-326) was demolished in the 16th century, but we can see what the original interior looked like by viewing the large fresco executed by Raphael's pupils in the Stanze in the Vatican. Painted between 1520-28, it depicts "the Donation of Constantine", which was supposed to have taken place in this very basilica (fig. 27).

Before approaching the sepulchral monument, the *romei* paid homage to the ancient statue of Peter, following the old adage: "when in Rome, do as the Romans do", (fig. 28). This maxim referred to the statue whose exten-

28. *Bronze statue of St. Peter*, possibly from the 5th century. Even today the faithful kiss its outstsretched foot. Engraving by S. Bassutti, 1850.

ded right foot was to be kissed or at least caressed out of reverence for St. Peter and his successors. Experts still disagree about its authorship. The fact remains that the work is made of antique bronze and has been in St.Peter's from at least the thirteenth century, more or less in the same place where it is now, that is, on the right-hand side in the central nave. Seated in stern majesty upon a marble throne, which was added in a later period, he holds in his left hand the two keys given him by Christ, one to bind and one to loosen, to open and close the kingdom of heaven. The right hand is raised in a gesture of benediction in the old Greek manner: two fingers raised to signify the two natures of Christ, human and divine, and the other three fingers put together signifying the Trinity. Not only does this hand bless, but it seems to be admonishing, teaching and passing judgement as well. Everything that a pope must do is summed up in this one, simple and still majestic gesture of Peter. On important feast days and in particular on that of SS. Peter and Paul, the 29th of June, the statue is dressed up as if it were a real live pope, garbed in a precious brocade cope, costly tiara and golden fisherman's ring. When not adorning the statue these objects are to be found in the Treasury of St. Peter's. When the reigning pontiff goes to kiss the statue's foot it looks as if the bronze Peter were blessing his living successor.

The center of attraction in the old basilica was, however, Veronica's veil. The name Veronica probably comes from a compounding of the Latin attribute *vera* with the Greek word *ikon* meaning, therefore, a true image; in other words, the true likeness of our Lord and Redeemer. In Holy Scripture the name of Veronica is never mentioned, but popular devotion conceived of her amongst the weeping women Christ encountered as he carried his heavy cross towards Golgotha. Veronica, moved to compassion, took off her veil from her head and offered it to Christ so that he could wipe his face of the blood and sweat. When he handed the veil back to her, it had been miraculously imprinted with the image of his face.

66

29. On feastdays the statue of St. Peter is adorned with a brocaded cope, tiara and the fisherman's ring, just as the pontiffs were in former times.

30. *St. Veronica's Veil* is displayed before the faithful in St. Peter's. 15th century woodcut.

According to the legend, Veronica brought the veil to Rome and with it cured the emperor Tiberius of leprosy. The veil's presence in Rome was first documented by Pietro Mallio in 1160 in his history of the Vatican basilica. The veil is a small white cloth with some dark spots upon it, kept under glass with a wooden frame. The more devotion in the Middle Ages delved into the human nature of Christ and meditated upon his Passion, the more important this image became. During the first Holy Year it was shown to the faithful every Sunday and Friday as well as on particular feast days. Upon seeing it, the faithful fell to their knees in reverence, as we can see in an old woodcut (fig. 30).

The effect which the "Sacro Volto" or "Holy Face" had upon the pilgrims can be read about in Dante's *Paradiso* (XXXI, 103-108):

*Like a man who perhaps from Croatia comes to
see our Veronica,
And while it is shown, stares at it with never-sat-
ed-gaze,
And with his old hungry longing, thinks to himself,
"My Lord Jesus Christ, true God, didst Thou who
I see,
So look, was this then Thy true semblance?"*

That which otherwise would only be seen in heaven,
the pilgrims could already see on earth, in Rome: the true
face of Christ. It so impressed them, that they made the
veil of Veronica the symbol of the Rome pilgrimages. At
that time there were already so called "Veronica painters"
who painted the veil in miniature or made reproductions
in either wax or metal as well as souvenir dealers who
sold them to the pilgrims. The pilgrims worn them on
their hats or cloaks in order to show that they had been in
Rome and had seen the likeness of Christ, which for
everyone else would be possible only in heaven.

The sacred or true image was depicted in many wood-
cuts, engravings and also in famous paintings, e.g., by El
Greco. Christ was always shown with dark medium-length
hair, small mustache and a short pointed beard, quite similar to the shroud of Turin, except that in the shroud his
eyes are closed because it shows the dead body, while in
the veil they are open, showing the living, suffering Christ.

Today during the Lenten period, the veil is still displayed from "Veronica's pier" which is one of the four
piers supporting St. Peter's dome. Under the Veronica bal-
cony or loggia stands a statue of Veronica sculpted in marble by Francesco Mochi in 1646, which depicts her as running forth, holding her veil high in order to show us
Christ's image (fig. 31).

* * *

At the same time as Constantine was engaged in
costructing St. Peter's basilica, that is to say around the

31. Statue of St. Veronica in St. Peter's. She comes rushing forth in order to show us her veil which has been impressed with Christ's image. Francesco Mochi, 1646.

year 320, he was also building St. Paul's as well. As this latter church was to stand over the actual grave of the apostle, it necessarily had to be built far from the city; the strictures of Roman law prohibiting burial within the city walls and also forbiding any subsequent removal from the chosen burial site. For this reason the church came to be called "St. Paul's outside the Walls". According to legend, both Peter and Paul had been incarcerated in the Mamertine prison, the Roman city jail located at the foot of the Capitol hill. Here, Peter converted his jailers and wished to baptize them. There not being any water in this underground vault, he struck the rock and water gushed forth. This spring still exists today and can be seen (fig. 32). When the two apostles were taken to be executed, they would have walked together for a short while along the Ostian Way passing the pyramid of Caius Cestius, but shortly afterwards they were forcibly separated. Upon the spot of their separation was erected a chapel and eventually a small church called *della Separazione* refering to the separation of the two apostles. This stood here until 1900, but today is only remembered in a bas-relief which depicts the scene of the farewell embrace on the front of the building at number 106 of Via Ostiense. Peter was then taken to the Circus of Nero on the Vatican hill and crucified there. Paul, on the other hand, as a Roman citizen, could "only" be beheaded; the legend continues by saying that he was taken further along the Ostian

32. The *Mamertine Prison*. Both apostles are said to have been fettered to this column. Water rises to the level of the opening in the floor. Tradition has it that Peter caused this water to emerge in order to baptise his prison masters.

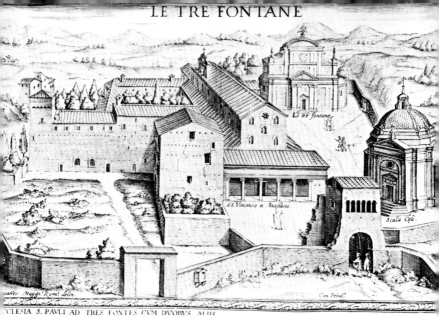

'CLESIA S. PAVLI AD TRES FONTES CVM DVOBVS ALIIS

33. *L'Abbazia delle Tre Fontane.* The abbey complex has three churches. The oldest was built on the site where St. Paul was beheaded and contains three fountains with the three springs which are said to have issued forth where the apostle's severed head touched the ground. Engraving by G. Maggi, about 1600.

Way to a point presently known as "Tre Fontane", a place kept by Trappist monks in an almost mystical silence (fig. 33). It is said that as it fell, his severed head hit the ground three different times and at these spots three springs miraculously issued forth. Upon the three springs, three fountains were built and, eventually, a church to house all three. Paul was then buried in the nearest cemetery, a pagan necropolis built in the open and near the banks of the Tiber. Remains of this cemetery can still be seen today. About a hundred years after Paul's martyrdom, a small monument was built over his grave. It most likely resembled the *aedicula* above St. Peter's tomb. About 150 years later, Constantine would build a memorial church over it; this was transformed in 390 into a grand basilica and is still today the most beautiful example of an early Christian basilica. It imparts a sense of the monumentality, the solemnity and the purity of the language of ancient architecture. The word "basilica" comes from the Greek word *basileus* or king, and the basilica was originally a royal hall or throne room. In Roman architecture all public buildings were built in the shape of a basilica, that is, a long great hall in which one could walk its length back and forth. When the Christians were finally given religious freedom they employed the basilican plan in building their churches. The greater parts of St. Paul's are, however, reconstructions that were effected after the church was almost totaly destroyed by fire in 1823; work began almost immediately to rebuild it as it had been, except that the original marble columns, which under the great heat had burnt down to lime, were substituted with fire-resistant granite.

One enters a great forecourt surrounded by a colonnade which allows the faithful either to seek the shade of the columns or the warmth of the sun (fig. 34). In place of the fountain which originally stood in the center of the court and served for the ablutions, a statue of a somewhat fierce St. Paul now stands brandishing a sword, which is his attribute and recalls his death by decapitation

The façade is covered with mosaics after the fashion of the early Christian churches even if these are nineteenth century imitations. Christ is seated on high upon a throne, while underneath stands the mystical lamb in the heavenly Jerusalem, and lower still, four prophets announce the coming of Christ. The mosaic is of the gold glass type typical of Byzantine art, used in symbolizing the glory of heaven. When the sun hits the façade, the gold shimmmers as if it were melting, while the white columns, the green palms and the azure sky together make a vivid impression of solemnity to those who are about to enter the house of the Lord. In the past, when the pilgrims, who made the journey up the Tiber by riverboat from Ostia, espied its brilliant gold façade, they knew that they were finally nearing their destination, the "golden Rome".

The main portal formerly boasted priceless bronze doors from Constantinople, the work of two artists,

73

Theodoros and Staurachios, who finished them in 1070 (fig. 35). This was exactly sixteen years after the Great Schism which still divides the Greek from the Roman Church, but in those days the Christians of East and West still considered themselves as one and worked for each other, as attested by these doors made by Greek artists for Rome and for the abbot Hildebrand, later Pope Gregory VII. These are, therefore, truly ecumenical doors. They consist of fifty-four panels with silver intarsia which show figures and episodes from both the Old and the New Testament, as well as from the lives of the apostles and martyrs. They shine as if made of antique gold, as if they were truly the "golden door" of which the medieval pilgrims gave ecstatic accounts. During the fire of 1823 the doors were severely damaged, and were not restored until the Holy Year of 1975, when they were re-employed, no longer as the main portal, but as the Holy Door of the basilica.

34. The forecourt of St. Paul's outside the Walls with colonnade, mosaic façade and statue of St. Paul. Rebuilt in the mid-19th century.

35. The *Holy Door* of *St. Paul's outside the Walls*. A Byzantine work in bronze with silver intarsia. Made in Constantinople in 1070, it was originally the main door of the basilica. Badly damaged in the fire of 1823, it is today used as the Holy Door.

Upon entering the church we are surprised how long, empty and dark it is (fig. 36), but this is the look that most Early Christian churches had. We are in a forest of eighty columns, which divide the church into five naves, the central one being higher than the side ones which are suc-

36. St. Paul's outside the Walls is a five-nave basilica with about a hundred granite columns above which run the portaits of all the popes. The triumphal arch of Galla Placidia (c. 450) frames the altar.

cessively lower. All Early Christian churches were conceived for the procession of the entire community moving towards the altar to make their offerings in *naturalia*. For this reason the central nave had to be empty, no obstacle was to be in the way of the faithful.

As most everyone knows by now, rows of papal portraits run above the columns. Originally they were painted in fresco, but they have been completely redone in mosaic and show all the popes from Peter to the present pontiff, whose portrait is always lit. There are still another twenty-eight roundels waiting to receive the images of future popes, so that, even if each one were only to reign for ten years, there will be still sufficient space for the next three centuries. The windows above are made of thin alabaster panes and allow only the subtlest of golden-yellow light to pass through. Transparent window glass was unheard of in antiquity.

76

A triumphal arch frames the altar area. Following the example of the ancient Romans who built triumphal arches to honor victors, the early Christians wanted to erect arches but in honor of the true Victor, that is Christ. These were not erected in public squares but rather in churches and were made of mosaic instead of marble. The inscription upon the arch at St. Paul's tells us that it is dedicated to the pious Empress Galla Placidia (386-450), who was most likely its donor, it is therefore of quite ancient date (even if heavily restored) and belongs to the generation immediately preceding the collapse of the Roman Empire, whose end came about when the last emperor of the West was deposed in 476. On the arch we see the same scene we find described in the fourth chapter of the Book of Revelations of John: the twenty-four elders dressed in snowy-white garb who approach Christ and hold up crowns in homage. At the top of the arch we see a bust of Christ framed within the spheres of the universe, as solemn and severe Lord of the universe, named *Pantokrator*, Lord of all things.

The altar stands alone and faces the congregation (fig. 37). In front of it is the *confessio*, a crypt similar to that in St. Peter's. A small red light constantly burns inside the altar, behind a grilled opening. Beyond this grillwork one can look down to a marble sarcophagus cover. In this sarcophagus it is believed that Constantine enclosed St. Paul's remains. To assure us, the stone bears the inscription: "To Paul, apostle and martyr". As in St. Peter's, the cover was later bored with holes to permit contact with the interior of the tomb. Rising above both altar and tomb is a splendid ciborium or tabernacle supported by four porphyry columns. The ciborium, by Arnolfo di Cambio, is made of white marble with gold mosaic decoration and is one of the few surviving works of Gothic art in Rome.

A transept lies behind the papal altar, but is not wider than the total width of the five naves, which means that in plan the transept does not extend beyond the rectangular form of the basilica. In the apse is the papal throne (a modern work) and above it a mosaic which is not as ancient as is that of the triumphal arch. It dates from the Middle Ages, to be exact, from the years 1216-27. We know this since the donor had himself portrayed small and humble at Christ's feet but with his name in large letters: *Honorius PP. III*, which proves that he donated this mosaic not only for the greater glory of God but also for his own. The mosaic is in Byzantine style, which was in vogue in Rome at that time. Christ sits in majesty upon a golden throne as *basileus*, as king, as the church is in a literal sense his basilica, his royal hall. The apostles stand on either side of Christ, as steadfast as officials had to stand at the Byzantine court. The palm trees between them symbolize the just, for the just flourish like the palms in the desert. In the lower row, standing between two angels, is a Greek cross, i.e., a cross having its four arms equal in length as opposed to the Latin cross which has a longer upright. The Greek cross is covered with gold and bestutted with gems as an emblem of Christ's victory.

We now turn our attention to the right of the papal altar. There stands the oldest, tallest and most precious paschal candlestick that exists anywhere. It is a white marble column in Romanesque style, a work of Nicola d'Angelo and Pietro Vassalletto; it depicts the Passion of Christ in a setting contemporary with the artist's own time. The soldiers wear chain mail armor which was in use in the twelfth and thirteenth century; no Roman soldier ever looked like these, but the artists certainly would not have known that. Especially noteworthy is the scene of the Crucifixion. In Early Christian art, Christ was never shown upon the cross, he was seen instead as an infant in his mother's arms, as teacher of his disciples or as the Good Shepherd. It would certainly have been abhorrent to the Christians to see their Lord and Savior suffering upon an ignominious cross. This was true in the Byzantine Church as well, where Christ was never depicted upon the cross but always in his full might and glory, as Lord of the

78

37. *St. Paul's outside the Walls.* Confessio, papal altar with ciborium by Arnolfo di Cambio and apse mosaic. The donor, Honorius III (1216-27) is kissing the foot of Christ who is enthroned as *Basileus* and surrounded by the apostles.

universe, as we have just seen in the apse of this church. Crucifixion scenes originated in the West during the Middle Ages (with some exceptional antecedents, e.g. Santa Sabina in Rome). Here on St. Paul's candlestick Christ is still standing upright on the cross without a sign of suffering. A long tunic covers him, he has neither wounds nor crown of thorns, and is almost smiling. The artist seems to have wanted to emphasize that Christ proved his divinity even upon the cross. The crosses of the two thieves stand under the outstretched arms of Christ, as if saying that Christ will save all of sinful mankind.

The Benedictines, who are the custodians of this church, live in the adjacent monastery; there is a cloister here as there is in every abbey, and it is the most beautiful in the city, a true "corner of paradise" as it is deservedly

79

38. St. Paul outside the Walls. Marble Paschal candleholder displaying Christ's Passion. Nicola d'Angelo and Pietro Vassalletto. About 1200.

39. Cloister of St. Paul's outside the Walls. Cosmatesque work. 12th-13th century.

named (fig. 39). This cloister was built in the 13th century. The small columns which run along its perimeter are in different styles and shapes. They are decorated with small mosaics which glitter and sparkle as if they were fashioned of pure gold, rubies or lapis lazuli. They are, however, made of glass paste and were fired in a kiln; being a rather inexpensive art form it found quick success in Rome. This style, developed by a family of stonecutters, named Cosma, is therefore named "Cosmatesque".

There are always roses in bloom in this "corner of paradise".

* * *

In the bull of indiction for the second Jubilee, Pope Clement VI proclaimed that in order to obtain the Jubilee indulgence it would be necessary to visit not only the two above mentioned churches of Ss. Peter and Paul, but also the church of the *Lateran*. This name comes from the site's original owners, the noble Laterani family. Their property had been confiscated by Nero. Later, Constantine gave part of this land to Pope Militiades (311-314) or perhaps to his successor, Sylvester I (314-335), for the purpose of building there the official residence of the bishops of Rome, who up until that time had lived with relatives or friends, often in hiding, in prison or in exile. Here, Constantine erected a grandiose five naved basilica (fig. 40). It was at first dedicated to the Redeemer and later re-dedicated to St. John, but is more commonly refered to as the Lateran. The name of St. John indicates both the Baptist and the Evangelist. Being the oldest church in the West and still now the cathedral church of the bishop of Rome, it is still the highest church in ranh. It stood at the center of papal life for more than a thousand years up until 1377 when the papal residence was transferred, first to Avignon and then to the Vatican. For this reason one reads the proud inscription written at both sides of the entry: *Sacrosancta Lateranensis ecclesia omnium urbis et orbis ecclesiarum mater et caput,* "This is the most holy church of the Lateran, head and mother of all churches of the city and of the whole world".

Over the high altar there were (and still are) two gilt silver reliquary busts of Peter and Paul (fig. 41). In the Middle Ages it was believed that the heads of the two main apostles were contained here. Since the importance of a church at that time depended not on the works of art but upon the relics it possessed, it was necessary either to procure or invent them. So it came to be believed that emperor Constantine had removed the heads of the two apostles from their graves and brought them here to dignify his church, since it did not stand upon the tomb of an apostle or martyr, like St. Peter's or St. Paul's. It was in fact built upon the former barracks of the imperial horse guards who had fought against Constantine; he vengefully dissolved them, razed their barracks to the ground and built the church on the site — certainly a unique location for-

40. Palace and Church of the Lateran shortly before its rebuilding. On the far left is the Sancta Sanctorum, while on the far right the baptistery can be seen. Lafrèry. Engraving. 1575.

the first and most venerable of all Christian churches! It is no longer believed that the heads of the apostles are kept here; nevertheless, there are certainly some relics which have touched their holy graves.

A wooden board is enshrined in the papal altar. This is said to have come from the house of the Roman senator Pudentius on the Esquiline hill. St. Peter is supposed to have been guest there and to have celebrated the holy eucharist on this table. It was eventually brought here so that all popes could say mass upon the same altar table that had been used by the apostle Peter himself. This was to enhance the concept of the continuity of the office of Peter.

The Lateran also houses a larger and even more important table, that is, the table of the Last Supper from Jerusalem. Held to have been rediscovered by St. Helen and brought here at her command, it is kept above the altar of the Blessed Sacrament, behind a bronze relief depicting the Last Supper. Rising mightily in front of this altar are four gilt bronze columns which originally came from the temple of Jupiter on the Capitol hill and now pay homage to the true God.

The most outstanding feature of the Lateran is the apse mosaic. High up in the vault of the apse, is visible Christ with dark medium-length hair, moustache and short pointed beard.[34] This was the first image of Christ to be seen in public and became the model for all other likenesses that followed. The Romans were so impressed by this image that they believed that Christ had actually come here in person when the church was being built and had left his facial impression upon the apse wall, just as he had done with the veil of Veronica. This can be understood if one considers the fact that before that time Christians had only been able to catch glimpses of the image of Christ in the half-light of the catacombs, in primitive, roughly executed wall paintings. Here, suddenly, they saw him against a golden background, great and powerful, solemn and severe, as Lord and judge of the universe.

This head of Christ is, as a matter of fact, much older than the mosaic beneath it, which was made at the time of the Holy Year of 1300. The date can be deduced from the name of the donor, who, as usual, had his portrait included — we see his small figure kneeling at the feet of the Madonna, who holds her hand protectively over his papal tiara. The inscription at the bottom reads: "Nicholas IV, servant of the Holy Mother of God". This pope was a Franciscan and so too was the artist of the mosaic, Jacopo Torriti. That is why we find a figure of St. Francis standing behind the pope and on the other side, standing behind St. John the Baptist, we see St. Anthony. The two figures are smaller than the others since they do not belong to the scene. To be more specific, the two saints do not figure in the repertory of the copy books of the Greek painter-monks, as they were born after the standard images in Byzantine art had long been established. In any case, Nicholas IV and Torriti both wished to include them as the two greatest saints of their religious order.

41. Interior of the Church of the Lateran. The high altar contains busts of Peter and Paul. The apse displays the oldest mosaic image of Christ (4th century), beneath which is the glorification of the Cross with the donor, Nicholas IV (1288-92), at the Madonna's feet.

85

In the center of the apse there is a brilliant gem-studded gilt cross, Constantine's victory cross. The emperor himself narrates how on the eve of the decisive battle with his rival, the emperor Maxentius, he had seen a cross appear in the sky and heard a voice which said: "In this sign thou shalt conquer!" We have already mentioned this in chapter four, but it is good to remember it: Constantine's victory took place in the year 312, on the 28th of October near the Milvian bridge north of Rome; he then granted the Christians religious freedom and built this first church in a gesture of thanksgiving. Four rivers spring forth from the cross; they are the four rivers of Paradise, which two deer drink from. They represent the man's soul which yearns for God just as deer yearn for running streams (Ps 42).

In the Holy Year of 1350 the church of the Lateran was in a state of neglect and disrepair; the papal palace had been sacked on various occasions during the long absence of its rightful inhabitants and an earthquake in 1349 completed the damage. Despite its sorry condition, Pope Clement VI prescribed visiting the Lateran as well as the two formerly mentioned churches in order to obtain the Jubilee indulgence. He justified this decree with the necessity of venerating the image of the Redeemer and Constantine's baptistery as well. This last was the first baptistery in the Western world; as long as the Christians had lived under the persecutions they could build neither churches nor baptisteries. The baptismal font is wide and deep enough to allow waist high immersion and to be walked through as was the practice in the first centuries. The circular basin is surmounted by two tiers of columns; the lower ones are of solid porphyry and the upper ones in fine white marble. Pope Clement VI believed like all of his contemporaries that Constantine himself had been baptized in this font. Only today do we know that in order to go straight to heaven, the emperor waited to receive the sacrament of baptism until he was on his deathbed and no longer able to sin.

One portal in this octagonal baptistery is known as the "singing doors", because when they are opened or closed, they emit notes of the musical scale.

42. The *Baptistry of the Lateran* with its great circular font
which allowed those to be baptized to stand in the water. Reputed to have been built by Constantine.

They sound like the sighs and moans of antiquity longing
for the waters of rebirth. As a matter of fact, the doors
originally came from the pagan baths of Caracalla. Their
being incorporated into the first Christian baptistery is,
therefore, highly symbolic.

Equally famous as the baptistery was the former private chapel of the popes which had earned the title of
Sancta Sanctorum, the most holy chapel, on account of
the great store of relics which was kept there (fig. 43). It
had been renovated by Nicholas III (1277-80) and embellished with porphyry columns, cosmatesque mosaics and
important frescoes. The very ancient and most revered image of Christ upon the altar, is considered an *acheropita*,
i.e., an image painted not by human hands, but by angels.
The inscription above the altar proudly proclaims: *"Non est
in toto sanctior orbe locus"* (There is no holier place in the
world than this). This is justified by the fact that it is the
oldest papal chapel and contained the greatest number of

87

43. The *Sancta Sanctorum*, the popes' private chapel in the Lateran, decorated with mosaics and frescoes of the 13th century. The Byzantine image of Christ over the altar is called *acheropita*, i.e. painted by no human hand.

relics. It is laden with a particularly mystical air; a "small place filled with heavenly graces", as earlier quoted in Petrarch.

One comes to the *Sancta Sanctorum* by means of the *Scala Santa* or Holy Stair (fig. 44). It was brought to this spot in 1589 when Sixtus V had the ancient papal palace demolished and replaced with a new one. The twenty-eight marble steps are covered with wood for protection. Legend has it that the stair was originally part of Pilate's court of justice in Jerusalem and that it was walked upon by Christ in the course of his passion: once at his trial, then when he was led out to be scourged and finally when he was taken away to be crucified. They were believed to have been brought from Jerusalem and installed in the Lateran palace by St. Helen. In the course of time, the Romans started to ascend them upon their knees out of reverence for Christ's Passion.

Eventually it was altogether prohibited to mount the steps on foot, this being looked upon as disrespectful. It was only permitted to go up them on bended knee, praying as one contemplated Christ's suffering. A plenary indulgence was also attached to this pious practice. There are two modern staircases on either side which allow one to descent. Even if we can never ascertain that Christ actually walked upon these steps, they are in any case a reminder of the suffering of Christ, and for this reason the pilgrims, still today, climb up them on their knees.

* * *

For the third Holy Year a visit to yet another church was added to the pilgrims' list of required churches: *Santa Maria*

44. The *Scala Santa* or Holy Stair in the Lateran. It is said to have come from Pilate's court in Jersusalem and that Christ ascended it during his trial. Even today the faithful climb it on their knees out of reverance for Christ's Passion.

Maggiore, St. Mary Major (fig. 45). It had been founded by Pope Liberius (352-366) upon the site of an ancient market-place, the *mercatus Liviae*. The legend went that the Blessed Virgin had appeared in a dream to both Pope Liberius and the patrician John and told them that she wanted a church built in her honor on the site where snow would fall that night. In fact, the legend assures us that on the next day there was snow upon the Esquiline hill, the highest of the seven hills of ancient Rome. This was said to have taken place on the 5th of August 352 (or 358). If it was not actually snow, it might possibly have been hail, which even in the hottest month of Roman summer is entirely possible. The Pope went up to this spot and drew the outline of the church in the snow, therefore, the feast of Our Lady of the Snows was introduced and is still celebrated every 5th of August in the whole Catholic world. To commemorate the miracle of the snows on this feast day, during high mass, a snowfall of white flower petals issues from the roof, both inside as well as outside the basilica. The original edifice built by Liberius was demolished less than a hundred years after its construction, in order to make way for an even bigger and more beautiful church: St. Mary Major, the greatest of the Marian churches.

It is indeed the first and most ancient church to be dedicated to the Vergin and was built at the time of the Council of Ephesus in the year 431. The council had proclaimed the dogma of "Mary, Mother of God". This was to emphasize the divine nature of Christ. Consequently, Mary had not only given birth to Christ the man, but also to the Son of God. In reality, the dogma was more concerned with Christ than with Mary, but naturally some of the glory of the Son of God fell upon His Mother, and enlarged devotion to Mary and in turn inspired Marian art. St. Mary Major was built, as we can read in the dedicatory inscription upon the triumphal arch, by "Bishop Sixtus for the people of God". This was Sixtus III (reigned 432-440). If it was not this pope who initiated construction, it was at least finished and adorned with mosaics by him. His words "for the people of God", again serve to remind us that Christians form the people of God who are on their way to the heavenly Jerusalem, as is depicted figuratively upon the triumphal arch.

Naturally, the late Baroque façade did not yet exist, but was added in the 18th century and hides almost completely the Byzantine mosaics of Christ seated in glory upon his heavenly throne. There was not as yet the marvelously curved apse, nor the two domed lateral chapels, nor the gilt coffered ceiling which was completed for the Holy Year of 1500; but the Romanesque campanile had already been built and is still the highest in Rome. The church interior already looked as it does today (fig. 46): a three naved basilica with thirty-six white Ionic columns. Over these runs a mosaic frieze with grapevines upon a golden background. Still higher are the original ancient mosaic panels which depict, on the lefthand side as one enters, the lives of Abraham and Isaac, and on the righthand side the stories of Moses and Joshua. In the beginning the basilica must have been flooded with light as the clerestory windows were placed one next to another, but today every other one is bricked up, so that it is hard

45. *St. Mary Major* as it looked in 1600 with its Romanesque bell tower and early Baroque domes, but still without its late Baroque façade (see fig. 127). G. Maggi, Copperplate, 1600.

to make out the mosaic pictures. The splendid baldachin over the high altar obstructs our view of the triumphal arch and the apse mosaic. Beneath the altar, in a niche, is a reliquary case which contains some pieces of wood. These are said to be what remains of the manger that held the infant Jesus in the stable in Bethlehem. Who found them and brought them here is not known, but due to their presence the sculptor Arnolfo di Cambio in 1300 created a beautiful group of figures for a nativity scene which can be seen beneath the altar of the chapel of the Blessed Sacrament on the right side of the nave.

Let us look up above the high altar and see the triumphal arch that Sixtus III had decorated with mosaics depicting the infancy of Christ. Starting up left is the scene of the annunciation with not just one but six angels around Mary and Joseph, who is included in the scene, which is quite noteworthy. Mary is dressed as a princess and sits in front of her house which is securely locked up, symbolic of her virginity. The house of St. Joseph is instead opened up, as it was believed that Joseph was a widower with grown children when he married Mary at the order of the high priest. The middle level shows the three Magi standing before the throne of the infant Jesus, while Mary in golden attire sits on the left. But who can the female figure be who is dressed in mourning and sits on the right side next to the throne? It is most likely Rachel, the mother of Israel, who (as it is written in Mt 2:18) weeps for her innocent children massacred in Bethlehem on the orders of Herod, a scene which is depicted upon the third and lowest level. At the base of the arch six lambs move towards the golden gates of the heavenly Jerusalem, representing the people of God moving towards their eternal goal. On the right side of the arch, starting at the top are the stories of the Presentation in the temple, the Flight into Egypt and the Magi before Herod. Six lambs also stand upon this side and together with the other six make up the holy number of twelve. All of the mosaics are original and were executed about one generation before the fall of the Roman Empire in 476, and are most miraculously preserved.

46. *St. Mary Major,* a fifth century three-nave basilica. The mosaics along the sidewalls and on the triumphal arch are contemporary with its construction. The coffered ceiling was commissioned by Alexander VI for the Holy Year of 1500.

The apse mosaics are not quiete as old but date from the Middle Ages and were realized during the pontificate of Nicholas IV (1288-92), whose captioned figure is kneeling in the garden of paradise. Therefore, it was made a few years before the first Holy Year. The artist, Jacopo Torriti, also depicted himself in the mosaic. We have already encountered both of them in the Lateran's apse mosaic. As fitting for the first church dedicated to Mary, the apse is decorated with stories of her life. The most important scene is the one in the center (fig. 47). This shows Mary laid out on her deathbed with the apostles bent over her with sorrow; an angel too, is drying its tears. In art this scene is called *dormitio* (sleep) or *transitus* (passing), because Mary is not truly dead. Christ in his almond-shaped nimbus appears from behind the bier and takes his mother into heaven. The scene is the reverse of the

93

norm; it is not Mary carrying the Christ child in her arms but rather the son who now carries his mother in his arms as if she were a little child. Yet a closer look tells us that this figure is of an old woman wrapped in a funeral shroud, not a baby in swaddling clothes. Here we see a representation of the doctrine of Mary's bodily Assumption into heaven, even though it did not become dogma until the Holy Year of 1950. The mosaic is proof that in Rome this doctrine was already held at that time. We also see that Mary did not "ascend" into heaven like Christ but is carried up by him. In heaven she can sit with her son on the same throne but not at the center. Nor does she crown herself but is crowned by her son. The difference between human and divine beings is therefore faithfully maintained. Mary is beautifully attired, just like a Byzantine empress, no amount of adornment being good enough for her. The idea was that the Lord had chosen the most beautiful woman upon the earth to become the mother of His son. Thenceforth, Mary's heavenly coronation became the favorite theme in Marian art, a theme that did not originate in the East, but had its origins here in Rome and precisely at the time of the first Holy Year.

In St. Mary Major we have, therefore, the entire history of salvation, beginning with the Old Testament on the side clerestory walls; going on to the New Testament represented upon the triumphal arch and culminating in the apse with Mary's Assumption into heaven which signifies the promise and expectation of the resurrection of all mankind.

Before leaving the church let us stop to look at the last chapel on the lefthand side. It is the Borghese chapel, named after Pope Paul V Borghese who had it commissioned. Here, upon the altar we find the most beloved of the miraculous images in the city, venerated as the *Salus Populi Romani*, the salvation of the Roman people (fig. 48). It is obvious that it is an icon in Byzantine style. The Romans attributed its authorship to St. Luke as he was believed to have been not only an evangelist and physician but a painter as well; for this reason he is the patron saint

94

47. *St. Mary Major.* The apse mosaic is by J. Torriti (about 1290) and illustrates the life of the Virgin. On the lower border Mary is seen lying on a bier while behind it Christ carries his mother into heaven where he crowns her as Queen of Heaven.

of painters. It was even said that Mary herself had posed for the original painting that was venerated in Byzantium, and that this one and another six in Rome were copies and re-tracings of that original. This miraculous image was always a pilgrim attraction and on special occasions is still carried in processions through the city. It used to be tradition to have two processions starting at the same time: one from the Lateran with the image of the Redeemer and the other from St. Mary Major with the miraculous icon of the Madonna. When they met, the two images bowed devotedly to each other, then they were put together as if to give each other a kiss and after having bowed a second time they returned to their respective churches.

Henceforth it was obligatory to visit four churches in order to obtain the Jubilee indulgence: St. Peter's, St. Paul's, the Lateran and St. Mary Major. They are called the four "patriarchal" basilicas, and belong to the Holy See. From the year 1500 onwards they each have a Holy Door, which we are going to talk about in greater detail later on.

48. The miraculous image of the *Salus Populi Romani* in St.
Mary Major. It was said to have been painted by St. Luke.

VI

The Holy Years
of the Late Middle Ages
1390 - 1400 - 1423

The first two jubilees were a great experience for all peoples of the Christian Western World. They had been wrought with a strong bond of unity. This cannot, however, be said for the two jubilees that followed, overcast as they were by the shadow of the Great Schism of the West.

To be sure, the papacy had finally returned to Rome in 1377 with Gergory XI but then he died the following year. His successor was Urban VI (1378-89), a Neopolitan whose harshness and temper quickly made him unpopular, so that the francophile cardinals elected an antipope, Robert of Geneva, and together with him returned to Avignon. This brought about the Great Schism of the West which was to last thirty-nine years and produced six antipopes. Urban VI wanted at least to gain the favor of the Romans and decided therefore to celebrate a Holy Year, which had proved to be a good way of combining spiritual with worldy gain. In 1389 he determined that the Holy Year should be celebrated every thirty-three years, taking as a measure of interval the presumed number of years that Christ had lived on earth. According to this, the year 1383 should have been a Holy Year, but as it was already past he decided to make up for it by holding a Jubilee in 1390. He fell short of his calculations, however, as he died before the opening of the Holy Year, and it was for his successor, Boniface IX Tomacelli (1389-1404) to take charge of. The new pope was a Neopolitan as well but shrewder and more prudent than his predecessor. He wanted to emulate Boniface VIII, the pope who had reigned during the first Holy Year, and therefore took the same name. The Holy Year for this pope signified a wonderful chance to reap profit and prestige, which in that moment were both sorely lacking. This Holy Year turned out, however, to be a fiasco as it attracted only pilgrims from those countries who backed the Roman pontiff, i.e. Germany, Hungary, Bohemia, Poland and England. The antipope in Avignon, Clement VII, forbade his followers to journey to Rome. The Schism continued therefore to divide Christians of the entire Western World.

* * *

Ten years later Boniface IX celebrated yet another Holy Year in compliance with the directive of his predecessor and namesake, Boniface VIII, who had prescribed back in 1300 that a Holy Year was to be celebrated at the turn of every century. Apart from this, he also wanted to attract pilgrims from the countries that had sided with the Avignon pope and had not come to Rome in 1390. There was by this time a religious unrest akin to that of a hundred years earlier. Penitents and flagellants and religious fanatics, beggars and nobility all left southern France and swarmed towards Rome. Having donned a white cowl, they went around shouting out: "Peace and mercy", whipping themselves until they were bleeding. This procession of *bianchi* ("whites" - so called from their white habits) awoke amazement and fear wherever it went, since it was accompanied by mystical prophecies and odd miracles. It had started as a movement of peace and reconciliation, freeing prisoners and placating the enemy. When they arrived in Rome it is estimated that they were 120,000 men strong. They were said to have a secret book in their possession that could only be opened in St. Peter's. In it was written who the rightful pope was and who the next pope would be; this we learn from the Roman agent of the

99

49. The procession of the *bianchi* in 1400. Dressed in whilte robes, they are seen flagelating themselves as they enter Rome's city gate. Illustration by G. Sercambi from his book *Chroniche* published in 1420.

"Merchant of Prato" Francesco di Marco Datini. The Pope, both hesitant yet at the same time moved, gave them his blessing, granted them the "great pardon" and showed them Veronica's veil.

Also of interest is another letter from the Datini archives. A friend in Rome wrote him: "For this pardon of the Holy Year come countless numbers of people and of every ten of them, nine are French".[35] Here for the first time we find the Italian term *Anno Santo*, "Holy Year". From this point it would gain currency, although the original names of "Jubilee" and "Jubilee Year" would still remain in use.

Giovanni Sercambi (1348-1424) of Lucca, published a universal history entitled *Chroniche*, which contained small, cartoon-like illustrations. In one of these we can see the *bianchi* with their images and crosses, whips snapping in the air above their shoulders, entering the city gates of Rome (fig. 49). He notes, "Thus, it can be said that everyone eveywhere was moved by them".[36] The Black Death, however, which was always lurking wherever masses congregated, suddenly broke out in their ranks, and the lack of hygienic care brought about their total demise.

Many historians are still at odds as to whether the year 1400 can be truly counted as a Holy Year, since a bull of convocation is totally lacking. In the chronicles and in the "General Prospects" of the Holy Years we find no mention of it until the last century. There are however, two documents in the Vatican archives which are dated the 14th and 15th of March 1400 and speak of this "jubilee year".[37] In a pontifical brief, Boniface IX proclaimed that the alms given by the pilgrims be put at the disposal of the Apostolic Chamber, and in another brief he condemns both Nicol' and Giovanni Colonna for having made the streets unsafe and for attacking pilgrims, robbing and even killing them. Just how much the city was afflicted by the feuding of the noble families Colonna and Orsini can be seen in the Chroniche by Sercambi, already cited: "It can be said that whoever comes to Rome comes into wild woods... there is no justice, no common sense, no love nor peace".[38] Sercambi deplored as well the fact that there were fewer Italians than there were foreigners who came for the "perdono", the great pardon. There was, however, good reason for this: the Italians had already celebrated a jubilee ten years earlier and adhered to the dictates of Urban VI, according to wich the Holy Year was to be celebrated only every 33 years.

Although passports were not necessary, those who could brought credentials given to them by their home parish or where possible from their bishop or a letter of safe-conduct from their municipality. These letters were of value in case of emergency, for example, in arranging the freeing of kidnapped pilgrims. It was also possible to make a pilgrimage by proxy. If a wealthy man was indiposed by either illness or approaching death and wished nevertheless to keep a pilgrimage vow, he could "rent" a pilgrim. He would pay someone, who on his own would never have been able to afford such a journey, to go on his behalf to Rome or to some other sanctuary. It was also possible to bequeathe money in a will to defray the cost of pilgrimages for other

50. The *Roman Forum*, once the center of the ancient world. In the middle ages it was reduced to a cow pasture, as can be seen in this print by G. Vasi (1750).

persons. To the Christians of this era, who considered themselves to be part of the mystical body of Christ and believed in the communion of saints, in heaven as on earth, the idea of substituting one Christian for another to make a pilgrimage was easily arrived at.

Needless to say, there were a good share of adventurers and vagabonds in these numbers. They followed the slogans: "Pilgrimages set you free" and "Pilgrimages know no bounds". Nevertheless, the true motivation remained a religious one.

* * *

Martin V (1417-31), who had been elected pope at the Council of Constance, found a city in shambles. Added to the ruins of antiquity, there were the ruins from the Middle Ages. The *Forum Romanum*, once the center of the ancient world, had become a cattle market (fig. 50). The Romans had aptly named it *Campo Vaccino* or cow pasture. At the edge of the Forum and next to the arch of Titus, stood and still stands the church of *Santa Maria Nova* which is now named *Santa Francesca Romana* (fig. 51). Every Holy Year has its saints. What would a Holy Year be without saints? It would be a contradiction in terms. Francesca Romana (1384-1440) was the saint of the Holy Year of 1423, just as Bridget had been of the Holy Year of 1350. She was a wealthy and prominent widow. She founded, right in the midst of the Forum's ruins, a convent for women who were called "Oblates". Her body is preserved in the church which bears her name and can still be seen in a glass casket in the crypt. Standing above this, in the *confessio*, is a statue of the saint by Giosuè Meli, sculpted in 1866. An angel kneels before her as it is said that she was blessed with the constant vision of her guardian angel, that is why she has been named patron saint for Roman motorists. On her feast day, the 9th of March, a public blessing of motor vehicles takes place outside her church. The church also possesses the oldest known icon of Mary; it is painted on canvas and is in all

51. The *Roman Forum* as it appears today. In the foreground is the house of the Vestal Virgins. In the background, the Basilica of Maxentius and Constantine. On the right is the white façade of *Santa Francesca Romana*.

probability a work of the fifth century. The Madonna's sad dark eyes seem to have witnessed the decline and fall of the ancient world.

Martin V started to eliminate the autonomous but inefficient city administration. After the last uprising of the Roman populace in 1434 the popes would become the temporal rulers or Rome until 1870. Martin V also thought of ways to bring new luster to the delapidated city and remembered the decree of Urban VI which had stated that a Holy Year was to be celebrated every thirty-three years. The last Holy Year had been in 1390, and by simply not counting the Holy Year of 1400 this would make a Jubilee Year due in 1423. The opportunity was by far too good to be passed over. There exists, however, no bull of indiction and nor firsthand written accounts of this Holy Year. Participation was very low, the times being too unstable.

Some modern writers of history erroneously persist in setting this Holy Year in 1425. They unwittingly fall into the trap of applying to those times the present scheme of twenty-five year intervals between the jubilees. This system was not as yet in use; the thirty-three year cycle still being in effect. In the "General View of the Holy Year", the date 1423, is clearly visible (see fig. 136). Furthermore, the papal documents speak quite clearly as well.[39] Martin V conferred upon the duke of Lithuania and his councilors in 1423 *praesenti anno Jubilaei*, (in the present jubilee year), the privilege of enjoying the jubilee-indulgence in their homeland. In another letter, he instructed his two nuncios in England to reprimand the archbishop and chapter of Canturbury for having imitated the pope in declaring a jubilee for all those who would come to their cathedral in England. Obviously, this was an exclusively papal prerogative.

Martin V holds a place of honor in the Church of the Lateran. His grave lies in the *Confessio* in front of the high altar (fig. 52). Upon the bronze plaque that covers his tomb is written that he was "the happiness of his time"

52. Bronze funeral monument of Martin V (died 1431) in front of the high altar in the Lateran church.

(*temporum suorum felicitas*). The old custom of tossing a coin upon tombs is still practiced here by those visitors who wish to leave a small token for the church.

Unfortunately, the Holy Year of 1423 did not bring about the desired effect; instead of promoting goodwill, it aroused a mutual animosity between the Romans, who lamented the general disorder and unrest caused by the *romei*, and the pilgrims who complained about bad treatment and the excessively high prices everywhere. This distrust and antipathy grew worse over the years and eventually would constitute two of the many factors that contributed to the outbreak of the Reformation.

VII

The Holy Year
in the Early Renaissance
1450 - 1475

Mid-15th century Florence saw the begining of a new cultural movement which came to be known as the Renaissance, which literally means "rebirth", rebirth of antiquity. With the rediscovery of ancient manuscripts and classical statuary, Greek philosophers and Latin writers, the enthusiasm for antiquity was such as to wish to bring that age to life again. The humanists, the learned men of the time, sought to combine Christianity with antiquity, learning with religious devotion and the love of God with the love of life and beauty.

Under *Nicholas V* Parentucelli (1447-55) the Renaissance came to Rome and made conquest of the papal throne. After the abdication in 1439 of Felix V (the last antipope in history), the legitimacy of the Roman pontiff was universally recognized. Nicholas was a man without "a coat of arms", i.e. a man of the bourgeoisie. His father had been a doctor. He had done his studies in Florence, the cradle of the Renaissance, and combined his love of books with a passion for building and was the first humanist to ascend the papal throne. Very quickly he began to transform the Vatican, which until that time was nothing more than a dreary fortress, into a colorful Renaissance palace. The artist-friar Fra Giovanni da Fiesole, better

53. Nicholas V as Pope Sixtus II entrusting St. Lawrence with the chalice and the treasures of the Church. Fresco by Fra Angelico in the Chapel of Nicholas V, Vatican.

known as Fra Angelico, since he lived and painted angelically, embellished the walls of the papal residence with colors both bright and unusual. In the Pope's private chapel he painted the Pope in the act of entrusting the deacon Lawrence with the chalice and the treasures of the Church (fig. 53).

Nicholas, together with the great architect Leon Battista Alberti (1404-72), began planning the complete refurbishing and rebuilding of the city: "in order to raise the prestige of the Holy See", as he declared. A Holy Year was again due in 1450. The pope, a good Latinist, drew up the bull of indiction by himself. He made provisions that the pilgrims would be able to see the heads of Peter and Paul in the Lateran on Saturdays and the veil of Veronica on Sundays in St. Peter's. It was he who started the traditional papal blessing still given in St. Peter's

Square on Sundays and feast days. The throng of pilgrims was so great that St. Peter's Square which, far from being the spacious oval shape that it is today, was incapable of holding all of them. An eyewitness, Paolo dello Mastro, tells us that the pilgrims stood upon "Nero's hill and in the vineyards", in order to get a glimpse of the Pope.[40]

When on the evening of December 19th, the papal blessing was not given owing to the late hour, the crowds of disappointed pilgrims began to swarm back into town over the narrow Sant'Angelo bridge, where they ran into a horde that was rushing towards St. Peter's, intent upon attaining the papal blessing. In this press some horses took fright and in the ensuing fracas 170 people lost their lives. After this tragedy, the access to the bridge was widened and the triumphal arch of the emperors Gratian, Valentinian and Theodosius, the ancient church of Saints Celsius and Julian and the many shops upon the bridge itself were all torn down.

This year saw the birth of the custom of holding canonizations and beatifications during a Jubilee Year. Three thousand Franciscans came to Rome to attend the canonization of Bernardine of Siena. Among them were three future saints: John of Capestrano, James della Marca and Diego of Alcalá.

The Pope stationed a militia along the pilgrims' route to make it safer and set up what could be called information stands in the most trafficked areas. Every home was turned into a boarding house yet there was still not enough space. Bread was in short supply and then the plague broke out. The Romans fled the city as did the Pope himself. In order to make it easier on the pilgrims, only a five day stay was now required to obtain the indulgence. Cosimo de' Medici was papal banker at the time. Being a shrewd businessman he had commemorative gold coins minted that the pilgrims bought as souvenirs. Many other moneychangers set up their *banchi* along the street that led to the Sant'Angelo bridge, thus it became the business district of Rome. A great amount of the money that flowed into the papal coffers was earmarked for sending buyers abroad to locate and aquire Greek and Latin manuscripts for the papal library.

The pilgrims who now came to Rome were no longer just simple country folk; there were also those educated in the humanities who combined sincere religious motivation with a love of learning. *Giovanni Rucellai*, a wealthy Florentine cloth merchant and humanist as well, was perhaps the best example of this type of pilgrim. He came to Rome with his brother and son-in-law and kept a diary in which he reports how they visited the important churches in the mornings, the ancient monuments in the afternoon and spent the evenings making notes of the day's events.

Certainly the most distinguished figure after the Pope during this Holy Year was *Nicholas of Cusa*, from Kues on the Mosel, also known as Nicolaus Cusanus (1401-64). He had already played a role at the Council of Basel as advocate of the idea of the supremacy of councils over popes. Later he became a zealous defender of the Pope who sent him to Constantinople to bring about the union of the Greek-Orthodox with the Roman Church. He was raised to the cardinalate and made bishop of Brixen. Like the pope, he was a man from a bourgeois background. When with his new office he needed a coat of arms, he chose the sign of a red crab, because "Krebs", (i.e. crab) was his family name. He was a true Renaissance man gifted with a universal mind; and great scholar of Greek and Roman antiquity; and equally well-versed in theology, philosophy and the newly born natural sciences. He himself personified the *docta ignorantia* (learned ignorance) and the *coincidentia oppositorum* (coincidence of opposites) which were terms coined by him in his writings. With his treatise *De Pace fidei* (On the peace in faith), he can be considered a precursor of modern ecumenism.

What Cusanus did for the Holy Year in Rome or during that time is not known. We do know, however, that he was in the Roman countryside busying himself with his studies, and that in November he celebrated holy Mass upon the papal altar in St. Mary Major. His most important commission came on the last day of the year, December

31, 1450, when he was sent to Germany as papal legate in order to bring the Jubilee indulgence to all those who were unable to make the journey to Rome. Up to that time, this privilege had only been extended to certain individuals in the past, as can be surmised from various papal briefs; e.g. to Konrad Rok of Vienna and his wife Dorothea, in 1390. In this case a large sum of money equivalent to the cost of a pilgrimage to Rome had to be put towards good works such as the construction of churches and hospitals, campaigns against the Turks or simply devolved to the papal treasury. From then on it became customary to extend the Holy Year to other nations in the year following the Roman Holy Year. Cusanus traveled all over Gemany for the entire year preaching, instructing, settling disputes and checking ecclesiastical abuses. In response to a query to whether a monk could make a pilgrimage to Rome without the consent of his superior, he gave the classic reply: "*Melior est oboedientia quam indulgentia*" ("Obedience is better than indulgence").[41]

Nicholas Cusanus died while travelling to Todi in 1464 and was intered in his titular church *San Pietro in Vincoli* (St. Peter in Chains) in Rome. Every cardinal "possesses" a church in Rome and bears the name of this church in his title (hence the terms "cardinal titular" and "titular church"). As "possessor" of a church he is incorporated in the diocese of Rome and as such has the right to be buried in his church. The name "St. Peter in Chains" refers to the two chains on view in this church with which St. Peter is said to have been fettered while imprisoned. One chain comes from the jail in Jerusalem and the other from the Mamertine prison in Rome. On his funeral monument by Andrea Bregno, Cusanus has been portrayed kneeling humbly before St. Peter who is holding his chains (fig. 54). Underneath is his cardinal's hat and his coat of arms with the crab device. Next to it is his marble gravestone upon which his distinctive face appears once more. His hands extend beyond the frame around his effigy as if he wished to reach beyond his time, which he has in fact done. Although his mortal remains repose here, his heart,

54. Tombstone and monument of *Cardinal Nicholas Cusanus* (died 1464) in his titular church of *San Pietro in Vincoli*. Beneath his cardinal's hat is his heraldic device, the crab, from his name Krebs ("crab"). Relief, possibly by Andrea Bregno (1418-1503).

according to his wishes, is kept in the church of the Cusanus Hospital which he founded in his native Kues.

* * *

Pope Paul II Barbo (1474-71), a Venetian, is known to most visitors to Rome as the builder of *Palazzo Venezia* which gives its name to Piazza Venezia, the square which is the center of Rome (fig. 55). He is important to our study as he issued the bull *Ineffabilis Providentia* which stipulated that all Holy Years would be celebrated at twenty-five year intervals, starting with the year 1475. Originally, as will be remembered, it was only to be once a century, then every fifty years, with the intervals being reduced later to thirty-three years and finally to twenty-five. The reason Paul II gave was "the shortness of human existence" and "to allow each generation in its lifetime of obtaining the Jubilee indulgence". The motivation behind all of this was, however, the Pope's personal desire to celebrate a Holy Year during his pontificate. Ironically, the pontiff died suddenly, leaving his successor to harvest what he had sown for himself, the Holy Year. This had already happened to Urban VI who did not live to see the Holy Year of 1390 proclaimed by him. Now with Paul's II death the honor fell to *Sixtus IV* della Rovere (1471-84). He came from Savona and of humble background, but due to his erudition and great religious devotion he rose from general of the Franciscan order to cardinal and finally to pope. With Nicholas V he shared a passion for building and the love of books. In *Melozzo da Forli's* famous fresco, we see Sixtus IV appointing the humanist

55. *Palazzo Venezia* built by the Venetian Pope Paul II (1464-71) as his residence in Rome. From there he proclaimed that the Holy Years were to be celebrated every 25 years.

56. *Sixtus IV* appointing the humanist Platina as head of the Vatican Library. Between them stands the pope's nephew, Cardinal Giuliano della Rovere, the future Pope Julius II. Fresco by Melozzo da Forlì. 1477. In the Vatican Pinacoteca.

Platina as prefect of the Vatican Library founded by the Pope (fig. 56). The person standing proudly before the Pope is his nephew Giuliano della Rovere, the furture Pope Julius II.

Every visitor to Rome has heard of Sixtus IV as he gives his name to the *Sistine Chapel* which he built in 1473 as chapel of the papal court. Let us admire it for at least a little while (fig. 57). The entire history of mankind is illustrated in this single space. It starts on the left side wall with the stories from the life of Moses and on the right, with scenes from the life of Christ. Not just one painter, but all the more important Renaissance painters labored here in competitive zeal, and eventually there came the greatest of all, Michelangelo, who painted on the ceiling the story of Creation. However, he "corrected" the Bible, if we may say so, in two respects. This he did by showing Adam receiving the spark of life directly from God through the touching of their fingers and not by having life breathed into him, as is told in the Bible (fig. 58).

113

Eve looks out from under the other arm of God the Father, who has laid His arm tenderly around her shoulders. Eve, however, does not gaze upon God, instead she looks away with curiosity towards her husband to be, as if she had been destinated from the very beginning just for him and is interested only in him. Adam is not as yet concious of Eve but yearns for God and life. The other "correction" is in the panel of original sin where Eve does not give Adam the forbidden fruit, rather, Adam picks it from the tree himself, which, by the way, is a fig, not an apple tree.

57. The *Sistine Chapel*, called after Pope Sixtus IV (1471-84) under who it was built. The frescoes on the ceiling illustrate the Creation, while on the left side are scenes from the life of Moses and on the right scenes from the life of Christ. The Last Judgment is depicted on the altar wall. The screen separates the space reserved for the Pope and his court from that reserved for guests. On the right wall is a *cantoria* or choir loft.

58. *Sistine Chapel.* Adam being awakened by God's touching his finger. Fresco by Michelangelo (1508-12).

Above the windows twelve mighty figures of the prophets and the sibyls indicate that all early history was to lead up to Christ's coming, not only the Hebrew prophets but the pagan sybils announce his advent as well. For the same reason, Michelangelo placed the ancestors of Christ above the windows, as they prepare the coming of Christ the Savior. Thus, the fresco cycle starts with the Creation of heaven and earth and leads us through the Old Testament, the prophets, the sybils to the ancestors of Christ, then through the New Testament until the Last Judgement: the entire history of salvation in a single glance.

The Last Judgement was painted by Michelangelo in the third period of the chapel (1534-41). It is a pictorial representation, verse by verse, of the medieval hymn or sequence, the *Dies Irae* ("Day of Wrath"). Michelangelo who had worked all alone for six years on this huge wall, felt so expended like St. Bartholomew who had been skinned alive, that he decided to paint his own portrait on the skin of the martyr. After Rome had been looted in the terrible *Sack of Rome* in 1527 and the glories of the Renaissance reduced to dust, Michelangelo hoped with this vision of the end of the world, to make man aware of his ultimate destiny exhorting him to repent and return to Christ. Yet the dark terror of the Last Judgement is transformed by the brilliant blue sky into the refulgent light of eternity, and the ressurected bodies now bask in the light of transfiguration. In the middle of this whirl of bodies Christ comes forth from his throne of clouds as the supreme judge of mankind (fig. 59). With his left hand he seems to be beckoning the resurrrected figures to him, while, with his right hand, he casts the unrepentant sinners into hell. Christ, as God made man, has a powerful muscular body to emphasize his incarnation. For the body Michelangelo took his inspiration from the Greek statue of the *Torso del Belvedere* which he used to study from all sides. The youthful face of Christ, however, with its curly hair, reminds us of the antique statue of Apollo, the Greek sun god, also standing in the Belvedere courtyard. With this, Michelangelo shows us that Christ is the true sun, the *sol invictus* of the Romans, the "sun of justice" of the Bible. The only other figure standing in his nimbus of glory is his mother. Mary stands mute at his side, in complete deference to his divine will which alone can reconcile punishment with pardon, justice with mercy and transform all into an act of love. Thus, the divine history of salvation is brought to an end.

The Sistine Chapel is still used for the election of each new pope. This election is called "conclave", from the Latin *cum* and *clavis*, meaning that the cardinals are shut up in the Vatican "under lock and key". The stove that is used to burn the ballots is not normally found here as it is installed only during conclaves. The outside world can tell by the color of the smoke that rises from the chimney, just what has been decided within. If black smoke comes out this signifies that the cardinals have not yet reached an agreement, which requires a two-third majority vote. If, however, white smoke is emitted then a new pope has been elected. "*Habemus Papam*" is then proclaimed from the main loggia on the façade of St. Peter's.

Sixtus IV was also responsible for the complete rebuilding of the *Santo Spirito* hospital, which much earlier on had been richly endowed by Cardinal Stefaneschi, who we remember from the Holy Year of 1300. Botticelli

116

59. *Sistine Chapel.* The Last Judgement. Christ in glory as judge of the universe sending the unrepentent to Hell while Mary stands by his side, in silent assent. Fresco by Michelangelo (1534-41).

60. *Sistine Chapel.* The Temptation of Christ by Botticelli, painted in 1480. In each episode the devil is dressed in Franciscan robes. The temple is the Roman hospital of *Santo Spirito* which Sixtus IV had built for ailing pilgrims and which is still in use today as a hospital.

turned it into the temple of Jerusalem when he painted the Temptation of Christ panel which faces the papal throne in the Sixtine Chapel (fig. 60). In this way the pope would have a reminder of his good deeds right before his eyes. In the same panel, Botticelli in three different places depicted the devil dressed in a Franciscan habit as if to say that the devil can even disguise himself as a monk. This was quite audacious on Botticelli's part as the Pope himself was a Franciscan, and moreover, had been general of the Franciscan order.

Sixtus IV also built the bridge named after him, *Ponte Sisto,* in order to relieve the Sant'Angelo bridge of its heavy flow of traffic. Now the pilgrims would journey to St. Peter's via the Sant'Angelo bridge and return into the city via the Ponte Sisto. The marble dedicatory plaque is still upon the bridge and states that the bridge was built, "for the use of the pilgrims of the Jubilee 1475" (fig. 61). The churches of *Santa Maria della Pace* and *Santa Maria del Popolo* were both built by this pontiff. He also had streets widened and paved; in short he ensured that the city was worthily renewed for the jubilee of 1475. As a matter of fact, Holy Years have always been a great incentive in getting the city cleaned up, improved and beautified.

A novelty in this Holy Year was that the bull of indiction was not written by hand but printed by a printing press. This new invention had been introduced in Rome by two Germans. For the duration of the Holy Year the Pope nullified all other indulgences so as not to diminish the importance of the jubilee indulgences. This practice was followed by all popes until Pope Paul VI. Monetary offerings were put towards financing the war against the Turks, the necessity of which was becoming ever more urgent.

61. *Ponte Sisto*, the bridge constructed under Sixtus IV in 1475. As the inscription confirms, it was built to carry pilgrims over the Tiber.

62. *Queen Carola of Cyprus* with her consort, Louis of Savoy, listening to the Sermon on the Mount. Fresco by C. Rosselli (1480) in the Sistine Chapel.

The guest of honor for this Holy Year was the former Queen of Cyprus, *Carola* or *Carlotta Lusignano*, who had been forced off Cyprus by her step-brother with aid of the Venetians and had found refuge in Rome. She brought an oriental allure to the papal court. We can see her in the fresco panel by *Cosimo Rosselli* in the Sistine Chapel as one of the listeners intent upon hearing the Sermon on the Mount (fig. 62). She stands out as she is dressed in regal attire and also because of the look of suffering and resignation on her face. Owing to her great devoutness and also to the large bequest she left to St. Peter's church, she was buried in 1487 in the Vatican grottoes. Leaving aside the grave of the legendary St. Petronilla (reputed to have been St. Peter's daughter), there are buried in St. Peter's, next to 147 popes, three queens, one countess and a princess. The princess is Agnesina of the noble Roman house Colonna; the countess or margravine is the famous *Matilda of Canossa*; and the three queens without lands are the just mentioned *Carola of Cyprus, Christina of Sweden* and *Maria Clementina Stuart of England*. Later on we shall get better acquainted with the last two.

VIII

Alexander VI
and the Holy Door
1500

We must dedicate an entire chapter to *Alexander VI* (1492-1503) since he did much for the Holy Year in starting the custom of opening the Holy Door at the beginning of a Jubilee Year and the closing of the door at its end.

Naturally in the first Jubilee Year there was no Holy Door, since it came into being by means of a spontaneous folk-movement to which Boniface VIII gave his blessing only subsequently and retroactively, too late, therefore, for any kind of preparation. In any event, the idea of a Holy Gate as sign and symbol were already well known to the Christians through Holy Scripture. One knew of the "gates of saving justice" of the psalmists (Ps 118:19) and the "narrow gate...", that according to the gospels of Matthew (7:13-14) and Luke (13:24 25) " ..leads to life". The Christians knew of the vision of the "gate of heaven", that Jacob had seen at the end of the ladder to heaven (Gn 28:17) and also what had been revealed to the evangelist John (Rv 3:8;4:1). However, the gate was above all a symbol of Christ himself, as he had said: "I am the gate. Anyone who enters through me will be safe" (Jn 10:9).

In the first centuries of Christianity, the gates played a special role in the liturgy and in the practice of penance. A public sinner was not allowed to pass through them. The repentant sinner, however, would be met at the portal by the bishop and then led over the threshold by him.

Later, the image of the door appeared quite often in the vision of the mystics. It is said that Pope Clement VI, who proclaimed the second Jubilee Year, twice saw a door in his dreams. An venerable elderly man holding two keys bade him: "Open the door, and a fire shall issue forth that will light and warm the world".[42] In spite of this vision Clement VI opened no holy door for the simple reason that he stayed in Avignon while the Jubilee Year took place without him. The Holy Year which followed, that of 1390 gives no mention of the existence of a special door. The first indication made is in a report to the earlier mentioned "merchant of Prato", Francesco di Marco Datini, from his agent in Rome and dated the 28th of March 1400. It reads: "A door in St. John Lateran has been opened that hasn't been opened in fifty years. Whoever goes through it three times, from one side to the other, obtains the pardon of all guilt and punishment; and it is wondrous how the people go through these doors. During the Jubilee of ten years ago, this door was not opened as the Pope didn't want it so. Therefore, if you wish to go to heaven, then come hither! Christ be with you!"[43] This letter, which is extremely important, shows us that as early as the year 1400 there was a door of special importance, at least in the Lateran, and that it can be infered that there had already been one in 1350. There is, as yet, no mention made of a papal ceremony for the opening of the door. This would be introduced only later, as we shall see, during Christmas of 1499.

A second mention is made in *Nicola della Tuccia's* chronicles of Viterbo: "Pope Martin made this the year of pardon and had the door of San Giovanni Laterano opened, and the pardon lasted for the year 1424, and many came to Rome for the pardon".[44] We read here the term *porta santa* or "holy door" for the first time. Yet, Niccola errs in citing 1424 instead of 1423. In this instance, there is a lack of accuracy as he was reporting from second-hand accounts. He was, however, present in person for the next Holy Year and wrote: "When the year 1450 came, Pope Nicholas V held the Year of Pardon...

and had the doors of all the aforesaid churches opened",[45] namely St. Peter's, St. Paul's, the Lateran and St. Mary Major. Our chronicler does not make mention of any opening ceremony of a particular door, rather he makes general reference to all doors.

Another observer present at the 1450 Jubilee was *Giovanni Rucellai*, a prosperous and well-educated merchant of Florence. We have already mentioned him, and must do so again in this connection. He came to Rome and kept a travel diary for his children. This diary is named *Lo Zibaldone* and was a mixture of facts, legends and stories of miracles, written in the style of the pilgrims' book *mirabilia urbis*, "Marvels of the City of Rome", a book which enjoyed great popularity at that time. These handwritten annotations contain an interesting paragraph dealing with the church of the Lateran: "Of these five doors, there exists one that is always sealed up, except in a jubilee year. It is unwalled at Christmas time when the jubilee year begins, and the devotion is such on the part of the people that not a brick nor a piece of plaster remains once it is unsealed, and those who come from beyond the Alps take them back home as holy relics. It is said that the figure of our Lord Jesus Christ passed through this door and went to imprint itself upon the apse of the church. Because of this devotion, all who come for the pardon pass through this doorway, which is walled up when the jubilee comes to its end. It is also said, that the palace of the emperor Constantine was on this very spot where the church now stands and that a door in this palace enjoyed such pre-eminence that whosoever had commited homicide or theft or any other dishonest thing and went through this door would be freed of his misdeeds. At the time of Pope Sylvester it was established that just as a sinner was at one time freed of his temporal misdeeds by passing through this door, now everyone would be freed of their spiritual sins by doing the same".[46] From this somewhat confused report it can at least be discerned that in popular legend there were supposed to be two

123

doors, one in the palace and the other in the church of the Lateran, and that both of them dispensed pardon.

At the same time, if not already in the preceeding year, a Swiss provost, Dr. *Felix Haemmerlin*, wrote a *Dyalogus de anno jubileo*, in which for the first time there appears the expression *porta aurea* or "golden door" which supposedly was opened every fifty years in St. Peter's and in the Lateran. The earlier mentioned Nuremberg patrician, *Nikolaus Muffel*, came to Rome in the retinue of Emperor Frederick III for the coronation of the latter in 1452. In his *Description of the City of Rome*, Muffel writes: "Going behind the altar on the right as one enters, where Veronica's veil is kept, there is a golden door through which Christ himself carried his holy cross. It is made of precious marble and was brought to Rome by Titus and Vespasian, and in the days when it was open if one who had committed murder passed through it, he would be pardoned of the sin and the crime. Later came the pope and had it walled up and said: "No one should tempt the Lord thus, for this reason it shall remain immured forever".[47]

The "golden door" Muffel makes reference to should have come directly from Jerusalem and was later walled up by order of the pope to prevent the spreading of the superstition that made it sufficient to walk through it in order to obtain pardon for ones sins. Since according to Muffel, the door had been walled up forever, it therefore could not have been opened and then shut again for the Holy Years. Muffel also reports of three sets of doors in the Lateran palace that were said to have come from Pilate's palace and that Christ had walked through. An anonymous German author published a book on Rome in 1472, entitled *In dem puechlein stet geschrieben wie Rome gepauet ward* ("In this Booklet is written how Rome was built"). It contains the same legend already found in Muffel, only much more elaborated; "At this altar (Veronica's) is the golden door which is walled up, built up and it is forbidden to open it, because at one time a certain Roman killed his father, mother, brothers and sisters so that he came to possess all of their belongings, and later went through this door and in his wickedness yelled out: 'Today God is so full of love and compassion that he must pardon me my sins.' Then a voice was heard to reply: 'Today for you and never to anyone else!' These words were heard by a cardinal who relayed this to the Holy Father, the pope. The pope thereupon had the door bricked up and placed a malediction upon whosoever should want to reopen it. The pope decided that when he died, he would be buried right before the door as sign that it should never be opened, except it be revealed by God Himself".[48]

In the Lateran there were, so stated the "Booklet", as many as three doors, and people went through all three of them in order not to miss going through the right one. If this was done in a state of sincere repentance than one was so cleansed as to be exactly like someone newly baptised. It was also possible to go through the doors to aid the departed souls.

As we have seen, in the due course of time the holy doors increased in number. From all these different quotations it is easy to discern that there were all sorts of conflicting and unclear stories about the golden or holy doors. These ideas were so beautiful and romantic, that they were constantly being elaborated and re-elaborated by the pilgrims and the Romans themselves. In truth, they were nothing more than pious legends, as we learn from Master *Johann Burckard.* Master Burckard was from Strasbourg. The present-day *Largo Argentina* (Strasbourg Place) in the center of Rome takes its name from him, as he built a house near by which is still standing there. A man of distinction, he was ambitious and wealthy as well and had bought the position of master of papal ceremonies. A diary kept by him, called the *Liber notarum,* lists in excruciating detail all the goings-on of the papal court between the years of 1483 an 1506. He too, had believed in the existence of a golden door in St Peter's that was only opened at the end of every century. As Christmas of 1499 was approaching and with it the Holy Year, Burckard suggested to the Pope that this door be opened in great pomp and ceremony. The Pope came to St. Peter's on the 18th of December and Burckard showed him where, according to the chapter of canons this immured door should have been, that is, under the portico to the extreme right, in a line with the far right-hand nave, were the Veronica chapel is. The Pope, taken by this idea, immediately gave instructions to Tommaso Mataratius, the master mason, that the immured door be freed. It appeared however: *"quod in eo loco nunquam fuit porta prius, sed murus undique altera parte ejusdem muris equalis et collegatus"*,[49] i.e. that on this spot there had never been a door, than in fact the walls were alike on both sides and neither had any opening or breach through it. The only thing that might be taken for an opening was a sort of altar niche which was, of course, that of the Veronica chapel.

As to the basilica of St. Paul's, there was even less there to be found. When the cardinal legate, who under the Pope's orders, came to open the holy door on Christmas night, neither the abbot nor the monks knew about any such door. Burckard was indignant that the monks of this abbey knew nothing about such an important matter: *"tantam rem ignorarent"*.[50] To be on the safe side, the cardinal had not just one but three walled-up doors reopened.

Alexander VI had the entrance wall of St. Peter's at the extreme right side of the portico pierced through and a door installed. He loved pomp and ceremony and took his duties as *pontifex maximus* very seriously. Together with his master of ceremonies, he planned all of the particulars of the event in advance. On the afternoon of December 24, before Vespers the Pope crowned with the tiara, had himself carried in the gestatorial chair into the portico of St. Peter's. His retinue and the gathered assembly of cardinals carried long lit candles while outside all of the church bells of Rome rang. As the choir sang the words of the psalmist (Ps 118:19-20): *Aperite mihi portas justitiae. Haec porta Domini, justi intrabunt in eam, Introibo ad domum tuam* (Open for me the gates of saving justice, this is the gate of the Lord...), the Pope rapped three or more times against the walled-up door with a hammer. He then reseated himself upon his throne under the baldachin and waited until the workers unwalled the door. At this point there was a noteworthy mishap. The Pope had given strict orders that under pain of death no one was to go through the door until he, the Pope, had. For this reason the workers worked from both inside and outside. In the excitement, however, one of the crew forgot the ban and passed over the threshold to retrieve a hammer. He was reprimanded by Burckard but it is not known if he suffered the death penalty or not.

Once the door was finally freed of wall, the Pope knelt and prayed for the length of half a *Miserere*. He then walked, braced by Burckard himself, over the threshold of the Holy Door, carrying a lighted candle in his left hand and giving his blessing with his right. At this point he should have recited the *Te Deum*, but "so great was the crush and excitement of the crowd that the Pope as well as we ourselves, quite forgot about it".[51] The prayers that followed just as those recited previously, were taken from Holy Scripture and the Hebrew jubilee year. They were personally composed by Burckard of Strasbourg, so it was his idea, but it was to the credit of Alexander VI to have introduced this beautiful ceremony into the liturgy of the Church. With this he gave that solemnity to the inauguration that had been lacking in the previous Holy Years, succeeding in combining the beauty and pageantry of papal ceremony with a profoundly religious and biblical significance. He ordered that thenceforth all Holy Years shoull begin in this way. While Alexander VI was opening the Holy Door in St. Peter's three other cardinal-legates were opening at the same moment and in the same manner a holy door in each of the other three basilicas.

For St Peter's, Alexander VI had a door made of precious marble. It was about 3.5 meters high and 2.2 meters wide (11 ft. × 7 ft.). It was later sacrificed when the church was rebuilt. A new marble door was installed in 1618 which, too, was eventually replaced by a bronze door in 1950 of which we shall speak later on. Whoever wishes to receive the grace of the Holy Year must from now on pass through this smaller door on the right end of the portico as an act of humility and penance and not go, as the tourists do, through the larger central doors. The Holy Door represents the "narrow gate" that leads to Christ and everlasting life. The Pope prescribed that the Holy Door be kept open day and night to accomodate the flow of pilgrims and that it be watched over by two members of the clergy, prohibiting beggars, the infirm and crippled to loiter before the door as they used to do in front of other churches.

News of the pontiff's initiative spread like wildfire and awoke great excitement throughout the Christian world. A chronicler from Halle wrote that the news traveled from mouth to mouth, "moving persons who otherwise would never have journeyed to Rome, to go there instead".[52]

The romanticism in the notion of a "golden door" is felt in a verse from Schiller's poem (which was set to music by Schubert) *Der Pilgrim*, who, "in the springtime of his life", set out "upon his light pilgrims' staff":

> *... till you reach a golden door,*
> *there you enter,*
> *since the profane will there*
> *divine and everlasting be.*

* * *

Instead of adhering to the order of Boniface VIII to end the Holy Year on the 24th of December in memory of Christ's nativity, it was closed this time on the 6th of January. Veronica's veil was shown once again, but instead of the Pope, two cardinals proceeeded in procession after vespers through the basilica and walled the door up, one from inside with a silvered brick and the other from outside with a gilded brick. Then they waited and prayed while the building workers walled up the door in front of

63. Two commemorative medals of the Holy Year of 1550. Both medals bear a portrait of Alexander VI on the obverse. On the reverse of one, the pontiff is seen opening the Holy Door and upon the other side sealing it up once more. Both medals were struck at the end of the 16th century by G. Palladino.

them. The cardinal legates performed the same ritual in the other three major basilicas. The Jubilee Years that followed would see the Pope himself walling up the door with three gilt bricks, a tradition which continued until 1975 when Pope Paul VI simply pulled it shut. The Pope is always the first person to pass through the portal and the last to close it, in fulfillment of the words of Isaiah (22:22): "When he opens, no one will close, when he closes, no one will open".

Two commemorative medallions of the Jubilee Year of 1500 exist (fig. 63). They show on the obverse side the rotund and unattractive profile of Alexander VI. On the reverse, one medallion shows him striking the Holy Door with the hammer, causing it to crumble, while upon the other we see how he places a brick upon the threshold to wall it up again. The medallions are, however, not authentic, that is to say, they were not struck in the year 1500 but instead much later, towards the end of the sixteenth century by the Roman designer of medals, Giovanni Paladino, as Giulio Berni has shown.[53] The first medallion to be struck contemporarily with a Holy Year was that of 1525 and was possibly designed by Valerio Belli. Upon the earlier medallions there is often a door to be seen and this has led some historians to the false conclusion that a Holy Door had already existed in the fourteenth and fifteenth centuries. Berni has, however, proved that this should not be taken as the Holy Door but rather as the door of the *Sancta Sanctorum* in the Lateran. As has been stated, it is to the great credit of Alexander VI that the opening and closing of the Holy Door was introduced as a ceremonial element of profound symbolic import. He did, however, also prescribe that adjacent to the Holy Door of St. Peter's (and most likely in the other three basilicas as well) a huge chest of solid oak be placed. This was provided with three locks, each of which had its own separate key and each key was kept by a different dignitary of the papal court as is specifically reported in Master Burckard's diary. By this method the Pope quite wisely ensured that one key would not open all three locks and that no one person would be able to open the chest without the knowledge of the other two. It now became an unwritten law that every pilgrim who stepped through the Holy Door was to leave an *obulus*, an offering, in this chest which being so large that it was impossible not to notice it. This gave rise to the false impression that one could and ought to buy the indulgence and roused the ire of the pilgrims. It was this protest that led to widespread indignation in regard to the trafficking in indulgences. This sentiment gained ground and in less than seventeen years led to Luther's famous ninety-five theses against indulgences which triggered off the Reformation.

According to an old custom, half of the alms belonged to the basilicas where they had been recieved, while the other half went to the Apostolic Chamber and were used for the needs of the Church at large, and especially for the wars against the Turks. In this year however, the greater part of this money wound up in the pockets of Cesare Borgia, the Pope's son, to finance his military ambitions.

130

* * *

Alexander VI, before becoming pope, was already the father of many children, something not unusual for the time. Nor was the fact that he brought them along with him to the Vatican and sought to procure crowns and realms for them. He was particularly fond of his delicate and beautiful blond daughter, *Lucrezia Borgia* (1480-1519), who is depicted in the *Appartamento Borgia* by Pinturicchio. Here we see her as St. Catherine of Alexandria as she defends her Christian faith before the pagan Emperor Maximian (fig. 64).

Lucrezia during her father's absence was the *custode* in charge of the Apostolic Palace and presumably was present at all celebrations. We know from Burckard that on January 1 she rode out with a great retinue in order to gain the jubilee indulgence. Her father hurried up the Castel Sant'Angelo that he might better see the procession as it passed by. A hundred horsemen rode before her, bishops and barons. On her left was her young consort, the marquess Alfonso of Bisceglie, illegitimate son of the king of Naples. The noblewomen of Rome followed accompanied by their ladies in waiting. A squadron of soldiers brought up the rear of the parade. All this, as Burckard writes: "to the praise and honor of the Holy Roman Church".[54] What he really should have said was that it was to the praise and honor of the Borgias; of penitence there is neither hint nor mention.

Not everything has been holy in the Holy Years. In the very same year and in the same *appartamento Borgia* where we admired the beautiful portrait of Lucrezia Borgia, her brother, the violent Cesare Borgia, had her second husband, the young and innocent marquess Alfonso, killed leaving Lucrezia free to make an even greater alliance, this time to the hereditary-prince and future duke Alfonso d'Este of Ferrara. In Ferrara she became very devout and was greatly loved by her husband and her people; she

131

64. *Lucrezia Borgia* as St. Catherine of Alexandria confessing her faith before the emperor Maximinian. Fresco by Pinturicchio, before 1500. In the Borgia Apartments in the Vatican.

gave birth to seven children and died in a premature child-birth in 1519 at only thirty-nine. Her second son, Ippolito d'Este, achieved fame through the building of the *Villa d'Este* at Tivoli.

The *Pietà* of Michelangelo was completed for the Holy Year of 1500 and placed in a side chapel of "old" St. Peter's (fig. 65). In the new St. Peter's church it welcomes every pilgrim as he comes through the Holy Door and beholds it there, immediately on his right. The Italian word *pietà* comes from the Latin *pietas* and means piety as well as pity, commiseration and compassion. In the history of art it denotes the portrayal of the Blessed Virgin as she mourns, holding her dead son in her arms. In beholding this image one should be moved to compassion for both mother and son; for this reason it was a favorite subject in art and devotion of the late Middle Ages. In Michelangelo's version it found its greatest expression. He was only twenty-five years old when he finished this marvelous piece. With justifiable pride he inscribed his signature upon the belt that runs over the breast of Mary. Unfortunately, the name is not easily made out, since a glass partition now separates us from the statue. This has been so ever since 1972 when on Pentecost a deranged man attacked the *Pietà* with a hammer. We can, therefore, no longer walk around the statue nor examine the face of Christ. Were this still possible, we would be able to note a contradiction: that Mary appears markedly younger than her son. She should have been about fifty years old at the time of her son's death. When criticized for this seemingly obvious error, Michelangelo was ready with a deeply theological retort. He said that he had deliberately portrayed the Vergin young and beautiful because her pureness had kept her so. This is the basic reason why, despite her age, Michelangelo portrayed the Mother of Christ as a maiden in the flower of youth, thus emphasizing her purity of heart, mind and body. The bowed head and her entire posture express loving devotion, no word of lamentation is upon her lips, no gesture of despair, not even a tear is in her eyes, for Mary knows the significance of Christ's sacrifice by his death. To fur-

133

65. Michelangelo's first Pietà and the only one brought to completion, in 1500. It was placed in a side chapel of Old St. Peter's and today is in the first righthand chapel.

ther illlustrate the bond between mother and son, the two figures are executed from the same block of the purest white Carrara marble.

Michelangelo took part in three Holy Years and, as we learn from his friend, companion and biographer, Giorgio Vasari,[55] went from church to church devoutly making his pilgrimage. We can see his portrait in

Raphael's fresco of The School of Athens in the *Stanze* of the Vatican (fig. 66). Here Raphael has represented him as the pessimist philosopher Heraclitus. Michelangelo was indeed quite melancholic, unsocial and introspective, just as he appears here. He was ugly-looking and shabby dressed, his nose broken, his eyes deep-set, his hair unkempt and he wore high boots which he left on - even while asleep. Here Raphael has captured his great rival perfectly. Raphael himself was the exact opposite: young, handsome, joyful and charming, but he died prematurely at the age of thirty-seven, while Michelangelo lived to be nearly ninety.

In 1500 the building of the German Nationals' Church, *S. Maria dell'Anima,* was begun under the supervision of Master Burckard, and a solemn *Te Deum* was held to celebrate the birth of the Hapsburg prince Charles, the future emperor Charles V, "upon whose empire the sun never set". The church is built in the form of a German hall church,

66. Michelangelo depicted as the philosopher Heraclitus in Raphael's fresco *The School of Athens.* Stanza della Segnatura. Vatican.

135

67. German nationals' church *Santa Maria dell'Anima*. The fanciful spire is said to be by Bramante. Watercolor by E. Roesler-Franz from his series of scenes of "Vanished Rome", painted between 1870-1880. Museo di Roma.

with its original bell-tower covered with yellow, green and blue glazed roof-tiles and spire surmounted by the Hapsburg double-eagle (fig. 67). The church possesses a beautiful altar painting by Giulio Romano (1520-21) showing the Holy Family with the donors, two brothers of the banking family Fugger; one of whom had himself portrayed as a pilgrim.

On the righthand side of the prebytery is the tomb of the infelicitous Pope Hadrian VI (1521-23). He came from Utrecht in the Low Countries, was extremely pious, erudite and of great austerity. He advocated the Church's reform *in capite et in membris* ("from its head to all its members"), but he found no support for his cause. This is why his epitaph laments: "Alas, how much depends on the times into which the life of even the most worthy of men chances to fall" (fig. 68).

Little by little, each of the great nations came to have a nationals' church. The Spanish church, *San Giacomo degli Spagnoli*, is in the immediate vicinity of the Piazza Navona. Building had gotten under way during the Holy

68. *Santa Maria dell'Anima* church with its altarpiece of the Holy Family by Giulio Romano and the tomb of Hadrian VI of Utrecht (died 1523) designed by B. Peruzzi.

Year of 1450, but was only brought to completion under Alexander VI. The French nationals' church, *San Luigi dei Francesi*, was founded shortly afterwards, in 1518, by Cardinal Giulio de' Medici (the future Pope Clement VII) who would reign during the following Holy Year of which we are now going to speak.

IX

The Holy Years
in the Shadow
of the Reformation
1525 - 1550

The Holy Year of 1525 came at the most inopportune moment imaginable. Many were those who went before the Pope to try to convince him not to call a Holy Year so as not to give the Protestants further pretexts for protest. Yet he did not wish to give up the idea but did, however, forbid any request of money for the Jubilee indulgence. This measure was taken to avoid giving any further impression of trafficking in indulgences. With the aim of emphasizing the religious nature of the Holy Year, passion plays were enacted in the Colosseum (fig. 69). There, on the delapidated steps where once the Roman pagans had watched the bloodthirsty games of animals and gladiators, the Christian pilgrims now sat to re-live the recounts of the Passion of Christ and of the martyrs. The religious confraternities vied with one another to put on the most realistic performances. It was commonly believed in those times that the early Christians had been martered in the Colosseum. Today we know that this was not the case, as the Colosseum did not even exist at the time of the first persecution. The first Christians were martyred in fact in Nero's Circus and later in the Circus Maximus. To the thinking of antiquity, the Colosseum was "too small" to serve as a

69. The Colosseum built as an amphitheater for gladiators between 72-80 A.D. It has been in ruins since the Middle Ages and
once provided a setting for Passion plays and for the devotion of
the Way of the Cross. According to an old prophecy, Rome will
stand as long as the Colosseum does and the world as long a
Rome does.

place for the execution of Rome's enemies. They were always executed "en masse" in order to please the crowd of
spectators; but this does not rule out the possibility of individual Christians coming to combat here with wild animals
or gladiators in a fight to the finish.

None of the measures were of any help at all in quiet-
ing the protest against the Holy Year. For the first time a
total refusal to participate was noticed. True, there had always been voices of dissent warning against pilgrimages
since they were wont to degenerate into a vagabond existence. The most popular devotional book of the time, *The
Imitation of Christ*, maintained: "Too many pilgrimages

140

seldom lead to holiness" (I, 23). As we already know, Nicholas Cusanus, replying to the monks who wanted to journey to Rome without the consent of their superior, had answered: "Obedience is better than Indulgence". Now, however, at least in Germany, the Jubilee was openly under attack. The two Jubilee bulls of Clement VII were published by Luther in German translation with added prefaces and marginal notes. He exhorted the Pope to spare his "lead and parchment" as no one would be coming from Germany: "We shall no longer pay so dear for Roman lies". He also asserted: "The Golden Door is so called since it brings much gold to the pope".[56]

The first pamphlets made their appearance. The gratuitously reciprocal abuse of these pamphlets was typical of those times. This was due in part to the newly invented printing press whose easy use often led to wantoness and misuse. An example of such a defamatory leaflet by an anonymous German writer is kept in the *British Museum Library*. Upon the frontispiece runs the following verse:[57]

> *Concerning the Jubilee Year,*
> *This little book speaks very clear,*
> *The questionable Jubilee Year,*
> *The one of Our Lord Jesus Christ is sure,*
> *The other of the Pope is commerce pure,*
> *So he who of this little book takes heed,*
> *Will not go to Rome for pardon, but only need*
> *Know that Christ will pardon concede,*
> *To all sinners abroad or at home,*
> *Needless then, t'roam hither t'Rome.*

It can be seen from this verse just how misunderstood the Holy Year was.

The few pilgrims to undertake the journey, found themselves in the midst of the peasants' uprising in the Tyrol, and soon in the theatre of war of the two great rival powers, France and Spain. Emperor Charles V and King Francis I had brought their campaigns into Northern Italy. The Pope was caught in the middle. Wanting to preserve his independence and the balance of political power in Italy, he vascilated between the two great powers and when he finally sided with one, his choice sealed Rome's fate.

* * *

Clement VII (1523-34), was a member of the wealthy and art-loving Medici family of Florence. Their coat-of-arms contained six balls or "pills", since (as is said) their forbears had been farmacists who manufactured pills. Medicine was already a profitable business back then! They achieved fame and fortune, becoming lords of Florence and giving four popes to the Church: Leo X, Clement VII, Pius IV and Leo XI. We have already seen Clement VII portrayed in the last of Raphael's "stanze", the Hall of Constantine, in the scene of the Donation of Constantine. The emperor is shown giving the symbolic statue of Rome to Pope Sylvester I, who in reality bears the features and beard of Clement VII (see fig. 27).

As had been foreseeable, only a few pilgrims made their way to Rome. We know the name of only one personage from Germany, Albrecht von Brandenburg, archbishop of Mainz and Magdeburg, who traveled via Venice with his retinue of twenty-two men. Machiavelli, who was anything but saintly, came to Rome in the same year to present his "History of Florence" to the Pope. The celebrated and witty Isabella d'Este, duchess of Mantua, heedless of all danger, did not want to miss out on the chance of obtaining the Jubilee indulgence. Mention should also be made of another famous woman, *Vittoria Colonna* (1490-1547, fig. 70). As a princess of the powerful noble family Colonna, she enjoyed a position of social prominence. As a poetess of numberless sonnets, she was a

142

70. Vittoria Colonna with her husband the Margrave d'Avalos of Pescara. Oil painting by Sebastiano del Piombo, before 1525. Columbus Museum of Art, Ohio.

celebrity with her contemporaries, and as Michelangelo's *grande amico* (sic!) her name has gone down in history. Her husband, the marquess Ferrante d'Avalos of Pescara, was a famous military commander under the emperor. He died in the Holy Year of 1525, from wounds received in the victorious battle of Pavia. Vittoria Colonna who up until this time had lived between Naples and Ischia much in adoration of her husband, experienced a religious change of heart. She withdrew to the convent of S. Silvestro in Capite in Rome. It is interesting to note that the Pope gave the strictest orders to the mother-superior not to receive her into the order. Perhaps he felt that a woman of such standing could be made better use of in a matrimony for further political alliances. Vittoria, however, never remarried, nor did she become a member of any religious order, but spent the rest of her life in various convents. She gathered around her a circle of men who desired internal reform of the Church in the spirit of the Gospels, but without breaking with Rome, therefore this movement is called "Evangelism" rather than "Protestantism". Even

Michelangelo made up part of this circle and it inspired his work and sonnets. Many were the reform movements of this period, such as the Capuchin and the Theatine. Many prominent prelates gathered together in the Oratory of Divine Love in order to combine common prayer with acts of charity. Yet Rome would first have to experience a terrible shock before the reform movement would take a firm hold.

The atmosphere in Rome was already tense during the Holy Year. The members of the Colonna clan battled in the streets with the Orsini. A "Christ's fool" arrived from Siena and roamed the streets prophesizing the imminent destruction of the city, and as a warning sent pouches filled with bones to pope and prelates. Clement VII eventually sided with the League of Cognac against the emperor, and thus engendered the emnity of the latter and his punitive reaction. Imperial troops took the city by storm and laid it to plunder. They rampaged murdering priests and nuns, destroyed priceless books and art treasures and laid siege to Castel Sant'Angelo whither the Pope had fled to safety. This was the horrific Sack of Rome of 1527, which brought about an end to the splendor and glory of the Renaissance, as well as an end to its licentiousness. From its ashes would slowly arise the Catholic Counter-Reformation.

* * *

Since few Geman pilgrims were to be seen in Rome during the Reformation, more notice was taken of the "Moors" or "Indians". In reality these people were Abyssinians, but the Romans' knowledge of geography was somewhat confused. In 1525, the Arabian historian, Johannes Africanus, wrote of these folk: "From Ethiopia come certain monks whose faces are marked with fire. One sees them in all parts of Europe, but especially in Rome".[58] The description, "faces marked with fire", could have meant either that their skin was sunburnt or that

144

they had been branded with hot irons. This was sometimes done to Christian pilgrims when they fell into the hands of Moslem Arabs. They came from the most southerly geographic extremity of Christianity. Abyssinia was a Christian enclave in Africa, surrounded and closed in by Moslems and pagans. The Abyssinians, however, would not renounce their link to Rome, and particularly not the pilgrims. They faced incredible dangers and hardships, first through the desert to Jerusalem, then by ship to Rome and often they journeyed on foot as far as Santiago de Compostela. It was they, the monks and sometimes women as well, who kept contact with Europe alive. Once in Rome, they stayed months and even years at the expense of the Apostolic Chamber (there are still expense receipts on file). In 1480, Pope Sixtus IV put a hospice and church at their disposal just behind St. Peter's. The small church still stands and by its name, *Santo Stefano degli Abissini*, recalls these early pilgrims, who lie buried here. In their pilgrim-home an active life prevailed. Its most important occupant was the rector, Abba Tesfazion, called Fra Pietro Indiano. Highly erudite and knowledgeable he was so influential at the papal court as to belong to the intimate group of the *famigliari* of Pope Paul III.[59]

* * *

It was this Pope, Paul III Farnese (1534-49), who after many attempts and negotiations summoned the Council of Trent to effect a "reformation in head and members". This reform, which had been demanded so ardently by the reformers, was finally to be made without their collaboration. The Council lasted eighteen years (1545-63). Falling between the Reformation and the Counter-Reformation, the Holy Year of 1550 duly suffered the tensions of this transitional period.

Paul III died shortly before the end of 1549. After a lengthy struggle in the College of Cardinals between the

71. The golden hammer of the Holy Year of 1550. Possibly made in Augsburg. Nationalmuseum, Munich.

pro-French and pro-Hapsburg factions, a successor was elected, *Julius III del Monte*. He was the last "Renaissance pope". Even in this very Holy Year he celebrated Carnival and allowed the performance of an ancient pagan comedy by Plautus. Vignola built a new summer villa for the pontiff, the beautiful *Villa Giulia*, at the foot of the Pincian hill which today is home to the National Etruscan Museum.

No sooner had Julius III been elected on the 22nd of February 1550, then he proclaimed the Holy Year. For the opening of the Holy Door he used a gilt hammer, which still exists. The hammer had as profound a significance as the Holy Door, and took its inspiration from biblical imagery. Just as Moses had struck the rock in the desert and water had gushed forth, giving drink to the Israelites who were dying of thirst (Ex 17:6 and Nm 20:11) so too the Pope would now strike the Holy Door with a hammer so that a stream of grace and great pardon might shower upon the contrite sinner.

This symbolic gesture was another idea of Master Burckard. Alexander VI only used a simple hammer, "similar to that used by common masons", as Burckard noted in his diary.[60] We learn from Domenico Manni that Clement VII was the first to use a golden hammer, although we do not know anything else about it.[61] On the other hand, we can see the hammer of Julius III on display in the National Museum of Munich (fig. 71). The Pope made a gift of this hammer immediately after its use to Cardinal Otto von Truchsess, bishop of Augsburg (who had perhaps donated it in the first place). Later, in 1554, Cardinal Truchsess in turn donated it for the founding of the University of Dillingen which was in his diocese. The hammer acquired a new connotation: "so that orthodox teaching shall be brandished like a hammer and ready to strike against heresey".[62] For this reason the hammer of the Holy Year of 1550 figured in the coat of arms of the University of Dillingen. With the dissolution of the university in 1803, the hammer passed through various hands until finally it was bought by the National Museum in Munich. There are other hammers in the Louvre and the Vatican Museums, but they are either of later date or were never used by a pope.[63]

Although the Holy Year of 1550 did not attract many visitors, with the exception of some Italians, two saints did participate: *Ignatius of Loyola* and *Philip Neri*. Ignatius (1491-1556) was a Spanish nobleman and knight and one of the most important Rome pilgrims of all time. His coming to Rome decisively influenced the development of history and the growth of the Church. Just as in former times St. Francis had come to Rome seeking papal approval for his new concept of life, so now came Ignatius. At the last stage on his way to Rome, in the locality of *La Storta* (where a memorial chapel stands) Ignatius had a vision of Christ and heard the promise: *Ego vobis Romae propitius ero*, i.e. "I will be benevolent to you in Rome". This was in November of 1537. It makes us automatically remember the promise heard two hundred years earlier by

72. *Tomb of St. Ignatius* (died 1556) in the church of *Il Gesù*. It is made of bronze, silver and gold. The world globe is in lapis lazuli. The life-size figure of the saint is by Antonio Canova and the allegorical figure of Truth chasing away heresy is by P. Legros, about 1700.

St. Bridget: "Go to Rome... where the road to salvation is shorter". Was Ignatius as disappointed as Bridget had been when he got to Rome? Whatever the case, the promise he heard in *La Storta* was made good. In that same Holy Year of 1550, Pope Julius III gave final approbation to the Society of Jesus and its constitution was drawn up.[64] Ignatius saw as his first task the spiritual revival of the Romans through preaching, education of youth and pastoral work. Rome should no longer be the moral stumbling block, but would become an exemplary model of holiness. In 1551 he founded the *Collegio Romano*, a public school for the children of the Roman bourgeosie, and one year later the *Collegium Germanicum* for the seminariens which still exists. Ignatius stayed in Rome until the end of his life. Today, the cell where he lived and died can be visited and *Il Gesù*, the church which played an important role in the development of Jesuit Baroque, houses his tomb. No emperor nor pope has ever had as magnificent a monument as St. Ignatius (fig. 72). The life-sized statue of the saint was executed in silver by Antonio Canova and is bestudded with precious gems. It stands as a visual manifestation of the Counter-Reformation sentiment of triumph over false doctrines. Quite explicitly, we see on the right-hand side a fierce allegorical Truth as she pursues heretics to the edge of a precipice. Luther and Calvin trip over volumes of their heretical works, (their names, upon the spines of the various books, used to be easily legible, but now the outlining has been erased). At the bottom a putto rips apart the heretical books with unabashed glee. This marble group is a work of the Frenchman Pierre Le Gros (1666-1719) and expresses the staunchly polemical spirit of those times which, fortunately, is quite unthinkable today.

The second saint was *Philip Neri* (1515-95), native of Florence and therefore not a true Roman but a newcomer. He came to the city for his studies, but seeing the need of the unprotected and homeless pilgrims, he decided to dedicate himself to their care. To accomplish this he founded the Confraternity of the *Santissima Trinità dei Pelligrini e Convalescenti*, and somewhat later, the church and hospice of the Most Holy Trinity near the bridge of Sixtus IV. It is thought to have given shelter to as many as half a million pilgrims in that Holy Year. Often bed tickets had to be issued in order to ensure that no one stayed longer than was absolutely necessary. The temptation to do so

73. *Tomb of St. Philip Neri* (died 1595) in the *Chiesa Nuova*. The portrait above the altar is by Guido Reni and was painted only after the saint's death.

was great, because the accomodation and the food were free. Every pilgrim was considered as a "guest of God". He was waited upon, cared for and washed. He would receive a warm and clean bed in a large dormitory hall. In the morning he would be given warm milk soup, during the day he would be accompanied to the pilgrimage churches and be given provisions for the road. In the evenings he got a bowl of soup, 250 grams of meat, some salad, a pitcher of wine and a loaf of bread. If they were priests they enjoyed an unlimited allotment of bread and wine with a special after-dinner plate of figs and nuts. We know all this in detail as the daily menus are still extant. St. Philip went as far as the Milvian bridge to meet the new pilgrims and to show them the way into Rome and to invite them to stay in his hospice. He washed their feet, and soon afterwards popes and queens would do the same imitating his example. Philip Neri also organized concerts of sacred music, the so-called oratorios. He became the favorite saint of the Romans. They nicknamed him "Pippo Buono", as he was always in good spirits and constantly surrounded by a throng of children; he gently chided them to be good: *"State buoni - se potete!"* i.e. "Be good, if you can".

Philip Neri, is buried in his church, the *Chiesa Nuova*. Above his tomb is a radiant mosaic copy of *Guido Reni's* (1575-1642) portrait of the saint (fig. 73). His cell can be visited on his feast day the 5th of May. In 1740, the famous copperplate engraver *Giuseppe Vasi* (1710-82) made an engraving of the church and hospice; a group of pilgrims are heading towards it, dressed in typical garb: the scallop shell affixed to their pelerins, a broad-brimmed hat and a pilgrim's staff (fig. 74). Another engraving which is dated 1650 depicts various acts of charity and religious instruction which the archiconfraternity practiced (fig. 75). The members of the archiconfraternity (both men and women) go to meet pilgrims, to receive them and lead them to the pilgrims' hospice, once there they seat them on high benches and wash their feet and then feed them. Finally they are shown to a dormitory hall where each pilgrim is given a freshly made bed. On the following day they are accompanied to the four major basilicas where they will be shown Veronica's veil and the heads of Peter and Paul. They receive the Pope's blessing. In the evening they listen to more preaching in the church of the Most Holy Trinity, as the archiconfraternity tends not only to the pilgrims' physical well-being but even more to their spiritual formation.

Upon the exterior wall of the pilgrims' home, a marble plaque informs us that Goffredo Mameli, the composer of the Italian national anthem, died here from injuries received in the battle of the Gianicolo in 1849. The hospice functioned until the dissolution of the Papal States in 1870. Until very recently it was used as a billiard club, and the popes and benefactors whose portraits and busts still line the walls of the entry hall, looked down as if taken aback by the young game opponents who stood either anxiously or bored around the billiard tables (fig. 76). A short while ago the hall was given back to the archiconfraternity which still exists. There are today only a few elderly members, and the church, which has a beautiful façade by Francesco de Sanctis and contains a number of paintings by Guido Reni, is only open for early morning mass.

74. Pilgrims on their way to the pilgrim-home and the pilgrims' church of Santissima Trinità dei Pellegrini. Copperplate by G. Vasi. 1740.

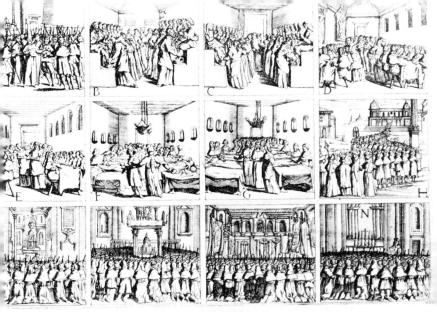

ZIONE DELLE FVNZIONI PRINCIPALI, CHE SI ESERCITANO DALLA NOBILISSIMA
Archiconfraternità della S.ma TRINITA di Roma nell'albergare i Peregrini l'Anno del Giubileo 1650.
AL MOLTO ILLUSTRE, E MOLTO REVERENDO SIGNOR MIO PADRONE OSSERVANDISSIMO
IL SIGNOR' ABBATE GIROLAMO CASTALDI.

75. The good works of the Archiconfraternity of the Holy Trinity. Copperplate 1650.

76. The pilgrim-home as it was when transformed into a billiard
club. The busts of the former benefactors and patrons seem to
be gazing in astonishment.

X

"Roma la Santa" and the Seven Pilgrimage Churches 1575

Unlike the Prostestants who saw in Rome the new Babylon and prophesized its impending fall, those who, in the period of the Counter-Reformation, which we are about to enter, remained faithful to Rome saw in the city the embodiment of sanctity. A most interesting engraving bears witness to this. It is entitled *Roma la Santa* and is by *Giovanni Battista de Caballeriis* (Cavallieri), dated Holy Year of 1575 (fig. 77). A copy of this is to be found in the *British Museum Library* in London. It was published by Thurston in his book which was a standard work on "The Holy Year of Jubilee".[65] Rome is depicted standing in the center as a personified saint: *Sancta Roma*. In one hand she carries a chalice and host and in the other a processional cross, she is as the same time treading upon symbols of superstition and paganism. In twelve small scenes all her good works are represented, for Rome is the model of all virtue: she gives comfort to the distressed, gives alms to the poor, preaches truth, prays and fasts and does penance, she is the instructress of humility and the model of piety, the liberator of those who are imprisoned, the nurse of those who have fallen ill, and it is she who gives the pilgrims shelter and feeds the poor. Framing this picture, there runs a river which is constituted of seven tributaries

77. *Roma la Santa*. Copperplate by G.B. de Cavallieri, engraved for the Holy Year of 1575. British Museum Library, London.

like the seven gifts of the Holy Spirit. God the Father hovers above in the clouds. In the frame, the words from the Psalm 46 are written: "There is a river whose streams refresh the City of God, and it sanctifies the dwelling of the Most High". At the very top are the words from Psalm 65: "You crown the year with your bounty". In the four corners of the engraving are seen the four major basilicas (St. Peter's is still without its dome) and moving towards them in processions are the pilgrims dressed in their costume.

What makes this print even more interesting for us is the coat of arms and family name of Cardinal *Stanislaus Hosius* (1504-78) to whom this engraving is dedicated. Hosius came from Ermland in East Prussia. His surname was extremely commonplace: "Hose" (in the sense of leg wear) and it is indeed possible that his father had been a breeches maker. As he rose to the rank of bishop and later cardinal he found his name too prosaic and had it latinized into "Hosius". He did, nevertheless, make a play on the original meaning of his name when designed his coat of arms using a leg as a device. During Holy Year of 1575 he was the Major Penitentiary in Rome and as such had to sit in St. Peter's on a tall wooden throne and tap every repentant sinner on the head with a long wand; a special indugence was connected to this. This practice was abolished with the reform of indulgences after the Second Vatican Council.

This engraving is indicative of the sentiment that possessed the pilgrim of the time. No Holy Year, before or since, has ever been celebrated with such pious fervor as this one was. It was the first Holy Year of the Counter-Reformation and was perhaps the holiest of all Holy Years. The Council of Trent had been brought to a successful conclusion in 1563 and the Catholic Church had come out the better for it, purified and strengthened anew, although it had lost many adherents and even entire nations. Now she went about regaining that which had been lost. In 1571 a definitive attack was made against the Turkish fleet

156

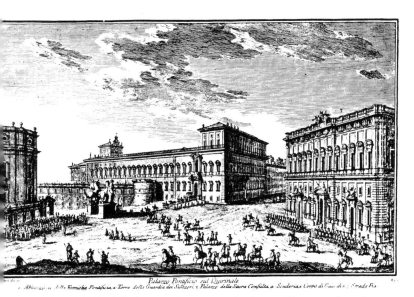

Palazzo Pontificio sul Quirinale
1 Abitazioni della Famiglia Pontificia, 2 Torre della Guardia dei Svizzeri, 3 Palazzo della Sacra Consulta, 4 Scuderia, 5 Corso di Guardia, 6 Strada Pia

78. The *Quirinal Palace* as it appeared when still a papal residence. Engraving by G. Vasi. 1750.

at Lepanto. The Jesuits departed from Rome spreading in all directions throughout the old and new world to strengthen the old faith and to found new missions. It was a period of upsurge and change, where everything was in need of renewal: the Church, the world and even the calendar.

Pope Gregory XIII Boncompagni (1572-85) introduced the new calendar in 1582. For this reason the calendar, which we still use today, is called the Gregorian calendar. He was a great lover and patron of natural sciences. He founded the papal Osservatory and the *Gregorian University*, the most prestigious theological institution in Rome. The *Via Gregoriana* also bears his name. He had the straight *Via Merulana* laid out to link the church of St. Mary Major with the Lateran. In order to show the pilgrim the best side of the city, Rome was now finally going to be restored and embellished after the damage it had suffered in the Sack of Rome of 1527.

Gregory XIII began by building the Quirinal Palace upon the Quirinal hill as a summer residence for the popes, but with time the popes came to prefer it to the Vatican and resided there permanently until Rome fall to the

157

King Victor-Emanuel II in 1870. It then became the residence of the kings of Italy and today is the official residence of the president of the Italian Republic. Churches of the new orders were also built in this period. The Jesuits built *Il Gesù*, the Theatines *Sant'Andrea della Valle*, and the Oratorians the *Chiesa Nuova*. The pilgrim hospice of the *Santissima Trinità* was enlarged and is said to have cared for 170,000 pilgrims in that year. As the city certainly did not have more than 40,000 inhabitants at the time, this meant that there were four *romei* for every Roman. The first price lists were introduced for lodgings and prices were frozen. It was also prohibited to evict any tenant in order to gain a higher rent from a foreigner. Even the prostitutes were banned from the streets, that is, at least, for the duration of the Holy Year.

Gregory XIII introduced the custom still practiced today, that is, the issuing of the bull of indiction for the new Jubilee Year on the feast of the Ascension, and having it subsequently read in the portico of St. Peter's on the fourth Sunday of Advent. This custom has a profound significance: "The feast day of the Ascension shall serve as a reminder, that through the grace of the Jubilee indulgence, the gates of Heaven will be opened to the repentant sinner; the last Sunday of Advent will indicate that in place of the Synagogue, the Church now stands and in place of the old year, the Jubilee year has come".[66]

The ceremonies for the opening of the Holy Door were held with the two churches of St. Peter in the background, as we can see in an interesting etching of that year (fig. 79). The first being the Constantinian basilica built around 320. It is recognizable by its rectangular atrium; standing out in its center is the *Cantharus*, the famous pine cone shaped fountain. Behind this, the new church of St. Peter's has been in the process of being built since Julius II laid the cornerstone in 1506. The drum of the dome is already visible, but the dome as such would be brought to completion only fifteen years later. The Pope in the gestatorial chair and under a baldachin is being carried

79. Gregory XIII passing through the atrium of St. Peter's (with the dome as yet unfinished) on his way to open the Holy Door at Christmas of 1574. Engraving by G.B. Cavallieri. 1575.

through the overcrowded atrium to the extreme righthand side of the church where he will open the Holy Door.

Torquato Tasso (1544-95) captured this scene in his great poetic work, *Gerusalemme Liberata* (canto XI):

> *They call to you, who like the mighty cliff,*
> *and guardian of the house, founded by God,*
> *wherein now his worthy successor*
> *opens the doors of grace and forgiveness.*

159

Duke Ernst of Bavaria presented the golden hammer to the Pope who swung it with such force that it broke. He then proceeded to strike the door three times (as ritual prescribed) with the handle that had remained in his grasp. The ceremony was accompanied by the polyphonic music composed and conducted by Pierluigi da Palestrina (1525-94) and sung by the famous boys' choir of the Sistine Chapel. Neither before nor since have so many princes been in attendance for the opening ceremonies and subsequent midnight mass as for this Christmas of 1574. By their presence the Pope wished to underscore the alliance with those nations which had remained loyal to him.

A detailed description of the pious atmosphere in Rome with all the ceremonies, the people's zeal and their good works is given by an English priest, Gregory Martin, who at that time was living in exile in Rome in the newly founded English hospice, later called the English College. The title of his book is in keeping with our theme: *Roma sancta.*[67] In this and in other late sixteenth century books on Rome, the new attitude of the pilgrim becomes evident. He not only wants to see and venerate the various holy places and gain indulgences, but rather first and foremost wishes to increase his faith and confirm his own Catholic conviction.

In truth, no Holy Year has ever been celebrated with such solemnity, in such fitting and fine fashion. Earlier on the pilgrims wandered to Rome on their own accord, alone or together with relatives. The greater part of them made the journey on foot, ragged and tattered, exhausted and destitute; filled with a touching folk-piety, often coupled with a fanatical fervor for penance (we need only remember the procession of the *bianchi* and the flagellants of 1400). Now, however, the pilgrims came already organized in rank and file. A new phenomenon came into view: the *confraternities*. Almost everyone at this time belonged to a confraternity or sodality. There were confraternities for every walk of life, for every object of veneration and for every town and region. All of these confraternities paraded through the city, both day and night, all year long, one after another. Each confraternity had its own outfit or habit, sodality colors, candles and torches, carried its own standard, pictures and sacred statues. They prayed and sang without interruption, accompanied or relieved by musical instruments. By traveling to Rome as part of a sodality the pilgrim had not only the advantage of greater safety while traveling, but also in having to visit the basilicas only once. But, by coming alone the pilgrim fell under the old rules of Boniface VIII under which a Roman had to visit the churches thirty times and a *Romeo* fifteen times.

* * *

In this Holy Year the number of pilgrimage churches was increased to seven. Since seven was a sacred number there should also be seven main churches. The first Holy Year had had only two, *St. Peter's* and *St. Paul's*. In the second Jubilee Year the Lateran was added and subsequently in the third Holy Year St. Mary Major. We are already familiar with these four basilicas. In order to achieve the sacred number of seven, the churches of *St. Lawrence outside the Walls, Holy Cross in Jerusalem* and *St. Sebastian* were added to the pilgrims' program. All of them date back to the time of the emperor Constantine or his sons, except for S. Major.

The fifth main or "patriarchal" basilica lies to the east, outside the city walls, hence its name *San Lorenzo fuori le Mura* (fig. 80). It was built upon the grave of the most beloved deacon of Rome, Laurentius or Lawrence, who was martyred upon a flaming gridiron which has become his symbol. In the same tomb there are said to be the relics of his "colleague", the arch-deacon St. Stephen of Jerusalem. He was the first Christian martyr and his remains were brought here some centuries later so that the two most beloved deacons could be venerated together. As the ancient two-storied building was in a state of decay a new church was added on in the Middle Ages. This last was not, however, as fine a building as the earlier one had been. The church suffered major damage from bombing in

80. *St. Lawrence outside the Walls.* This basilica was greatly damaged during World War II. The portico and bell tower date from the Middle Ages. A figure of St. Lawrence with his gridiron surmounts an ancient column in front of the church. In the background can be seen the city cemetry, *Il Verano.*

World War II and was rebuilt afterwards in its original style. Fortunately, its sixth century triumphal arch, the charming Romanesque cloister, square campanile and 12th century portico all escaped damage. Under the portico are the graves of the German Pope Damasus II (died 1048) and the Italian statesman Alcide de Gasperi (died 1954). As for the crypt of Pius IX, we shall speak about it later.

The basilica of St. Sebastian (fig. 81) lies on the *Via Appia Antica*, the ancient Appian Way. It is the oldest paved highway and is named after the censor *Appius Claudius* who began to build it in 312 B.C. The *Via Appia* was eventually extended to Brindisi. The Christian faith first came to Rome along this highway as we learn from the Acts of the Apostles. Many catacombs developed along the Appian Way and the most important catacomb is that of St. Sebastian, which has always been accessible, even in the

Middle Ages, as we know from the visits of St. Bridget. In earlier times, it had been thought that all catacomb graves were of martyrs, which, however, was not the case. It was the normal means of burial for the Jews and Christians who were for the most part poor people and not able to afford a lavish masoleum above ground; nor did they allow cremation of their dead as the pagan Romans did. When the available surface area was filled with graves, it was then necessary to dig deeper and deeper into the earth. The ground here was soft volcanic tufa and allowed for the easy digging out and development of maze-like tunnels with as many as four underground levels (fig. 82). The deceased were laid into hollowed-out slots called *loculi,* which lined the tunnel walls. The corpse was simply wrapped in a plain linen shroud and in most cases laid into the grave without a sarcophagus or casket. The *loculus* was sealed airtight with either a terracotta roof-tile or a marble plaque. It is impossible to know exactly how many graves there were, as much has yet to be excavated. About fifty catacombs surrounded the ancient city. The most

81. The *church of St. Sebastian* on the ancient Appian Way. The basilica, originally built by Constantine or his son, was completely rebuilt in 1609.

82. A corridor in the Catacombs of St. Sebastian. 3rd - 4th century.

83. Graffiti invoking Peter and Paul on the wall of the so-called *triclia,* a Christian meeting-place in the Catacombs of St. Sebastian.

interesting of all catacombs are those at St. Sebastian's, since they contain a room, the so-called *triclia*, upon whose walls the names of Peter and Paul are found in countless *grafitti* (fig. 83). This demonstrates that they were especially venerated at this place. The church which was built over this spot was, in the first instance, dedicated to the two apostles. Only later was it re-named after St. Sebastian, the famed Roman martyr, who was buried here. The church was originally built as a five-naved basilica with colonnaded ambulatory. It was later narrowed down to its present-day single nave; a few ancient columns are employed to support the portico outside. The beautifully carved and coffered wooden ceiling was commissioned by cardinal Scipione Borghese, as can be seen by his coat of arms. He had the church remodeled in 1609 entrusting the project to the Dutch architect Jan Van Santen, whom the Romans called Vasanzio.

As we proceed along the ancient Appian Way towards Rome, we come to a small, almost inconspicuous church the name of which is, however, very well known: *Quo Vadis* (fig. 84). Upon this spot the apostle Peter, who was fleeing Rome at the outbreak of the first Christian persecution, is

84. The church of *Quo Vadis* along the ancient Appian Way is built upon the spot where, according to tradition, Peter had a vision of Christ. As he saw Christ approaching, Peter asked: "Domine, quo vadis?", "Lord, where are you going?"

S.CROCE IN GIERVSALEMME.

Joanes Maggni Rom: delineauit

85. The *church of the Holy Cross* in Jerusalem is one of the seven pilgrimage basilicas. Built by Constantine upon the site of his mother's palace and upon earth said to have been brought to Rome along with the relics of the True Cross from Jerusalem.

said to have had a vision of Christ heading towards Rome. Peter, amazed and embarassed, queried: *"Domine, Quo Vadis?"*, "Oh Lord, whither goest Thou?" Whereupon Christ anwered him: "I go to Rome to be crucified once more". This near reproach made the apostle recognize the error of his flight, he repented and turned around and headed back to Rome. Legend would further have it that an impress of Christ's feet was left in a pavement stone of the Via Appia at this very spot. Indeed, the church conserves a white marble stone with the imprint of two large bare feet; hence, the church was built upon the spot where the stone was found and named after Peter's query *"Quo Vadis?"*. The stone that is found in this church is, however, only a replica, as the original is kept in a reliquary case in the church of St. Sebastian.

The church of the *Holy Cross in Jerusalem* lies near the Lateran on the former site of the palace of the empress Helen (fig. 85). The reason for this name is two-fold:

firstly, it supposedly stands upon earth brought back by Helen from Jerusalem and secondly, it possseses the greatest number of relics of Christ's Passion, all of which are said to have been discovered by St. Helen. The miracle of the finding of the true Cross is vividly depicted in the great apse fresco painted by Antoniazzo Romano around 1490 (fig. 86). The relics are preserved in a modern side chapel; they include a large fragment of the Cross, a nail, two thorns, three small stones (one from the grotto of the Nativity, another from the column of the scourging of Christ and one from his tomb). In the center is a large piece of a wooden board that Pilate had hung over the head of Christ upon the cross with the lettering: "Jesus of Nazareth, King of the Jews", written in three languages as one can still make out (fig. 87). This board, whether genuine or a fabrication, brings us to an almost frightening immediacy with Christ on the cross and induces us to kneel down in silent adoration.

From this time onwards it became customary to visit the seven basilicas on the same day, when possible on foot

86. The *Church of the Holy Cross in Jerusalem*. The scenes of St. Helen finding the True Cross were painted in the apse by Antoniazzo Romano in 1490.

87. *The Church of the Holy Cross in Jerusalem.* Reliquary case containing the greatest quantity of relics of Christ's passion.

and on an empty stomach, which truly made for an exercise in penance. All this was done, however, in processions with prayer and song, day and night, with candles, torches and standards, as can be seen in the famous print by Lafréry made in this jubilee year of 1575 (fig. 88).

The pilgrimage to the seven churches was especially advocated by St. Philip Neri, who unwittingly played a great role in this Holy Year owing to the charitable works that were done by the Confraternity of the Most Holy Trinity, founded and directed by him. In this year the already mentioned pilgrim hospice of the Holy Trinity was built and the Oratory, a community of secular priests also founded by him, received papal approval.

88. The confraternities as they march in process on, dressed in long robes, carrying banners, crosses and candles from one church to another. It is interesting to note the appearance of the churches at this time. For example, St. Peter's is still without a dome. Copperplate by A. Lafréry, 1575.

89. *St. Charles Borromeo*, nephew of Pope Pius IV and archbishop of Milan. Portrait by A. Crespi. 1575. Ambrosian Pinacoteca, Milan.

* * *

Two other men, who were later canonized as saints, attended the Holy Year, not to mention the many other unknown saints. Pope Gregory XIII had expressed his desire that *Charles Borromeo* (1538-84) would come to Rome for the inaugural ceremonies from his episcopal see in Milan (fig. 89). St. Charles had already worked for years in Rome under his uncle, Pius IV, as Cardinal Secretary of State. At that time he had presided over the humanistic "Academy of the Vatican Nights", so called because it met at night in the *Casino of Pius IV* in the Vatican Gardens. The simple reason for this nocturnal assembly was that the cardinal had no time during the day. Now almost daily he walked in procession through the city barefoot and with such reverence and repentent zeal, that his confreres in the College of Cardinals felt obliged to follow his austere example. He obtained from the Pope a Jubilee year for his diocese of Milan, that would be celebrated in the year that followed, and for which he would personally write a book of prayer.

The second saint of the Holy Year was *St. Camillo de Lellis* (1550-1614), nobleman, soldier and vagabond. After his conversion in 1575, he worked in the hospital of the incurables, *San Giacomo degli Incurabili,* in Rome and then founded an order of regular priests, who take a fourth vow, that of caring for the sick, and are distinguished by a red cross wear on their robes. They wore this as they first appeared on battlefields tending the wounded, being precursors of the modern International Red Cross. St. Camillo is in fact the patron saint of the infirm.

The Year of 1575 left a great and lasting impression. It demonstrated the new force of faith and the fervently religious zeal that typified the Counter-Reformation. It showed that the papacy, which Luther half a century earlier had pronounced dead, had been not weakened but, on the contrary, had been strengthened. The Jubilee, however, had not accomplished its final objective: to bring the Protestants back into the Catholic camp. It had instead served to do just the opposite, widening the gap between the Catholic and Protestant doctrines and their respective forms of devotion. Thus, the paths of Christianity diverged for centuries to come; yet, the Roman crisis had been overcome. Rome had become, once again, a religious center. Church life would take on a more unified form. The link between the Mother Church and her local churches would be tightened (by means of a standard cathechism and strict formation of priests, also through permanent nunciatures or apostolic delegations and frequent state visits). Just as she had done in the Early Middle Ages, Rome sent out her messengers of faith and in return received homage from peoples from all corners of the world as *Roma la Santa.*

XI

The First Holy Year of the High Baroque Age 1600

At the beginning of the new age, the Baroque, which we are now entering, a magnificent painting was created which is fitting to our theme: the Madonna of the Pilgrims by *Caravaggio* (fig. 90). Michelangelo Merisi, called *Caravaggio* (1569-1610), was the first Baroque painter in Rome. Other famous paintings of his can be found in the churches of *Santa Maria del Popolo, San Luigi dei Francesi*, in the *Galleria Borghese* and in the Vatican, but none of these is so venerated as the *Madonna of the Pilgrims*, which most likely was finished in 1604 and was placed in the first side chapel of the church of *Sant'Agostino* where it still hangs today.

Here the pilgrims can see themselves, in this picture of the old woman and young man. The two pilgrims kneel, with their walking staffs under their arms, their bare, dirtied and swollen feet, their hands folded in prayer as they look up at Mary with an expression of profound devotion. Here we have no longer the ethereal Queen of Heaven, that we know from Byzantine mosaics, nor the lovely Madonna of Renaissance paintings; we see instead a real flesh and blood Roman woman with black hair and simple dress, who appears at her front door and sympathetically leans forward towards the pilgrims, carrying a child in her

90. The *Madonna of the Pilgrims* by Caravaggio, 1604. Painted for the church of St. Augustine where it still hangs today.

91. The *Girondola*, the fireworks from Castel Sant'Angelo celebrating the arrival of the new century. Engraving by G. Maggi. 1600.

arms. The infant Jesus appears just as human as his mother and looks on in curiosity at the newcomers, who kneel here at the doorway, not as beggars but as worshippers. This painting beautifully interprets the piety of the pilgrims of this period.

This heartfelt piety is also attested to by the Austrian Rome-pilgrim *Hieronymus Marstaller,* abbot of the Benedictine abbey of St. Paul in Carinthia. He writes: "We were struck by the foreigner's devotion when visiting the churches. We saw people praying fervently, their eyes wet with tears. There was no lack of those from the Roman nobility and clergy, and in particular, noblewomen, who journeyed on foot to the holy sites often dripping with sweat, it would be therefore unfair in making the generalization: 'The nearer one comes to Rome, the worse it gets', as there was a devil amongst the angels in Heaven and a Judas Iscariot amongst the apostles, but their godlessness did not detract from either the angels or apostles. For my part, I saw nothing of a scandalous nature in Rome, on the contrary, I found great devotion".[68] One notes in these words the subtlely polemical tone which distiguishes the Counter-Reformation.

The new century was heralded by a magnificent firework display called *girandola* from the summit of Castel Sant'Angelo, as can be seen in a picture by *Giovanni Maggi* (fig. 91). Almost immediately afterward, on the 19th of February, the Holy Year was beclouded by the smoke that issued from another fire, from the stake where *Giordano Bruno* (1548-1600) was burnt alive. After leaving the Dominican order he expounded his pantheistic views at Oxford, Paris, Geneva and Wittenberg.

Yet he met with no success, and finally he fell into the hands of the Inquisition at Venice, was sent to Rome where he was condemned to death, not just for his false teachings but also for his reckless invectives against the Pope and the Church. The Pope would have reprieved him, had he been ready to recant, but Bruno prefered to immortalize himself on earth by going to the stake since he did not believe in immortality in heaven. While his death sentence was being read, he said to the judges: "Perhaps you tremble more in pronouncing this death sentence than I do in hearing it".[69] As Giordano Bruno's execution was taking place, the Pope, although suffering from gout, made the round of pilgrimage churches and climbed up *the Holy*

175

Steps praying for Giordano Bruno, in vain hope that he would have a change of heart in the last moment.

The square where he was executed ironically bears the name Campo de' Fiori ("field of flowers"). There amidst the brawl of the daily market his statue rises up. It is the work of *Ettore Ferrari* (1881) (fig. 92). Bruno stands just as defiantly as he did up until his death. He wears the Dominican cowl greatly covering his face and in his hand tightly holds a book containing his theories. On the three bronze reliefs are depicted the most noteworthy events of his life: his teaching at Oxford, his defense before the judges and ultimately his burning at the stake. Running around the pedestal are the portraits of eight predecessors or companions in faith (this according to whoever conceived the monument): Pierre Ramus, Giulio Vanini, Antonio Paleario, Michael Servet, John Wycliff, John Hus, Fra Paolo Sarpi and Fra Tommaso Campanella. Strangely enough, Martin Luther is not included; after all, he would not have desired to be represented on a monument to an avowed opponent of the Christian faith. The dedicatory inscription reads: "To Bruno, from the century that he foresaw, at the place where he burned at the stake".

There is a engraving from 1600 which depicts everything that was of interest to the pilgrim: in the middle is a city map of Rome, around this are the seven main basilicas, and underneath the Pope is shown in the act of opening the Holy Door at St. Peter's (fig. 93). The Pope during this Holy Year was *Clement VIII*, Aldobrandini (1592-1605). He entrusted Maderno with the building of the *Confessio* and the papal altar in St. Peter's as well as the chapel in the grottoes, the *Clementine Chapel*, which takes its name from him.

Clement VIII, despite the nepotism he practiced, was an otherwise very devout person; a duality some of his predecessors had known how to live as well. He would personally hear confessions and give holy communion in St. Peter's (one estimates circa 300,000 communicants in one year). He often invited twelve poor pilgrims to table with him and personally served them. He visited the Hos-

176

92. *Campo de' Fiori.* The statue of Giordano Bruno stands in the center of this market square on the spot where he was burned at the stake for heresy in 1600.

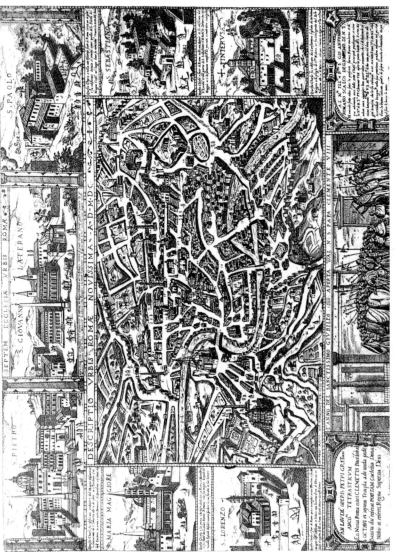

93. Clement VIII opening the Holy Door in 1599. In the middle a map of Rome surrounded by the

pice of the Most Holy Trinity where he gave alms and washed the feet of the pilgrims. He forbade the cardinals to wear the purple during the Holy Year. He founded two commissions of cardinals, the one to deal with the practical needs and the other to care for the spiritual needs of the pilgrims. These last were also divided into groups according to their nationality and language. The pilgrims who came from the Protestant countries of the North were treated with especial attention: The Roman Jews were required to furnish five hundred mattresses and bedcovers. Pickpockets were already at work back then; during the opening ceremonies, the Protestant Duke Friedrich I of Würtemberg was robbed of his pocket watch, which was a very rare object in those days.

Two erudite cardinals participated in the Holy Year of 1600. The first was the Oratorian, Cardinal *Cesare Baronius* (1538-1607), an important writer of Church history, who had just published his "Annals", a rebuttal of the Protestant interpretation of history as given by Flacius Illyricus and by the "Magdeburg Centurians". The second was the Jesuit *Robert Bellarmine* (1542-1621), who would later be canonized and raised to the rank of Doctor of the Church. He wrote a dissertation upon the Holy Year entitled *De indulgentiis & Jubilaeo*. The Calvinists celebrated the Holy Year as well, albeit in their own manner. The Calvinistic preacher Charles Drelincourt published his tract in Paris: *Du jubilé des églises reformées avec l'examen du jubilé de l'église romaine*, "The Jubilee of the Reformed Churches with an examination of the Jubilee of the Roman Church" in reply to the Roman Jubilee.

XII

The New St. Peter's
1625

The Jubilee of 1625 went by quite uneventfully, however, the pilgrims finally had the chance to see the new basilica of St. Peter's almost completed. Let us now try to enter it with their self-same spirit. It had taken over one hundred years to build the new church, which had been begun by Bramante in 1506, continued by Michelangelo (1546-64) and brought to completion by Maderno (1600-12) (fig. 94). For this reason the inscription on the façade proudly proclaims; IN · HONOREM · PRINCEPS · APOST · PAULUS · V · BURGHESIUS · ROMANUS · PONT · MAX · AN · MDCXII · PONT · VII · "To the honor of the prince of the apostles, Paul V Borghese, Roman and Pope, in the year 1612, the seventh year of his pontificate". The verb is missing and the inscription sounds as if Paul V had the church completed. In reality, it only refers to the façade. It was for his successor, Urban VIII (1623-44), to be able to consecrate the church and indeed, on the 18th November 1626, the very same day upon which the first basilica was supposed to have been consecrated in 326. Thirteen-hundred years distance one event from the other; in Rome one is used to thinking in terms of centuries and millennia. Urban VIII Barberini was the Pope for the Holy Year of 1625. Therefore, the three heraldic bees of his family coat of arms, "the busy bees of the Barberini", are found all over and remind us of this Pope.

St. Peter's Square was still unfinished, although the obelisk from Nero's Circus, which had witnessed the mar-

94. *St. Peter's Square* with the obelisk which in 1586 was moved to this spot from its setting in Nero's circus. The façade was completed by Maderno in 1612.

tyrdom of the first Christians, now stands as a silent memorial in the center of the new square. In 1586, *Domenico Fontana* moved the twenty-five meter high Egyptian obelisk (dating from 1935 B.C.) from the former site of the Neronian circus to where it stands today; a very daring and risky feat but a bold achievement symbolic of the Counter-Reformation, by which the Pope, Sixtus V, wished to impress the world. The inscription at the base of the obelisk heralds the triumph of the cross over the "enemy powers". Everyone is free to imagine just who was meant by these "enemy powers".

95. Fountain by Maderno in St. Peter's Square situated in front of the Apostolic Palace. Every Sunday at noon the pope appears at his study window and gives his blessing to the crowd assembled in the square below.

On the righthand side, that is northwards from the obelisk, stands the first of the twin fountains, created by Maderno in 1613 (fig. 95), while the second one on the other side of the square was made some sixty years later by Bernini. The only difference in the two fountains are the coats of arms; the first bears those of Paul V and the second is of Clement X. Many years later (1882), the view of these two fountains with their high water spray flowing over the three basins, resembling the lightest of bridal veils, would inspire the Swiss writer *Conrad Ferdinand Meyer* to write a poem. In its brevity it is complete; if we might jump ahead in time with this poem (written in 1882), this is a good moment to quote it:

> *The waterjet springs up, and falling fills,*
> *To the brim the marble basin round,*
> *Which in turn lets out a veil-like fall,*
> *Into a second basin's bottom,*
> *The second one gives, being too rich,*
> *The third one surging, with its flow,*
> *And each one gives and takes as well,*
> *And rushes and rests.*

The Apostolic Palaces rise up on the right side of St. Peter's square. It was built by Domenico Fontana (1585-90) in a simple cube-shaped form. On the top floor is the Pope's private apartment. The second window from the right is his study where he appears on Sundays at noon to give his blessing to those who stand gathered below in St. Peter's Square.

In 1625, the square had not yet had seen the addition of the colonnades, which today so festively frame the square. Bernini created them at the end of his long life. With them the arms of the Mother Church would be represented, who wishes to embrace and unite all mankind. Upon the nearly three hundred travertine columns, almost one hundred and fifty statues of saints make up a heavenly choir. The saints seem to be inviting us to enter into the church. On special feast days the Pope gives his blessing *urbi et orbi*, to the city and the whole world, from the benediction *loggia* above the main entrance. When he does this, it seems as if the statues from their heights and the pilgrims in the square, that is, the Church triumphant and the Church militant, are united in this blessing (fig. 96).

This magnificent view, however, should not let us forget the sad fact that it was precisely the construction of the

183

96. *Easter celebrations* in St. Peter's Square. After the papal
mass, which is held on the esplanade in front of the basilica, the
pope appears above the main portal at the festively decorated
loggia and imparts his blessing *urbi et orbi*, to the city and to
the world.

New St. Peter's which fomented the Reformation; in seeking to raise the money for its construction Pope Leo X in 1517 had granted a new indulgence which provoked Martin Luther's protest. Luther subsequently came out with his famous ninety-five theses against the trafficking in indulgences, setting the Reformation upon its path. Therefore, a tragic link exists between the building of St. Peter's and the Reformation, between this stone symbol of the greatness and universality of Catholicism and the breach in Christianity, which still has not been overcome.

Keeping this in mind, let us observe Giotto's famous mosaic which is found high up overhead under the portico (fig. 97). We mentioned it already in the first Jubilee Year (1300), when it was commissioned by Cardinal Stefaneschi. He is seen in the lower righthand corner as donor in the attitude of prayer. It is called the *navicella* or little ship, and refers to the boat of Christ's apostles on the sea of Galilee; at the same time it signifies metaphori-

97. *La Navicella*, or small boat of Christ's disciples on the Sea of Galilee. Peter is being held firmly by Christ who prevents him from drowning. The mosaic was designed by Giotto in 1300. Its donor, Cardinal Stefaneschi, can be seen on the lower righthand side. Heavily restored, it is now inside the portico of St. Peter's above the main portal.

cally the ship of the Church. Christ appears upon the water, Peter wants to rush to his side out of love, but fear overcomes him and he begins to sink. Christ, however, holds his hand firmly. It is hence the strength of Christ, that holds Peter up and with him the Church, so that she does not sink. This illustrates the whole theme and significance of St. Peter's: the Church continues to stand because Christ sustains her and holds her fast.

Carlo Maderno (1556-1629) built the portico and also lengthened the whole church changing its groundplan from a Greek cross into a Latin cross and by so doing turned it into the world's longest church; its 186 meter length (604 ft.) excludes the measurements of the thick walls and portico. It is not, however, the tallest church as it is "only" 136 meters (446 ft.) high. The magnificent central door, made in bronze by Filarete in 1440 was the first work of Renaissance art in Rome but seems to elicit little interest from the pilgrim. Perhaps on his way to Rome he has already seen similar doors in Florence at the baptistery there. The lateral portals were only outfitted with simple wooden doors, which awaited that moment when they might be replaced by bronze. The extreme righthand door was smaller than the other four, made new by Paul V in 1619. An inscription above tells us that this is the Holy Door. Overhead on the left a marble plaque records the bull of indiction of the first Holy Year in 1300. Many are the pilgrims who kneel and, moved by emotion, kiss either the threshold or the door frame. Processions pass through this doorway, singing and praying as they advance, watched over by members of the confraternities dressed in hooded robes and carrying staffs. Once inside, the three majestic naves open up in front of the pilgrim and leave him awestruck (fig. 98). But this sight is not at all oppressive, rather it is extremely uplifting as Schiller has the church of St. Peter's say:

> *Willst thou seek the immeasurable here?*
> *Then thou hast erred,*
> *My greatness is*
> *To make greater theyself.*[70]

186

98. Interior view of St. Peter's with light beaming through the central nave, begun by Michelangelo, completed by Maderno and decorated by Bernini. Upon entering the basilica, the *Cathedra Petri*, St. Peter's Chair, can be seen at the far end through the canopy with rises above the main altar.

99. *Gian Lorenzo Bernini.* Young self-portrait. About 1623. Borghese Gallery, Rome.

Gian Lorenzo Bernini (1598-1680) now began with the embellishment of the church interior (fig. 99). Similar to Michelangelo, he was a genius of all disciplines: sculptor, painter and architect all at the same time. He was as fervently religious as Michelangelo had been, and just as Michelangelo had brought the Roman Renaissance to a glorious climax, Bernini would now create the Roman Baroque. With his churches and palazzi, his squares and fountains he indelibly stamped the city with the Baroque look that still today constitute its glory and fascination. In one last regard can he be compared to Michelangelo: he lived to be over eighty, which at that time was very unusual. Although he had created magnificent tombs for popes and princes, he himself was laid to rest quite obscurely in the family floor tomb in St. Mary Major.

The interior walls of St. Peter's were now covered with costly marble, gilt stuccowork, as well as mosaics. The color spectrum ranges from gold-yellow to red. Bernini wished to give us a foretast of the splendor and

100. *Procession in St. Peter's,* 1775. Copperplate by G. Vasi.

magnificence of Heaven. He wanted to place before our
eyes a heavenly hall leading up to St. Peter's throne, the
Cathedra Petri, in the rear. Thus, he made a throne room
out of the mausoleum that St. Peter's had been from its
very beginning. Yet, the church of St. Peter's has always
been a house of prayer, where for more than 1700 years
the praise of the Lord has been sung. Shortly afterwards,
the piers were decorated with *putti* and portrait medal-

lions of canonized popes (not a gallery of all the popes as we find in St. Paul's). One by one, the empty niches were occupied by statues of the founders of religious orders. High overhead, running around and above the walls, are Greek and Latin quotations from Holy Scripture which refer to Peter. Everything which from a distance appears to be painted, is in reality made of mosaic. This applies to the altar pieces as well as to the decoration of the cupolas and to the main dome itself. These are works of the Vatican School of Mosaic which was founded for the express purpose of decorating the church in this medium which would not deteriorate as paintings would have done. This gave birth to a third period of mosaic art, the Baroque mosaic. Unlike the Ancient and Byzantine schools, it did not produce its own style, but merely copied famous paintings, e.g. Raphael's *Transfiguration* in the left transept.

There are no pews in the naves of the church. People walk about and talk to one another, perhaps a mother feeds her baby, but no one seems to be disturbed by all this. The pilgrims feel at home and do like the Romans do. "In Rome, Christ himself became a Roman", is an oft quoted comment of Dante's. This does not mean the Romans do not pray in St. Peter's, but the church is so big, that one loses sight of those who are praying. They are perhaps gathered around a side altar, where mass is being said, or are paying their respects to Michelangelo's statue of the *Pietà* or to a miraculous image, that had been rescued from the older church. Candles are ablaze throughout the church, and the air is perfumed with incense. From some recess singing is heard. A procession of canons or some sodality in choir gowns passes by. Even a dog is to be seen following them (fig. 100). Some pilgrims stand waiting to kiss the foot of the famous statue of St. Peter which we have already seen in the Holy Year of 1300 (see fig. 28). The foot has slowly been worn down from constant rubbing and kissing; everyone wishes with this gesture to honor St. Peter and his successors (fig. 101).

A few steps further ahead and we find ourselves in front of the *Confessio* (fig. 102). What is meant by this

190

Latin term is the grave of a confessor or a martyr, who by his death has confessed his faith; at the same time it is the place where we should confess our faith for which the martyr sacrificed his life. Between the two opened golden grilled doors, we can get a glimpse of the "pallium niche" which stands in relation to the first niche above the original grave of St. Peter. A Byzantine mosaic of Christ decorates the interior of the niche which contains a golden case. Many people wrongly assume that this holds the remains of the prince of apostles, but its contents are the

101. *Statue of St. Peter.* Its outstretched foot has been worn down by the kissing or touching of the faithful in reverence to St. Peter and his successors.

102. *St Peter's confessio and main altar* with the canopy by Bernini (1633). To the left, the statue of St. Veronica and to the right a
statue of St. Helen. St. Peter's Chair is visible in the rear.

palliums, the special woolen stoles, kept here until the
pope bestows them upon the shoulders of a newly appointed metropolitan. To the right of this niche, there is a small
wall clad in greyish-brown marble. Behind this is the famous *"wall g"* upon which the pilgrims of the third century scratched their names and invocations addressed to
Christ, Mary and Peter. In this wall there is a hollow

space in which the Emperor Constantine had the apostle's remains immured. After their re-discovery they were subjected to thorough scientific examination and eventually re-enshrined here in 1968 by order of Paul VI (fig. 103). These relics can be seen by taking a guided tour through the excavations of the ancient cemetery which lies under the church.

Only a few meters above this is the papal altar, and over this the 26 meter high ($85\frac{1}{2}$ ft.) partially gilded bronze canopy rises up like a giant crown. It rests upon four mighty bronze columns which are enlarged copies of earlier marble ones that encircled the original tomb built by Constantine. These are still in the church but now decorate the four balconies at the corners of the crossing. Bronze bees are seen swarming around on all sides of the

103. *The wall g.* This wall was built in the third century on the right side of the tropaion (see fig. 2). The names, prayers and invocations of those visiting St. Peter's grave have been scratched upon it. The wall contains a hollow area where some bones have been found. Research has shown that they could well be the remains of the apostle which were exhumed at the time of the building of the Constantinian basilica and sealed in this wall, thus preserving them until the present day.

canopy. The bees are the heraldic device of the Barberini family. Pope Urban VIII was, as we know, the most outstanding figure of this family. It was he who gave Bernini the task of taking the bronze beams from under the roof of the Pantheon's portico and melting them down in order to make this canopy. When the Romans saw this they were appalled and cried out: "What the barbarians didn't do, the Barbarini did!" Fortunately, however, that it was done, otherwise we should never have had this magnificent canopy. The only thing that mattered to this Pope was the decoration of St. Peter's interior and the glorification of his name. To show his gratitude towards his great patron, Bernini built his tomb which stands on the right side of the apse. The bees repose here from exhaustion, and the name of the deceased is being written upon a slate by a grim skeleton.

Let us cast our gaze upwards above the baldachin, and we see the immense *dome*, which is resplendent in its gold mosaics (fig. 104). Now we realize how it soars directly above the tomb of St. Peter, how a straight line rises from the level of the first to the second tomb of Peter up to the papal altar, to the baldachin and ultimately, up to the dome itself. With one glance we comprehend the entire history of the church. Michelangelo's dome has become the symbol of God's mercy, which bends over to mankind. Sadly, Michelangelo never saw this with his mortal eyes. He was already seventy-two when he was named chief architect of the "New St. Peter's". He declined any renumeration for the building of the church, as he declared he would do it, "... to the glory of God and for the salvation of my own soul". When he died in 1564, only the drum had been finished. It was not until twenty-six years later that the dome was completed. In the lantern which crowns the dome, God the Father hovers overhead in the clouds with his arms outstreched as if he would protect and bless the tomb of St. Peter, ever safeguarding it down to the present day.

194

104. Interior view of the dome of St. Peter's. This masterpiece by Michelangelo was completed in 1590 after his death. Later it was decorated completely with mosaics. God the Father is depicted high above in the lantern, with arms outstretched as if blessing the grave of St. Peter far below.

105. The *Cathedra Petri*, the so-called Chair of St. Peter, is a wooden throne (see fig. 7) enclosed by Bernini in 1665 in a gilded bronze case and set between clouds and rays of light. Underneath, four Fathers of the Church touch it ever so lightly with their fingertips. The Holy Spirit hovers above in the window and seems to indicate that the Holy Spirit illumines the pope when he speaks *ex cathedra*.

Looking through the baldachin to the rear of the church, we see the *Cathedra Petri* or St. Peter's throne, which at a medium height seems to float amidst clouds and rays of light (fig. 105). It is the perfect termination point for the historical development which has its beginning with the obelisk outside in the square, from the time of the first persecution of the Christians in Rome, passing through the portico and the long central nave over Peter's tomb, to the papal altar and finally reaches the throne of St. Peter, which is the focal point of the entire church.

The *Cathedra Petri*, so perfect in this context, did not exist at the time of the Holy Year of 1625. It was only created by Bernini some 40 years later in the high-blown Baroque style, which liked to combine many different elements and materials: architecture, sculpture, gold, bronze, stucco work and glass. The old and venerable wooden throne mentioned earlier (p. 20), which Emperor Charles the Bald had brought from Metz for his coronation (see fig. 7) was placed by Bernini in a gilt bronze case and lifted up over the altar. Four Fathers of the Church, two from the Eastern Church and two from the West, (the bishops Ambrose and Augustine, Athanasius and John Chrysostom), touch the legs of the throne, as if to express the collegiality of the bishops with the Pope. Naturally, the term "collegiality" did not exist back then, having only come into common usage during the Second Vatican Council, but Bernini has already illustrated the concept here. The bishops do not support the throne; they only touch it lightly with their fingertips, as if to say that the Pope does not reign without the bishops and they do not govern without him. The papacy is not something created by man but by God. Above all of this, the Holy Spirit hovers in a stained glass window, seeming to indicate that the Pope will be illumined by the Holy Spirit, when he speaks *ex cathedra*, that is from his throne, and solemnly pronounces a dogma. As was earlier done in St. Mary Major with the representation of the assumption of Mary, an artist has once again anticipated a dogma; in Bernini's lifetime the doctrine of the papal infallilbility had not yet been dogmatically defined but already believed — at least in Rome. It was not until 1870 that this dogma was finally proclaimed. In the afternoon, when the sun shines through this window of golden-yellow Bohemian glass, it glows and the dove seems to come to life and to waft through God's Church. No pope ever sits upon this throne. It is merely a symbol of the office of Peter and hence of the Pope. The pilgrim will search for a throne in vain, as there is no permanent throne. Only when special ceremonies require it is one installed, usually upon the *Confessio*; in this way the canopy not only frames the papal altar but the throne as well.

During Holy Week, the church's most important relics have long been displayed here from the four loggias in the crossing. They are: Veronica's veil; a large fragment of the True Cross, found by the empress Helen; the lance of Longinus which pierced Christ's side and the head of Andrew the apostle, which was restored to Patras in 1964.

Huge marble statues of these four saints stand under each of the loggias.

Behind each of these statues is a small staircase that leads down to the so-called, "sacred grottoes of the Vatican". This is a 2-3 meter high (7-10 ft) intermediate level which lies between the floor of the first basilica and the floor of the present day church. As these rooms were originally so dark and damp, they were given the name of "sacred grottoes of the Vatican" ("grotta" means cave in Italian). It was a subterranean realm of the dead in which popes, emperors and queens were buried. Today the grottoes have been enlarged and illuminated. Nevertheless, they have maintained their magical half-light and mystical atmosphere. One gets the feeling of going back into the early history of Christianity, to descend right down to its very roots. Through openings in the floor, one can look down and see the ancient necropolis which lies under this level. Constantine, as we know, had this filled in with earth, in order to build his basilica on top of the tomb of Peter. In our century the necropolis has been partially excavated in order to lay free St. Peter's grave. Above us, here and there, are grilled openings through which we can see up to the highest point of the dome. Song and prayer filter down through them from the church overhead. We can see up to the dome's summit.

We follow a narrow semi-circular corridor which leads us around St. Peter's immured tomb. At midpoint of this circuit, to one side, we find the vault of Pius XII (1939-58) and directly opposite this, the Clementine Chapel, also named Peter's Chapel (fig. 106). The reason for this second name is that the altar wall and the first monument to St. Peter are contiguous and stand back to back. In 1600, Clement VIII had this chapel richly decorated in marble and gilt stuccowork. Through the grillwork which is behind the altar one sees a white marble wall with porphyry stripes. This is the monument, as we already have learned, that Constantine placed upon the apostle's original burial site. Now we see this bit of it from the rear, but soon we shall also look at it from the front side.

198

106. *St. Peter's Chapel,* also known as the Clementine Chapel after Clement VIII (1592-1605) who had it decorated. Behind the altar is a gilded grill through which the back wall of St. Peter's funeral monument can be made out. This was built by Constantine and was covered with white marble and strips of porphyry.

In the corridor we pass by several national chapels, a Polish one, Irish, Czech as well as Lithuanian. Finally we reach a low-lit three-naved subterranean church, at whose sides sarcophagi of popes, emperors and queens are placed. The front wall of the central nave has recently been broken through so that we see the *Confessio* through a plate glass partition (fig. 107). This allows us to look straight at St. Peter's tomb. We have arrived; we have reached the heart of St. Peter's church, and with this the goal of our pilgrim's quest. Here, let us take a moment to meditate in thanksgiving.

Following the indications for the exit, we pass by the tombs of the modern popes: on the left side is the tomb of *John XXIII* (1958-63), while standing diagonally across are those of *Benedict XV* (1914-22) and *John Paul I* (1978). Again on the left side we see the tomb of *Paul VI* (1963-78). At the end of this side nave is the tomb of *Boniface VIII* (1294-1303), recumbent upon his bed of repose, a beautiful work by Arnolfo di Cambio (see fig. 13). We are quite familiar with this Pope, as it was he who proclaimed the first Jubilee Year in 1300. Looking across to the extreme opposite nave we can make out the gray stone sarcophagus of the only English pope, Hadrian IV, Nicholas Breakspear (1154-59). Further on in the same row is the sarcophagus of the last Catholic king of England, James III (died 1776). He lies buried together with his two sons; upon their deaths the royal line of Stuart died out. A bronze crown lies upon the tomb and represents the crown of England, which in reality was never worn by the father or by his sons.

In the rear can be seen Canova's marble statue of the kneeling Pius VI who died in 1799 in France as Napoleon's prisoner.

At the exit we meet yet another statue of St. Peter enthroned, similar to the one in the upper church. This one has his right foot outstretched as well, but no one kisses it, because it is a statue from late antiquity, which originally represented a pagan philosopher. It was found some-

107. View of the *Confessio* seen from the level of the lower Church. The frontal view shows the "pallium niche", so called because of the coffer containing the palliums to be conferred on newly appointed metropolitan bishops. The back wall of the niche is covered with a Byzantine mosaic of Christ. At the right side of the niche stands a small marble wall, behind which is the so-called *wall g*, which contains the relics attributed to St. Peter.

where nearby but with no head, and promptly turned (in 1565) into a St. Peter, by giving him his typical features: curly hair and short beard. To finish him off, his two keys were placed in his hand. This demonstrates how easy it was to transform a pagan philosopher into an apostle. We eventually come out into the open air and find ourselves in a Vatican courtyard with the mighty walls of the Sistine Chapel towering above us. From here we make our way back to the portico of the church and so to St. Peter's Square.

XIII

The Jubilee Years of the High Baroque Age 1650 - 1675

Although we have just gone ahead into the future in order to outline the building history of St Peter's all the way up until its completion, let us now return to the seventeenth century.

In the Baroque era, Rome was the artistic mecca and the model of all cities. Art and handicrafts flourished here as nowhere else, and merit is due to the popes and their courts who provided the great commissions. Without them we would never have had so many magnificent works of art, and we should, all of us, be the poorer for it.

The more Rome glorified itself with churches, palazzi, fountains and piazzas, the more ostentatious the Romans' religious sense became. Processions began to resemble carnival parades with floats decked out with allegorical themes and tableaux, accompanied by dazzling firework displays (these things were called *macchine* and even great artists, like Bernini, designed such *macchine*). Religious services became magnificent performances of theatrical piety. In the Baroque period there was a passion for putting oneself on display, vying for honor and preeminence during these ceremonies. The Pope had to expressly forbid the carrying of weapons at festivities as it seems that the fingers of certain pilgrims were more adroit at holding a dagger than the rosary beads.

108. *Innocent X.* Painting by Velázquez in 1650. Gallery of Palazzo Doria Pamphilj, Rome.

The Holy Year 1650 signified the high point of the Baroque era in Rome. It came two years after the Peace of Westphalia, which brought about the end of not only the Thirty Years' War, but also of the medieval concept of a "Holy Roman Empire of German Nation". Germany had ceded prominence to France. The principle of peaceful co-existence of nations would be recognized for the very first time. The Pope, for his part, made protests against the treaty through his nuncio, Fabio Chigi (later to become his successor as Alexander VII), since the Holy See's prerogatives had not been preserved, but his protests fell upon deaf ears. The States of the Church continued to exist but more through inertia, not on account of any new impetus.

The Pope at this time was an elderly, sickly, weak-willed man, *Innocent X* Pamphilj (1644-55). In the magnificent portrait of him, painted by the Spaniard *Velásquez,* his gaze is diffident and displays resignation (fig. 108). He had good reason for looking like this as he was totally dominated by his sister-in-law, his late brother's widow. Her name was Olimpia, but the people called her *olim pia* (once pious).

Thanks to the hefty dowry brought by *Donna Olimpia* (1595-1657), Innocent was able to make a career for himself in the papal court. Now that he was Pope, she was collecting interest. Just how energetic and power-hungry she was can be seen in the marble portrait-bust of her sculpted by *Alessandro Algardi* (1595-1654) (fig. 109). Her avarice knew no bounds. She took from the dying Pope his last money from under his mattress. She made sure she received the commemorative gold coins that were walled up at the end of the previous Holy Year in the Holy Door of the Lateran and should by tradition have gone to the Cathedral Chapter when again recovered at the door's re-opening at Christmas 1649.

Donna Olimpia did, however, demonstrate a devout religious as well as charitable zeal. She founded a noble-women's committee, that collected money and provided beds for the poor pilgrims. She personally oversaw the direction of the Pilgrims' Hospice of the Most Holy Trinity with which we are already acquainted. A malicious report of her role in the Holy Year was given by the Abbot Cesare Gualdi in a booklet which he entitled: "The life of Donna Olimpia Maidalchini, who ruled the Church during the pontificate of Innocent X". Concerning her role in the Holy Year we read: "Whosoever came to Rome wanted above all else to see Donna Olimpia. It seemed that the indulgence would be more easily obtained by gazing upon this woman than by visiting the prescribed churches. Many were those who zealously hankered to find a hotel near her palace and paid no thought to paying exhorbitant prices for such. Most pilgrims, especially the women among them, spent the entire day standing around her

204

109. *Donna Olimpia.* Marble bust by A. Algardi, 1646. Gallery of Palazzo Doria Pamphilj, Rome.

palace for no other reason than to see her but appear at the window. She, evidently, took great pleasure in being seen, and perhaps even more than the others took in seeing her".[71]

Small wonder then, that when a man of the lower classes, whether off-guardedly or intentionally derisive, said that he knew nothing about the Pope's Holy Year, just that of Donna Olimpia, he was jailed for three days.

Innocent X had to build a princely palace to please Donna Olimpia, *Palazzo Pamphilj* on *Piazza Navona*. At this point in time the piazza was the center of Rome, just as it becomes again today during the tourist season — especially so by night. The square has still preserved the shape of the ancient stadium that it once was. Its beauty is enhanced by three magnificent fountains. The central one is the largest and by far the most famous. It is called the *Four Rivers Fountain* and was created by Bernini in 1650 (fig. 110). Stone, water and air all come into fanciful play within the framework of the oblong piazza. The four male figures are personifications of the four most important rivers of the four continents, known at that time, Europe, Asia, Africa and America. Australia was not yet discovered. Three figures look away from the church which stands opposite, Sant'Agnese in Agone, as if they did not want to see the building. Only the Rio de la Plata looks toward the church, but with a horror-stricken gaze. He holds his hand up as if to protect himself, afraid as he is of the church falling down upon him. With this gesture Bernini is supposed to have expressed his criticism of Borromini's work. The anecdote goes further saying that when Borromini saw the evil trick that Bernini was playing on him, he placed a statue of St. Agnes upon the roof balustrade. She rests her hand quite calmly upon her breast as if to vouchsafe for the church's protection. Indeed, she has kept her promise, as the church still stands today, and the dialogue continues back and forth between the hand of the Rio de la Plata and that of St. Agnes. We see from this that in Rome the very stones speak. Even if it is not always a true story, it is at least a legend or, as in this case, an amusing anecdote.

In honor of the Holy Year a magnificent pageant took place in Piazza Navona for Easter of 1650. By today's standards it would seem to have been more of a carnival parade than a religious celebration (fig. 111). At both ends of the square were erected oversized altars with representations of Christ's resurrection and of the Assumption of Mary. Skyrockets were shot off from the center. The decorations and the processsion were arranged and paid for by the Spanish embassy, in the desire to show once more the glory of the Spanish empire. This was, however, to be a swan-song, as shortly thereafter Spain lost its hegemony,

110. The *Four Rivers Fountain* by Bernini in Piazza Navona. The church of *Sant'Agnese in Agone* by Borromini stands just opposite. The statue of St. Agnes placed on top of the façade rests her hand upon her breast as if to assure us that the church is not going to collapse, in contrast with the gesture of the river-god Rio de la Plata at the fountain below whose outstretched arm seems to indicate his fear that the building is about to fall down upon him at any moment.

111. *Easter procession in Piazza Navona in 1650. Engraving by D. Barrière, 1650.*

112. *Macchina* representing the adoration of the sacrifice of the Mass, built by C. Rainaldi in the church of *Il Gesù* for the Holy Year of 1650. Engraving by L. Rinaldi, 1650.

even here in Rome when the French faction in the Roman Curia won the upper hand. It is quite possible, that during these Easter festivities in Piazza Navona, *Calderon de la Barca's* religious drama *The Holy Year in Rome* was performed.

In the Jesuit church, *Il Gesù*, a religious play was enacted in the same year. For this event, the church interior was transformed into a gigantic stage set, as can be observed in an engraving (fig. 112). This *macchina* was made by Carlo Rainaldi, who ranked third as architect in Rome after Bernini and Borromini. The Sacrifice of Solomon was the theme. As Solomon was about to make his sacrificial holocaust, a monstrance with the sacred host inside floated overhead in the clouds. Higher still, God the Father encircled by angels, spread open his arms. The intent here was to draw parallels between the Old and New Testaments, between Judaic sacrifices and Christ's sacrifice on the cross, in a typical manifestation of the theatrical devotion of the Baroque era.

A memento of Innocent X and the Holy Year of 1650 is the church of the Lateran. He had it rebuilt in the new Baroque style; so much so, that it completely lost its look of an Early Christian basilica. We have already described the Lateran in the fifth chapter. The travertine façade was added later by Alessandro Galilei in 1735 and greatly resembles St. Peter's (fig. 113).

The Holy Year of Innocent X is especially well represented in several engravings. Let us look at just one of these (fig. 114). Here we have a bird's-eye view of the seven pilgrimage churches, the Tiber, the city walls and the church of *S. Maria del Popolo*, which at times was used to substitute the churches of St. Paul's or St. Sebastian's, if either of them were inaccessible on account of flooding or due to the danger of malaria. S. Maria del Popolo is located adjacent to the city gate Porta del Popolo which was entered by all pilgrims coming from the North. The church dates back to Sixtus IV, who we know as the builder of the Sistine Chapel. It still stands just as it did back in 1511 when Martin Luther as a devout monk

210

113. The new façade of the *Church of the Lateran* built in late Baroque style by A. Galilei in 1735. The modern statue of St. Francis, with hands raised up in prayer, stands opposite.

stayed there in the Augustinian monastery connected to the church and it is still run by the Augustinians. The Byzantine icon of Mary was there too, in its place over the high altar. It is one of seven icons attributed to St. Luke. Pinturicchio had already decorated the church with his fine frescoes, but in Luther's time, the moment had not yet arrived when Caravaggio would grace the church with his masterpieces of "The Conversion of St. Paul" and "The Crucifixion of St. Peter" (we have already seen his "Madonna of the Pilgrims" in S. Agostino: see fig. 90).

What is also interesting to note in Paluzzi's engraving is the third arm of the colonnade designed by Bernini, which was planned by him but never built. In addition there are two small churches to be seen in the upper righthand corner of the picture, that had been added just recently to the list of the seven main churches. They are *Tre Fontane* and *S. Maria Annunziata*. If the seven pilgrimage churches were not sufficient to satisfy the pilgrims' fervent devotion, they could continue over the open countryside to the site of St. Paul's execution, *Tre Fontane*.

211

114. Innocent X opening the Holy Door in 1650, with views of *the ten churches* which at that time were visited by the pilgrims. In addition to the seven churches on the pilgrims' itinerary, the churches of S. Maria del Popolo, Tre Fontane and L'Annunziatella also figure. St. Peter's Square appears with a third colonnade as originally planned. Engraving by G. Paluzzi, 1650.

Called "Three Fountains" after the three spring-fed fountains, the water is said to have sprung forth from the
spots hit by the decapitated head of the apostle. We have
already mentioned this ancient legend (see p. 72). From
here a country road led to the little church of the Annunziata, also called *Annunziatella* (a diminuitive form which
is quite sweet-sounding). It sits upon ancient ground,
where once Roman villas were and catacombs as well.
Around 1220, in order to safeguard the many relics which
were said to have been here, Honorius III had the church
built and dedicated it to the Annunciation. The cosmatesque flooring and the campanile both date back to
the thirteenth century. The fifteenth century saw the fres-
coeing of the apse which, of course, depicts the scene of
the Annunciation. During the Baroque era the façade was
painted and the interior was remodeled. In his artistic
guide *Le Nove Chiese di Roma*, published in 1639, the
painter Giovanni Baglione provides us with a good description of the church. So now instead of seven, there were
nine pilgrimage churches, and if *S. Maria del Popolo* was
counted, that brought the number up to ten. Some time
later the *Annunziatella* and its surroundings would fall into oblivion, but in the last few decades the area has
changed drastically due to the development of a new resi-
dential quarter called Grotta Perfetta. The once forgotten
chapel is today a thriving parish with 40,000 parishoners.

* * *

Upon the demise of Innocent X in 1655, Donna
Olimpia made her exit (by literally fleeing Rome) leaving
the stage free for an even more eccentric woman, by far
the most celebrated of all female pilgrims to Rome, *Queen
Christina of Sweden* (1620-89). The inner side of the city
gate of Piazza del Popolo was redesigned by Bernini as a
triumphal arch (fig. 115). To the Queen's "felicitous and
triumphal entry" proclaims the inscription above the arch.
Indeed, the magnificent parade around her, as she made
her entry into the city had impressed the Romans as if it

213

were a triumphal march glorifying the triumph of the true faith, that is of Catholicism.

Christina was the only child of King Gustavus Adolphus, who as defender of Lutheranism had fallen in battle during the Thirty Years War. When still a child, Christina had inherited the crown. By means of great study and secret instruction from Jesuit teachers, she came to be familiar with Catholic belief and wished to become a Catholic, which at that time in Lutheran Sweden was entirely impossible. She had to renounce her throne and leave her homeland. In 1655, on her way to Rome, she officially embraced Catholicism in the Hofkirche of Innsbruck. The papal legate, before whom she knelt while she made here solemn profession of faith, was himself a convert from the North, *Lukas Holstenius* (1596-1661). He was the son of a Hamburg dyer named Holste. Being an extremely learned man, Holstenius had risen to the position of Prefect of the Vatican Library. The high point of his career was this moment when, in the name of the Pope, he received the queen into the Catholic Church. From this point onwards, a unique friendship would grow up between the haughty queen and the unpretentious dyer's son. Both having come from the Protestant North, they shared the experience of converting to Catholicism and also the love of learning. Immediately after her conversion, Christina entered Rome with the splendor befitting a Catholic monarch. With the exception of some travel, she stayed and lived out the rest of her life in the Eternal City. She never married, never regained any kingdom, rather she dedicated herself to religion, art and science. She was an extraordinarily clever and learned woman, but also extremely ugly looking. She had a large hooked nose, a malformed body and a mannish voice. Arrogant and extravagant in her manner, she took sport in shooting off cannonballs to scare simple folk, and shocking the finer classes with her excentric attire. She was, of course, the center of attraction in Roman society and had her place of honor at all religious and social functions. Once she disrupted the solemn silence of a pontifical high mass when she loudly admonished one of her

214

115. *Porta del Popolo*, the city gate through which the pilgrims arriving from the north entered the city. Bernini transformed the gate into a triumphal arch to celebrate the entry of Queen Christine of Sweden. On the right is the church of *Santa Maria del Popolo*.

Protestant attendants to kneel for the papal blessing. At Eastertime she washed the feet of twelve impoverished pilgrims at the pilgrims' hospice of the Most Holy Trinity, and with tears in her eyes she mounted the Holy Steps on her knees. She asserted that she never regretted having renounced her kingdom for the sake of her faith, and as she lay dying in 1689 she uttered these proud words: "I was born free, I've lived free and I die freed". These words are written upon the wall of her death chamber in Palazzo Corsini. Since she made the greatest sacrifice which could be imagined at that time, renouncing her throne, she was buried alongside the popes in St. Peter's with honors worthy of a queen. Carlo Fontana designed her funeral moment which stands diagonally opposite the Pietà in the righthand nave (fig. 116). Her conversion is depicted on its side and the crown she renounced lies upon it. The realistic portrait is by G.B.

116. *Funeral monument of Queen Christine of Sweden* (died 1689) in St. Peter's. Designed by Carlo Fontana, the sarcophagus exterior shows the scene of her embracing the Catholic faith in 1655. The prelate who is holding the book up to her is the learned Lucas Holstenius of Hamburg.

Théodon. Christina's grave, however, is not here but below in the grottoes, next to the tomb of Pope John XXIII.

The seventeenth century was not only the age of Baroque but also the age of Jansenism, which threatened, especially in France, to create an internal rift in the Church through its rigorous moral doctrines, while the Romans busied themselves quarreling over Quietism, mystical speculations, theological casuistry and religious trivialities. In those times the famous French preacher and writer, *Jacques B. Bossuet*, bishop of Meaux (1627-1704), published his commentaries of the Holy Year and the Indulgences, *Méditations sur la rémission de péchés pour le temps du Jubilé et des indulgences, tirées principalement du Concile de Trente*. This treatise first appeared in 1696 and met with such success that it was subsequently expanded and published in different languages.

XIV

The Holy Years During the Enlightenment 1700 - 1725 - 1750 - 1775

The Holy Year of 1700 brings us into the century of the Enlightenment. A new secular and anticlerical attitude was developing in opposition to the excessive mysticism of certain exclusive circles and against the superstitious beliefs that prevailed amongst the common people. Matters of faith ought to be reasoned out through the individual's own understanding and be subject to criticism. In Rome, however, there was, at least for the time being, no trace of this new spirit.

"Of the Jubilee Year of the Year 1700" is the title of an engraving which shows "St. Peter's, the main church in Rome" in unusual perspective and filled with countless numbers of people (fig. 117). A magnifying glass is needed to make out the single figures. The print was made by the German engraver Hans Ulrich Crauss of Augsburg. This engraving was published in different languages and sold to the pilgrims as a souvenir.

Shortly before the beginning of the year 1700, *Queen Maria Casimira* made her appearance in Rome. She was the widow of the king of Poland, John III Sobieski, who had saved Vienna when it was besieged by the Turks in 1683. The queen wished to match the pomp and grandeur, as well as the piety, that had distiguished Christina of Sweden. Yet she was not of Christina's stature and therefore the Romans quipped: "She is a Christian but not a Christina!" Her journey to Rome with her enormous retinue resembled much more a triumphal procession than a pilgrimage, and was described by Antonio Bassani.[72] Her

218

117. *The Jubilee Year of 1700* in St. Peter's shown in an unusual perspective and with countless figures. German engraving by H.V. Crauss, Augsburg.

portrait is reproduced here from this book (fig. 118). She founded a convent in *Palazzo Zuccari* in the via Sistina, where she, at times, was wont to seek solitude. Today the building belongs to the Max Planck Institute and is the seat of the German library of art history, the *Hertziana*. Maria Casimira was responsible for the charming oriel which overlooks the square of *Trinità dei Monti* at the top of the Spanish Steps. When her resources had dwindled she quietly left Rome in 1714, and died two years later in France, in poverty and in solitude. Much later her remains were taken to Crackow where they were interred next to those of her famed consort, in whose glory she still shares.

219

118. *Queen Casimira of Poland* came to Rome for the Holy Year of 1700. Portrait by A. Odasio.

Yet another queen without a country was soon to attract attention. This was *Maria Clementina* (1702-35) a granddaughter of John Sobieski and the above mentioned Maria Casimira. While still quite young, she had been married to the last Stuart King James III who had to flee England together with his father when he was still a child and spent the rest of his life in Rome, where he lived from the Pope's munificence. Maria Clementina was an extremely devout woman, who felt uncomfortable with the pleasure-seeking lifestyle at court. She died at the age of thirty-three, worn out by a perhaps not unfounded jealousy and from constant penitential exercises. "With her death the eyeballs of the entire Catholic world wept", reads the funeral commemoration in the great pathos typical of court preachers. She can be considered the last Catholic queen of England and as such was interred in St. Peter's, unfortunately in one of the most awkward spots: standing directly above an entry to one of the dome stairways. It was executed by *Filippo Bargioni* in the taste of the late Baroque and displays cherubs and allegories of virtues (fig. 119). The personification of Charity holds the portrait of the queen, a typical lady of the Rococo age with powdered wig, painted by *Ignatius Stern*. The sarcophagus bears the proud

119. *Funeral monument of Maria Clementina Stuart* (died 1735), "Queen of England, France and Ireland" as is inscribed upon her sarcophagus in St. Peter's. She was the grand-daughter of Queen Casimira and wife of James Stuart, the Old Pretender, but she never set foot upon British soil. Her tomb was designed by F. Bargioni and her portrait is a painting by I. Stern.

inscription: "Maria Clementina, Queen of Great Britain, France and Ireland". In reality she never once set foot upon the soil of any of these countries. Chronologically speaking, she is the last of the six women who are buried in St. Peter's.

There was also a German princess who distiguished herself by her great piety during the Holy Year of 1725. This was *Beatrice of Bavaria*, the young and childless widow of the grand-duke Ferdinand of Tuscany. She later received the golden rose from the Pope in recognition of her virtues, with which she had tried to compensate for her lack of beauty and her unhappy lot.

The Pope in this year was *Benedict XIII* Orsini (1724-1730), a Dominican monk marked by a strong asceticism and unfamiliarity with the ways of the world; the exact antithesis of his predecessors. His excessive rigidity soon made him unpopular. For the Holy Year all games and festivities were suspended, even lotto, and this aroused the ire of the Romans. He wished to reform the Roman clergy, and for this purpose, in occasion of the Holy Year, called a *provincial synod* in the Lateran, which, among other things, forbade the current fashion among priests of wearing wigs and taking snuff during religious ceremonies. An amusing story can be told here which relates to these reforms: certain preachers, in a desire to follow the strict line sct down by the Pope, from their pulpits reviled the current women's fashion of silk dresses and silk bonnets. This, however, put the customs office of the Papal States into a state of alarm. Duties upon silk goods represented a considerable source of revenue; if no silk was sold, that would put the state into serious financial difficulties. A commission of cardinals (!) was formed to decide upon the matter and after much debate and consideration, the preachers were advised not to utter anything more against the silk fashion.[73]

Benedict XIII left the management of all temporal affairs to his favorite, the unworthy Cardinal *Nicolò Coscia*, preferring to find serenity in the monastery of *S. Maria Sopra Minerva*. He was later buried in this church, and his funeral monument, designed by C. Marchioni, has upon it a scene representing the Roman synod of 1725. The church itself dates back to the time of the first Jubilee

Year and enjoys the distinction of being the only church in Rome to possess gothic vaulting. It is duly famous for many other reasons, especially for the Michelangelo statue of the resurrected Christ (which holds a cross in its hand as symbol of victory). The tombs of *St. Catherine of Siena* (died 1380) patron saint of Italy and the painter and friar *Fra Angelico* (died 1455) are found here as well. In 1687, this church witnessed the solemn abjuration of Miguel de Molinos, the chief apostle of Quietism, which had created quite a following in Rome. In the adjoining Dominican monastery sat the Inquisition which brought Galileo before trial in 1633.

In the square before the church is a whimsical little marble elephant by *Bernini*. An Egyptian obelisk rests up-on its back; its hieroglyphs were thought to hide some magic formula (fig. 120). This is why the legend below tells us that it would take an elephant's strength to bear the wisdom of Egypt.

Under this otherwise stern Pope the exuberant *Scalinata di Trinità dei Monti*, the Spanish Steps, was completed. This is a work of the Roman architect Francesco de Sanctis who also designed the pilgrims' church of SS. Trinità dei Pellegrini, which is already familiar to us. The steps

120. *Santa Maria sopra Minerva.* A small marble elephant is carrying an Egyptian obelisk upon his back. The significance is that one must have an elephant's strength to bear the wisdom of Egypt. A fanciful invention attributed to Bernini, 1650.

121. *The Spanish Steps.* Built by Francesco de Sanctis in 1725. They lead up to the Church of the Holy Trinity and serve as a meeting spot for tourists and artists. In the period between Easter and Pentecost the steps are covered with azaleas. At the foot of the steps there is a fountain in the shape of a small boat. Water leaks out of it. Therefore it is called the "barcaccia" or broken boat.

are a masterpiece of Rococo design; they undulate with a complex series of curves and landings to form a link between the square and the Church of the Holy Trinity on the Pincian hill (fig. 121). The steps immediately became the favorite meeting place for artists, who now were coming to Rome in great droves, not for the indulgence as the pilgrims did, but rather to find inspiration or commissions. Just a stone's throw from here we find the famed Caffé Greco, where Goethe used to come to enjoy a sip of coffee in the company of fellow artists and countrymen.

To bring our theme to a close, let us go a step farther to the Trevi Fountain, whose construction had just gotten underway and would finally be completed by *Nicolò Salvi* (1697-1751; fig. 122). Not only tourists but pilgrims as well, continue the old and beautiful custom of taking their leave of Rome by throwing a coin into the fountain. This has to be done with your back to the fountain and throwing the coin over your left shoulder, making a wish to return someday to Rome. It is a small *obolus* or offering to the city of Rome, an act of thank's giving for the many splendours that you have enjoyed in Rome.

Ludovico Muratori wrote in his *Annali* of the Holy Year of 1725: "The participation of foreigners was not

122. *The Trevi Fountain* by N. Salvi was completed in 1762. Tradition has it that one's return to Rome is guaranteed by throwing a coin into the fountain.

123a. Twelve scenes depicting ceremonies of the Holy Year. Engraving by B. Picard, Amsterdam, 1723.

Les Pelerins vont en Procession visiter les Sept Eglises . | Les Pelerins montent à genoux LA SCALA SANTA.

Les PRELATS, et BARONS Romains, vêtis en Peniten- | Le PAPE benit les tables des Pelerins, et leur sert a manger.
lavent les pieds des Pelerins, et les *** *** . | avec les CARDINAUX, et autres PRELATS .

Le PAPE distribue aux Pelerins des Chapelets, Medailles. | A La fin du Jubilé, le PAPE pose la premiere pierre.
et Agnus Dei, et ils lui baisent les pieds . | pour fermer la PORTE SAINTE .

123b. Twelve scenes depicting ceremonies of the Holy Year. Engraving by B. Picard, Amsterdam, 1723.

227

great, due to the fact that many countries were in a state of war, but also because the novelty of this holy function had worn off.[74] In this year, however, a miracle occured which is worth mentioning, because it happened to a pilgrim, *Johann Kouvalski*, of Brünn in Moravia. This story shows in contrast to Muratori's assertion, the sacrifices made in order to come to Rome and the euphoria that was experienced by these pilgrims. Kouvalski, who as a soldier had fought against the Turks at Belgrad, had received injuries which had left him crippled. He could only move about by dragging himself with his hands. It was in this way that he made his way to Rome; driven all the while by an inner voice which assured him, that once there, he would be cured. In St. Peter's he asked some fellow-pilgrims to lift him up so that he might kiss the foot of St. Peter's statue. As he touched Peter's foot, he was instantly healed and once again able to stand upon both legs. Thus cured, he returned home. The case files of this miracle can be read in the Vatican Library.[75]

In 1723, *Bernard Picard* (1673-1733) published in Amsterdam two large volumes dealing with *Cérémonies et Coutumes Religieuses de tous les peuples du monde, présentées par des Figures dessinées de la main de Bernard Picard, avec une Explication Historique et quelques Dissertations curieuses.* In the first volume there are twelve scenes depicting the Holy Year, stage by stage (fig. 123): the Pope pronouncing the bull and opening the Holy Door; sending the cardinals on to the other three basilicas; the pilgrims receiving the tap upon their heads with the long rod and traveling to the seven churches and going up the Holy Steps on bended knee; prelates and nobles washing the feet of the pilgrims and serving them at their table; the pilgrims kissing the feet of the Pope and receiving medals from him; and finally the Pope sealing up the Holy Door. Picard noted in his commentary, that upon completion of the ceremonies, the cardinals accompanied the Pope to his private apartments where the Pope served them: "...a superb dinner, to help them relax after the day's fatigue".[76]

* * *

Next, we come to Pope *Benedict XIV* Lambertini (1740-58), who was the complete opposite of his stern and reclusive namesake, Benedict XIII. He was sociable, kind of heart and possessed both common sense and a sense of humor. He seems to have had the same effect upon people as Pope John XXIII had in our era.

Giovanni Paolo Pannini (1691-1765) painted a famous picture which, up until 1940, was in the private collection of the Modiano family of Bologna and which has, unfortunately, disappeared. Only one old photograph of the painting serves to show us with what splendor, with what richness of figures, color and movement, Pannini executed this picture of the opening of the Holy Door by Benedict XIV in 1749 (fig. 124). It was this Pope who made a requirement of receiving Holy Communion while prior to that time it had been only necessary to be confessed in order to obtain the Jubilee indulgence.

This year also saw the appearance of a famous preacher and saint: *Fra Leonardo da Porto Maurizio* (1676-1751), a Franciscan of the monastery of St. Bonaventure on the Palatine hill. His preaching enjoyed such success that he was named "the apostle of Italy". Since there was no church large enough to accomodate the great numbers who came to listen to his sermons, he preached in the open air of Piazza Navona, which we already know from the Spanish processions organized in the Holy Year of 1650. An anonymous painter of the time has shown Fra Leonardo as he preached; he holds his hand upon a large crucifix, and the assembly of people listen deeply stirred (fig. 125). All around the square prelates and nobles listen from windows and balconies. A sermon in those days was a sort of spiritual spectacle, during which one laughed, wept, trembled, applauded and enjoyed experiencing a vast range of emotions and changes of sentiment. Woe to the preacher who was too brief, as he would most certainly be unpopular!

Fra Leonardo brought a new inwardness to this Holy Year, propagating Franciscan forms of devotion, especially that of the Way of the Cross. During his lifetime he is re-

229

124. *Benedict XIV* opens the Holy Door on Christmas Eve 1749. Lost painting by G.B. Pannini, 1750.

125. *Fra Leonardo of Porto Maurizio* preaching in Piazza Navona. Anonymous. 1750. Museum of Rome.

ported to have introduced the stations of the cross in 576 different places. He reached his goal when, on the 27th of December 1750, he set up the stations of the cross in the Colosseum and Pope Benedict XIV consecrated it to the passion of the martyrs. This is recorded upon a marble plaque still found in the Colosseum. It finally brought an end to the wanton destruction of the Colosseum which centurylong had been used as a quarry, providing an easily available fund of building stone for the churches and palazzi of Rome. As early as the beginning of the sixteenth century the former gladiatorial amphitheatre had been used for putting on passion plays. Now the Colosseum was to become a site of Christian worship, an open air church, an ideal meeting place for pilgrims coming from all parts of the world, where torchlit processions and midnight mass would be held and the Christian martyrs would be remembered, they who were believed to have suffered and

126. On Good Friday the pope leads the Stations of the Cross at the Colosseum. It is the most moving ceremony of Holy Week.

bled to death here. Only in recent times were the stations of the cross removed and the central cross placed on the side of the arena. The arena itself has been excavated, making it impossible to congregate in its middle as was earlier done. The pope, however, still leads the Stations of the Cross on Good Friday. With the illuminated eerie ruins as a backdrop, this is the most moving event of Holy Week (fig. 126).

In 1750, *St. Mary Major* received a new stone facade executed in late Baroque style. Designed by *Ferdinando Fuga*, it unfortunately almost entirely covers the Byzantine mosaic of the original façade (fig. 127). At the same time, *Domenico Gregorini* completely remodeled *Santa Croce in Gerusalemme* (fig. 128).

127. Ferdinand Fuga's new façade for *St. Mary Major* for the Holy Year of 1750. The Romanesque bell tower rises up behind it. An ancient column and a fountain stand in the square before the basilica.

128. D. Gregorini's new façade for the church of the *Holy Cross in Jerusalem* built in Roccoco style for the Holy Year of 1750.

* * *

Towards the close of the age of Enlightenment, *Pius VI* Braschi (1775-99) ascended the papal throne. Goethe defined him as "the most beautiful and dignified figure of a man". He was the last Pope to build a palace for his nephews, the Palazzo Braschi at the *Piazza Navona*. He was also the last to have the Holy Year celebrated in full Baroque magnificence. Guest of honor was the archduke Maximilian, brother of Joseph II, emperor of Austria, whose goodwill the pontiff treasured. In his honor, a *macchina* was built at the base of Marcus Aurelius' column at *Piazza Colonna*. It was composed of artificial cliffs and caves and had allegorical figures upon it. No Christian theme was being represented though, rather a mythological one: Vulcan's forge. What made it sensational was, that it all went up in fire and smoke to the noisy and dazzling accompaniment of skyrockets; all this to the delight or fright of the Roman populace (fig. 129).

129. *Vulcan's Forge*, a *macchina* built at Piazza Colonna in honor of the visit to Rome of Archduke Maximilian of Austria for the Holy Year of 1775.

* * *

The eighteenth century was also the century of traveling for personal erudition. Now, instead of the pilgrims and penitents, who had been followed by princes and petitioners, and later by artists and craftsmen, came instead the sons of aristocratic or otherwise wealthy families. They came to Rome to complete their education and to acquire the latest social refinements. This type of travel was called variously: *Bildungsreise* (educational travel), *Kavaliersreise* (cavalier's journey), or more frequently the *Grand Tour*, since such an educational journey could last for months or even years, including visits to every European capital. In most cases the young "cavaliers" were accompanied by a mentor or at least by a major-domo and, of course, a suite of servants.

Such was the household that brought *Gotthold E. Lessing* (1729-81) to Rome. He accompanied the prince Leopold von Braunschweig throughout Italy on an eight month tour. Lessing was librarian in Wolfenbüttel and already famous as a writer of philosophical-theological works as well as of plays. He arrived in Rome in the Holy Year of 1775, but made no note of this fact whatsoever. He resided in the Locanda Stuart on the Spanish Square, which was at that time the center of the foreigners' area of Rome. But his stay was not the happy experience that Goethe's would later prove to be, as he was not free to pursue his own interests; instead he always had to accompany the prince to never-ending receptions and tedious banquets. Pope Pius VI received him with honors, spoke to him in German and bade Lessing to provide him with some of his writings which the pontiff had not been able to come by and desired for his private library. Lessing received permission to look at old manuscripts in the Vatican Library, which he found far more interesting than seeing churches or works of art. True, he did call St. Peter's "the most beautiful building in the world", but he makes no mention of the Pietà nor does he talk about the Sistine Chapel. Moreover, what is most striking is that he does not waste one word upon the statue of the Laocoön, in the Belvedere. It seems to have held no interest for him to look at the statue which nine years earlier had been the subject of his famous art-theoretical treatise: *Laokoon, oder über die Grenzen der Mahlerey und der Poesie* ("Laocoön, or On the Limits of Painting and Poetry").

Naturally, English noblemen came to Rome on their "grand tour" as well, and were most welcomed here because the English were believed to be the richest of all tourists. Rome had always attracted poets and artists from England starting with John Milton in 1683 and reaching its most glorious moment with the arrival of George Lord Byron in 1817 and John Keats in 1821. The latter died in Rome shortly after his arrival and lies buried next to his friend, the painter Joseph Severn, and near the remains of the poet Percy B. Shelley in the so-called English Cemetery next to the pyramid of Caius Cestius. But these men had nothing to do with our theme.

As regards pilgrims, there were no known English pilgrims who participated in this or any other Holy Year. The on-going political situation prevented English Catholics from making pilgrimages abroad. If they did so, it was because they were already living in exile, as we have seen in the case of Father Gregory Martin, who in his book *Roma Sancta* described religious life in Rome at the time of the Holy Year of 1575. We should also mention the English noblewoman Barbara Ward (1585-1645), a truly heroic and saintly woman, who attended all the religious functions of the Holy Year 1625. She had journeyed to Rome on foot seeking papal approval (just as St. Francis and St. Ignatius had done earlier) for the community of the "English Dames" which she had founded. They wished to adhere to the rules of St. Ignatius and be directly dependent upon the Holy See, live as non-cloistered nuns dedicated to the teaching of girls in public schools (something unheard of at the time) and to the Catholic apostolate amongst Protestants in their homeland. But the Holy Year of 1625 was instead a year of grief and tears for them; their school in Rome was shut down by the Church authorities who sent the sisters away from their home in via Monserrato. It was the beginning of the end of her great adventure.

XV

A Non-Jubilant
Jubilee Year
1825

The unusually lengthy pontificate of *Pius VI* (1775-99) came to a tragic end. Napoleon's troops had occupied Rome, made the Pope a prisoner and took him to France where he died in Valence shortly afterwards. Antonio Canova would later place a monument to his memory in the grottoes of St. Peter's (fig. 130). Thus, the new century began without a pope. It is true that in March of 1800 *Pius VII* Chiaramonti (1800-23) was elected Pope in Venice and was soon afterwards able to move to Rome but at this point it was too late to hold the Holy Year. No pilgrims would have come. The nineteenth century was a century without true Jubilee Years.

Relations between Napoleon and the new Pope quickly deteriorated. Napoleon occupied Rome in 1809 for the second time, but this time instead of a republic declared it "the second city of the empire" and named his small son "King of Rome". Then like his predecessor Pius VI the Pope was taken prisoner and forced to go to France. He stayed there for five years until Napoleon's new empire fell apart and he was able to return to Rome in 1814.

In 1815 the Congress of Vienna re-established the Papal States, though smaller than it had formerly been. Pius VII embarked upon a program of reconstruction, steered by the astute policies of his Secretary of State, Enrico Consalvi. On the 15th of July 1823, as the Pope lay dying, the

130. *Pius VI* who died in 1799 as a prisoner of the French. This statue by Antonio Canova (†1822) is in the Vatican grottoes and faces St. Peter's tomb.

PIVS VI · BRASCHIVS · CAESENAS
ORATE · PRO · EO

church of *St. Paul's outside the Walls* caught fire and burnt down. After St. Peter's, it had been the second longest church of Rome. Rebuilding of the edifice began almost immediately and in the same Early Christian basilican style. To substitute it, the basilica of *S. Maria in Trastevere* was used temporarily. This last was a church of ancient foundation, situated in Trastevere, i.e. on the other side of the Tiber, in what was at that time an impoverished area (fig. 131). This Marian church had already served the same purpose during the Holy Years of 1625 and 1700, when St. Paul's, far outside the walls, was deemed unsafe due to political troubles, epidemics or simply to the Tiber's flooding. When this happened the central door of the Trastevere church was declared a *Holy Door*, which is indicated in the inscription which can still be read above this door: "Open for me the gates of saving justice" (Ps 118:119). These are the words from the psalms recited by the pope or the cardinals when they strike any

131. *Santa Maria in Trastevere,* an early basilica which has been used in place of St. Paul's outside the Walls when this was inaccessible, as in the years 1625, 1700 and 1825. When used as such its main portal served as Holy Door.

one of the four Holy Doors with their hammers. The basilica is decorated with glorious medieval mosaics which pay honor to the Queen of Heaven. Christ sits enthroned in the center with his mother next to him and lovingly lays his arm upon his mother's shoulder, showing the love and honor he still bears her in Heaven.

* * *

"Let the Earth hear the words that issue from our mouth, let the whole world hear with joy the sound of the priestly trumpets, that announce the Jubilee of the people of God!" With these pompous words *Leo XII* Della Genga

240

132. A pilgrim kissing
the foot of Leo XIII.
Watercolor by F. Fer-
rari, 1825.

(1823-29) announced the Jubilee Year of 1825, which
turned out to be anything but a Jubilee.

Leo XII reigned in the era of the *Restoration*, which in
Rome as well as in Paris and Vienna was forcefully trying
to re-establish the pre-revolutionary *status quo*. The Pope
himself was the reactionary spirit incarnate, shunning with
dread anything innovative. We can see in a picture, how a
pilgrim threw himself upon the ground in order to kiss the
pontiff's foot; such was the awe and reverence shown to
the Pope (fig. 132). His cardinal Secretary of State and
some foreign powers as well, tried to talk him out of holding a Holy Year; they feared that revolutionaries and political agitators could infiltrate the pilgrims' number and so
enter the city. Each pilgrim was to be searched to see if
he carried any seditious literature with him. Even the
beloved statue of *Pasquino* (which by means of placards
affixed to it had always lampooned or criticized personali-
ties and events of the day) for once kept silent, fearing po-
lice and informers.

Just as in the Holy Year of 1600 Giordano Bruno had been burned at the stake, so now in this Holy Year two "carbonari" (coalmen) were executed as enemies of the state in the new *Piazza del Popolo* created by the architect Giuseppe Valadier (fig. 133). The *Carboneria* was a secret political organization of a pseudo-religious nature with the objective of overthrowing the little Italian states and forcibly bringing about the unification of Italy. The two *carbonari*, Angelo Targhini, a youthful fanatic, and the doctor Leonida Montanari, were condemned to death "without proof and without a trial" as can be read on a plaque in the square. They were buried at the *Muro Torto*, "the crooked wall", alongside heretics and prostitutes, not being allowed burial in sanctified ground.

There were hardly any foreigners, but there were some members of the Italian aristocracy, among whom the very

133. Execution in Piazza del Popolo, possibly that of the two *carbonari* in 1825. Anonymous.

134. *Princess Maria Cristina of Savoy* washing the feet of some women pilgrims in the hospice of the *Santissima Trinità*. Engraving by L. Barocci, 1825.

devout *Princess Maria Cristina*, daughter of King Victor-Emanuel I of Savoy, who soon became queen of Naples. During her stay in Rome, she kept a diary which reveals her very religious nature. A contemporary engraving shows the princess in the company of other ladies of the aristocracy, led by a priest in prayer while she washes the feet of some pilgrim women in the pilgrims' hospice (fig. 134). Other saintly men and women also took part in this Holy Year: Vincent Pallotti, Gaspare del Bufalo, Anna Maria Taigi, all of whom belonged to the *popolino* (common folk) of Rome and were later canonized. The piety of the simple folk of that time has been touchingly depicted in a picture by the Danish painter *Christoffer Eckersberg* (1783-1853). It shows a mother holding up her swaddled baby so that it might kiss the Holy Door (fig. 135).

This time, however, participation on the part of young men was entirely lacking; having turned to the ideals of the *Risorgimento*, the movement advocating the unification of Italy. The young poet and patriot *Massimo d'Azeglio*, in an ostentatious protest, left Rome for the duration of the Holy Year. He maintained that it was a "tragical comedy" during which Rome for twelve months

243

135. A Roman woman holding her infant child up so that it can kiss the Holy Door of St. Peter's. Painting by C. Eckersberg. 1815. Hage Collection, Nivaa, Denmark.

became a "great barracks for spiritual exercises". In actual fact, there was little of the original spontaneous enthusiasm of the first Jubilee Year nor of the intense passion of the Counter-Reformation. Now, instead, the state functionaries had to march in processions of compact groups, organized according to rank and station and dressed in their official attire, put up with sermon after sermon and line up to be confessed and to receive Holy Communion.

The Roman folk-poet *Gioacchino Belli* (1791-1863) composed a sonnet in Roman dialect on this Holy Year which closes with this verse:

> *You go to the churches,*
> *Singing in all seven*
> *Put ashes on your head,*
> *And so you go to heaven.*[77]

On the occasion of the Holy Year of 1825, the publisher P. Manna brought out a *General View of all the Holy Years* which made use of an earlier engraving of Giuseppe Vasi's (fig. 136). Here, upon a background of St. Peter's façade and at the very top Giotto's fresco in the Lateran (see fig. 10), are rows of effigies of all popes who celebrated a Holy Year, the dates of their pontificates, their bulls and commemorative medallions. The Holy Year of 1400 has been left out thus making an error in the final count. The Holy Year of 1825 was not the nineteenth, as reckoned in this print, but according to today's numbering would be the twentieth.

When at Christmast Eve in 1825 Leo XII sealed up the Holy Door, no one could have imagined that it would stay shut for seventy-four years.

* * *

In 1848 revolution was breaking out all over Europe and even Rome had been declared a republic. The Pope, *Pius IX* Mastai-Ferretti (1846-78), was forced to flee to Gaeta. Not long afterwards, on the 30th of June 1849, the papal troops were victorious at the battle of the Gianicolo where they defeated Garibaldi and his band of young patriots, who had risen in defense of the Republic. The Pope was able to return to Rome in April 1850 and re-established papal rule for the last time. However, it was now too late to proclaim a Holy Year and the atmosphere in Rome was in no way favorable to such a proposal. The Papal States held out for another twenty years, just long enough for Pius IX to proclaim the dogma of the Immaculate Conception in 1854, to convoke the First Vatican Council in 1869 and to promulgate the doctrine of papal infallibility in 1870.

Shortly thereafter, King Victor Emmanuel II of Savoy occupied the city of Rome, proclaimed it capital of the unified Kingdom of Italy and took up residence in the old summer palace of the popes, the *Quirinale*. Pius IX withdrew into the Vatican and declared himself a prisoner

245

PROSPETTO GENERALE DI TUTTI GLI ANNI SANTI

136. *General Overview* of all the Holy Years, against the façade of St. Peter's which is covered with the portraits of the popes, papal bulls and medals of the Holy Years from 1300 to 1825. At the top is Giotto's fresco in the Lateran church which shows the proclamation of the first Jubilee in 1300. Print by P. Manna from a

there. A sort of cold war went on between Pope and King for almost sixty years. Under these circumstances it was impossible to celebrate a Holy Year. Although Pius IX proclaimed a Holy Year, in his encyclical *Gravibus Ecclesiae et huius saeculi calamitatibus* on the 24th of December 1874, he immediately extended it to the whole world. Therefore, even if the Holy Year of 1875 counts as the twenty-first, it was not celebrated in Rome, no Holy Door was opened, nor did any pilgrim groups appear. Just some Frenchmen came, but not so much with the idea of obtaining the graces of the Holy Year but rather to show their solidarity with the "imprisoned" Pope. The old pilgrim organizations had been disbanded, the confraternities dissolved, the hospice of the Most Holy Trinity and many monasteries had been secularized. When Pius IX died in 1878, the hostility towards the Church was such that the Pope's nocturnal funeral procession, proceeding to the church of *San Lorenzo fuori le Mura* was attacked by a mob. San Lorenzo is one of the seven main churches and lies at the eastern city limits. The pontiff wanted at least in death, to leave the Vatican and ride once more through "his" city.

137. *Burial Chapel of Pius IX* (died 1878) in the basilica of St. Lawrence outside the Walls, completely covered with mosaics. The various coasts of arms seen on the walls are of the dioceses which contributed to its decoration.

Here in the lower church of *S. Lorenzo* a burial chapel was built for Pius IX (fig. 137). The surrounding walls are covered with colored and gold mosaics representing scenes from his pontificate and the coats of arms of the dioceses that contributed to its decoration.

XVI

The Holy Years in Modern Times 1900 - 1925 - 1933

Pius IX was succeeded by *Leo XIII* Pecci (1878-1903), the first Pope to open himself up to the modern world and especially to its social issues. He is known as the Pope of the first social encyclical *Rerum Novarum* (1891). He also began the "policy of the pilgrim parade" which served a double purpose. He wished to bring to the world's attention to exactly how difficult a position he found himself in, bereft of all means of support and shut up in the Vatican. At the same time he wished to display to the Italian government the honor shown to him by pilgrims from all nations. His strategy paid off and the atmosphere began to improve steadily until there was a willingness on both sides to make concessions, so much so that by 1900 a Holy Year could finally be celebrated once again, not only with the toleration of the Italian government, but with its endorsement. It pledged not to allow any demonstration of anti-clericalism, while the Church for her part had to confine religious gatherings to inside church doors. The only religious function celebrated in the open air was the eucharistic procession at the catacombs of St. Calixtus in conjunction with a congress of Christian archeology, a new field of study that was flourishing.

It was also the first Holy Year to be celebrated in the new technological era. Seventy-five years had passed since the last Holy Year and living conditions had radically changed. Pilgrims no longer came on foot, on horseback or by stagecoach but by train. Once here they no longer stayed in the old pilgrim houses, instead they found modern hotels with running water and central heating. They no longer needed to make the journey on foot from church to church but used the tram. Instead of sitting in dark candlelit rooms or finding their way through the gloomy streets by the light of torches or lanterns, they now found the city lit by gas or petroleum.

That the Church herself, in this new technological age, should want to take advantage of this technology for the strengthening and propagation of the faith is only too understandable. The other side of the coin was, however, that with all the modern comforts enjoyed during a pilgrimage much of the original spirit of sacrifice and penance had been lost. The spontaneous religious movements of earlier times and the services provided by the various religious confraternities were now replaced by national and international organizations, and a lay committee in Bologna assumed the responsibility of the Holy Year's entire organization. To replace the old hospice of the Most Holy Trinity the new St. Marta's in the Vatican was built, which took care of 40,000 pilgrims. As in the past, there was still little participation of youth and workers, and this time even less from the aristocracy. The Pope had invited the non-Roman Catholic Churches to come to the Holy Year, but they did not officially acknowledge the invitation, though some Protestants and members of the Orthodox Churches might have been unofficially present.

In his bull of indiction, *Properante ad exitum saeculo*, the ninety year old pontiff reminisced upon how he had participated in the previous Holy Year seventy-five years earlier. He could not disguise his regret of how over the years the situation had so deteriorated. In those days the Pope had been the ruler of Rome and of the Papal States, now he sat locked up in the Vatican and could not take part in the Holy Year festivities outside St. Peter's itself. Formerly, religious ceremonies could be held anywhere without any restrictions, now to the contrary, they had to

250

submit entirely to the discretion of someone else, i.e. of the Italian state.

The Holy Year started out quite smoothly and without any upsets. The Holy Door was opened to Palestrina's *Jubilate* which was conducted by another important papal music director, organist and composer: Lorenzo Perosi (1872-1956), who followed the tradition set down by Palestrina in the Holy Year of 1575. He would go on to be the conductor for the next two Holy Years.

On the 31st of December, for the turn of the century, the bells of all churches in the world rang and midnight mass was said in all churches. The Pope, a poet in his own right, wrote a poem in Latin, *A Jesu Christo ineuntis saeculi auspicia*, which was a greeting for the new century. Perhaps he wanted to emulate Horace who had paid homage to the turn of the century of ancient Rome in 17 B.C. with his famous poem *Carmen seecularis*.

Unfortunately, later on in that year, the young Italian state suffered a grave blow when on the 29th of July, King Humbert I was assassinated by an anarchist. The Pope sent neither a note of sympathy nor wired any inaugural wishes to the new king, Victor Emmanuel III. This provoked resentment in the Italian patriots and they held rallies in four so-called "lay-basilicas" of Rome as parallels to the four major basilicas of the Pope: in the *Pantheon* where there are the graves of the first two kings of Italy; on the *Capitol Hill*, where the town hall stands; on the *Gianicolo*, the site of Garibaldi's statue, and at Porta Pia, the city gate, where the Bersaglieri had made a breach in the city walls and seized Rome on the 20th of September 1870. When the first workers-strike in Rome took place and when the Tiber overflowed its banks, some reactionary minds saw this as divine punishment for the new temporal authority which now ruled Rome.

The only building erected in this Holy Year was the church of *Sant'Anselmo* on the Aventine. As the Pope was not able to leave the Vatican, he sent his Cardinal-legate Rampolla to officiate at the church's consecration. The *Aventine* is one of the seven hills of ancient Rome. Here,

251

138. *Piazza dei Cavalieri di Malta*. Designed by G.B. Piranesi. On the left is the church of Sant'Anselmo built for the Holy Year of 1900, and on the right the villa of the Order of the Knights of Malta with its famous spy-hole.

the great religious orders had established themselves: the Dominicans in *S. Sabina*, the knights of Malta in the *Villa of the Priory of Malta* and the Benedictines in *Sant'Anselmo*. This last church has little artistic worth, as it is only an imitation of the Romanesque style. The square outside was, however, elegantly designed by *Giovanni Battista Piranesi* (1720-78) who was famous as a copperplate engraver and also as an architect (fig. 138). The peephole in the garden door of the Maltese villa, offers us a charming view. St. Peter's dome stands at the end of a shady arbor, planted with laurel hedges, giving the impression that it stands at the end of the garden, when in reality it lies several kilometers away. Anywhere else it would be frowned upon to peer through a keyhole, but here even the most proper of pilgrims stands in line to do so.

The Italian poet *Giovanni Pascoli* (1855-1912) in his famous poem *"La Porta Santa"* describes how the Pope, "this mild servant of God", this "elderly man with trembling hands" closes the Holy Door. He bids him: "Keep hands away from the work, let us not stand in the portico before the shut door, awaiting cold death. We wish to enter there, where the silver trumpets break the graves asunder and herald the resurrection and eternal life. Let the door stay open!"[78] For the famous poet and the mere pil-

252

grim alike, the Holy Door is a symbol of the gateway to everlasting life.

Pope Leo XIII died three years later. He was buried according to his explicit desire in the Church of the Lateran, which he had renovated. His tomb is somewhat unhappily situated above the sacristy doorway. It does not vaunt the traditional allegorical figures of the virtues. It shows instead the first Pope to concern himself with social issues, standing here between a poor laborer and pilgrim and the symbolic figure of the Church in mourning (fig. 139).

* * *

The First World War brought the flow of pilgrims to a abrupt standstill. However, after the war, the Catholic Church was stronger and younger than before. It had in the meantime won over youth and intellectuals. Youth movements, liturgical and ecumenical movements were formed in many countries. In Italy, Catholics became quite active and founded the organization of Catholic Action and the Italian People's Party. The reconciliation of Church and State was imminent and in this favorable atmosphere

139. *Tomb of Leo XIII* (died 1903) in the church of the Lateran, designed by G. Tadolini. At the Pope's feet stand two allegorical figures which represent the mourning Church and the pilgrim.

the Jubilee Year of 1925 would be celebrated with renewed joy. *Pius XI* Ratti could observe with satisfaction that all countries were represented with the exception of Russia. For the first we have a precise statistical figure for a Holy Year: a total of 582,234 pilgrims had been in Rome in this year.

The disagreement over the exact number of Holy Years was solved by Pius XI when, in a speech given on the 14th of December 1925, he declared: "The twenty-third Holy Year is drawing to a close". He had included then the Holy Year of 1875 in order to number 1925 as the 23rd, as established by the official *Cronistoria* of the Holy Year of 1925.[79]

The theme of this Holy Year could be summed up in the motto: *pax Christi in regno Christi*. To achieve this goal, the Pope, at the end of Holy Year 1925, instituted the feast of Christ the King, which proclaimed Christ's dominion over men everywhere, over Christians by virtue of their baptism and over non-believers as an end.

In this Holy Year Theresa of the Child Jesus, Peter Canisius, the Curé d'Ars J.M. Vianney and John Eudes were canonized, while Bernadette Soubirous of Lourdes was beatified (to mention just the most important names).

Pius XI, a great scholar who formerly had devoted himself entirely to his studies, now as Pope took an active interest in promoting foreign missions. In pursuing this, he mounted in the Vatican an enormous exhibition dealing with the work of foreign missions. This was a "first" as far as being a Jubilee Year attraction. Each Holy Year since then has had a policy of mounting exhibitions to attach a cultural and educational significance to itself.

The Pope had provided for the systematic excavation of the catacombs and made them a part of the pilgrims' program. He introduced the weekly general audience, which since has become a "must" for every pilgrimage to Rome, and he revived the traditional blessing from the papal loggia, *urbi et orbi*, which had been suppressed in 1870.

140. *Pius XI* in the portico of St. Peter's for the opening of the Holy Years of 1925 and 1933.

Pius XI was the only pope who has ever opened the Holy Door twice (fig. 140). In 1929, the great "reconciliation" between the Pope and the King, together with Mussolini, took place. The terms of the Lateran Treaty were such that each side thought that it had had the better deal. The Pope officially renounced all claim to the Papal States which had already been lost in 1870, and in exchange, re ceived the small Vatican City which borders St. Peter's, as a sovereign state. Also included as possessions of the Holy See were the patriarchal basilicas, the catacombs, the pontifical institutes and universities in Rome and the summer residence at Castel Gandolfo.

The felicitous resolving of the "Roman Question" by means of the Lateran Treaty and the founding of the new Vatican State should be celebrated with rejoicing and the best way to do this would be to proclaim a Jubilee Year. The Pope sought a religious justification for this and brought the question to the rector of the Bible Institute. This was the well-known Father Augustin Bea, a German Jesuit priest and later cardinal. He was asked to draft a re port as to whether the year of the death of Christ could be commemorated in 1933 or not. Naturally, Father Bea replied in the affirmative, arguing that even though the exact year of Christ's death was not certain, there was nothing preventing the celebration of its memory. So it came about that Pius XI proclaimed an *extraordinary Holy Year* from Palm Sunday, the 2nd of April 1933, until Easter Monday, the 2nd of April 1934.

There had already been many extraordinary Jubilees for either special days, localities or occasions. There were even Holy Doors in places other than Rome, e.g. in Santiago de Compostela, which also has a "Holy Door of Forgiveness" which is opened and later closed with great ceremony. Just how many extraordinary Holy Years there have been is still uncertain, due to a lack of accurate dates. The first one we know was introduced by Leo X in 1518, in an effort to strengthen Poland in its war against the Turks. Still others were proclaimed for the conversion of Protestants, for the success of the Council of Trent, for England to re-embrace the Roman Church or for the preservation of the Papal States whose dissolution Pius VI sought to prevent with the only means at his disposal: with prayer. Pius IX for his part, celebrated two extraordinary Holy Years, one to celebrate the promulgation of the dogma of the Immaculate Conception in 1854 and the other for the convocation of the First Vatican Council in 1869. Later in 1929, Pius XI celebrated the 50th anniversary of his ordination to the priesthood with an extraordinary Holy Year and would proclaim yet another extraordinary Holy Year for 1933-34.

In his address with which he announced the bull *Quod nuper* (15th of January 1933), Pius XI explained that this would be: "...an extraordinary among extraordinaries, yet an extraordinary year among the regular Holy Years, since the term "extraordinary" seems as if it were in some way be inferior when instead it is greater, yes it is the greatest Jubilee corresponding to the magnitude, the dignity and the value of the events that are refered to by the century-old feast which commemorates the completion of the work of our redemption".[80]

The Holy Year originated as a celebration of Christ's nativity. Now, however, it was a commemorative year of

Christ's death and the "fulfillment of our redemption", as the Pope had said. It was celebrated with great pomp and ceremony and with the help of modern means of communications which had come into the service of the Church. For the first time ever, the Holy Door's opening ceremony was transmitted by radio. Its inventor, Guglielmo Marconi, had personally set up the Vatican radio station in 1931. Now the whole world could hear the triple hammer blows as they resounded via radio waves. The Pope, for the first time since 1870, was able to conduct solemn processions to the three major basilicas outside the Vatican. The newly forged link between Church and State remained strong for this year but not for much longer. Unfortunately, this "extraordinary Holy Year" was also the extraordinarily fateful year in which Hitler seized power, and this signaled the end of freedom and peace in many countries.

XVII

A True Jubilee Year 1950

1950 was a true year of jubilee and jubilation, as the Church had resisted the ravages of Fascism, Nazism and the Second World War, and could observe with reassurance that "the gates of hell had not been able to prevail upon it". The spirit of penance during the first Holy Years now was transformed into one of victory. The Holy Year 1950 was above all a manifestation of the greatness, the richness, the unity and universality of the Catholic Church. This manifestation enthused the participants themselves and transported them into a state of jubilation reminiscent of the first Holy Year of the Counter Reformation in 1575.

No Pope has ever been so highly revered as *Pius XII*, whose spare white figure inspired a sense of something almost other-worldly. He was called *pastor angelicus*, or the angelic shepherd, and the "Pope of Peace". After the horrific years of hate and murder, of the destruction of cities and the annihilation of entire populations, this was the time and place of reconciliation amongst peoples, where the former enemies (with the exception of the Communist states) met peacefully and rediscovered themselves as brothers in the name of the Catholic faith. On this occasion the Holy Year revealed its true nature: to be a means to and a sign of reconciliation between God and man.

It should be mentioned that for many pilgrims after the terrible war and the difficult post-war years, this was the first and only opportunity to make a trip abroad and those who could wanted to take advantage of this chance.

141. *Via della Conciliazione*, opened for the Holy Year of 1950. The name of this road refers to the reconciliation between the Church and the Italian State through the Lateran Treaties of 1929.

Among the French pilgrims the most famous was the poet Paul Claudel, who despite his eighty years, made the journey and said, *"Je ne suis plus capable de march*, mais je le suis encore de me mettre a genoux"* (I am no longer able to march, but I am still able to kneel). The pilgrims rarely travelled alone but rather in the company of their parish, or of some organization of their diocese. A great spirit of adaptability was essential, and given the fact that it was, after all, a pilgrimage and an exercise in penance, all discomforts were endured. In total, there were three million pilgrims who came. For young people a campsite was set up. Also a new profession grew out of this Holy Year, that of the tour-guide; this helped many students to support themselves during the period of their studies.

The *Via della Conciliazione* was finally completed for the Holy Year (fig. 141). It is so named to commemorate the reconciliation between Church and State with the signing of the Lateran Treaties in 1929. Work started almost immediately afterwards; the old buildings that had blocked the view of St. Peter's were torn down, and in some cases rebuilt, lining the newly created street. Widened and straightened it now leads from the Tiber river to St. Peter's Square. Neither plants nor trees decorate this stony

259

processional artery, just some curious obelisks that double as lampposts line the street on both sides. The buildings along this street house various ecclesiastical offices, for example the Holy See Press Office which is to be found at the end on the righthand side.

* * *

The prelate *Ludwig Kaas* of Trier, who presided over the administration office of St. Peter's decided to install a new Holy Door in bronze in place of the old marble doors which dated from 1749 and the pontificate of Benedict XIV (fig. 142). The commission was given to an artist from Siena, *Vico Consorti*. The diocese of Basel, Switzerland, funded the project at the suggestion of Bishop Franz von Streng of Basel and Lugano, as an act of thanksgiving for his country's having been spared destruction during the war; it would also honor the Pope of peace, Pius XII. In the dedicatory inscribed at the bottom of the door, prelate Kaas has imitated the medieval donors by including his own name: "Pius XII P.M. at the beginning of this Holy Year 1950, gave the commission to embellish the Vatican basilica with these bronze doors, while Ludwig Kaas was director of the administration of St. Peter's. Let the waters of divine grace flow copiously, purifying all those who pass through here. May they be filled with peace sublime and be instilled with Christian virtue, Holy Year 1950".

This door is a veritable illustrated Bible, a *Biblia Pauperum*, a poor man's Bible, for those who were not able to read or write and therefore had to learn the Bible stories by means of pictures. It is composed of sixteen panels which illustrate the theme of the Holy Year: "The great return and the great pardon". Beginning with the expulsion from the Garden of Eden, there are fifteen scenes from the Old and New Testament: The Annunciation, the Baptism of Christ, the Good Shepherd, the Prodigal Son, the Healing of the Paralytic, the Adulteress, Peter's query: "Lord, how often must I forgive my brother?", The Repentant Peter, the Good Thief, the Doubting Thomas, the

142. The *new Holy Door* of St. Peter's created by Vico Consorti for the Holy Year of 1950.

143. The Canonization of *Maria Goretti* officiated by Pius XII in St. Peter's Square, 1950.

Sacrament of Penance, the Conversion of Saul and finally the Opening of the Holy Door by Pius XII. Above the last scenes are written the words from Apocalypse 3:20, "Look, I am standing at the door and knocking". At the Pope's side two donors kneel and a Swiss guard stands by, which is a symbolic way of saying that the doors were paid for by the Swiss. The figure of the doubting Thomas who sticks his finger in the wound on Christ's side is the portrait of Kaas, while the figure watching from behind the door is the artist himself.

Running between the rows of pictures are the coats of arms of the 27 popes who have either opened or closed the Holy Door in a regular Holy Year. There are in addition nine empty blazons awaiting the coats of arms of future popes. Above the door on the interior wall is a mosaic of St. Peter in the clouds, made by Cirro Ferri in 1675 under Clement X.

262

We have already talked about the symbolic significance of the Holy Door when this ritual was first introduced by Alexander VI. The opening of the Holy Door was always effected on Christmas eve, on the 24th of December, and done in the same traditional manner.

* * *

In this year *Vincent Pallotti* (to mention just one name) was beatified, and *Maria Goretti* was canonized (fig. 143). The latter had died when only twelve years old in 1902, as "a martyr of chastity". Her mother was present for her canonization, a unique event in the history of canonizations. Equally unusual was the fact that Goretti's murderer was still alive. He had repented and made amends for his crime, and after his release from prison worked as a gardener in a convent.

The highlight of the Holy Year 1950 was the promulgation of the dogma of the bodily assumption of Mary into Heaven. This took place on the 1st of November in St. Peter's Square in the presence of 100,000 people (fig. 144). The dogma had long been taught by theologians and depicted in art, as we have already seen in the apse mosaic of St. Mary Major (see fig. 47). For this ceremony the most venerated icon of the Madonna, the *Salus populi romani*, was carried through the streets in procession from St. Mary Major, and at the moment when the dogma was proclaimed a tapestry hanging from the benediction loggia above the papal throne was unveiled to show an image of Mary's Assumption into Heaven.

Never before had a dogma been promulgated in a Holy Year and it may never happen again. The Pope, in raising this doctrine to dogma, had most likely deliberately chosen this particular moment to illustrate its profound significance. It was as if the Church wanted to respond to the horrible destruction of human life and the meaningless death of so many people in the last World War, as if the Church wished to console those who had survived by saying that at the end of all time, all men, even if their bodies have

263

144. *Pius XII* promulgating the dogma of the bodily *Assumption of the Virgin Mary into Heaven* on the first of November 1950.

been ravaged, burnt or scattered, will be resurrected and their souls be re-united with their transfigured bodies; they will be assumed into Heaven as had already happened with the Vergin Mary at her Assumption.

From the beginning of the 20th century, the Holy Years had turned into a cultural as well as a religious event. Therefore, once again there were many exhibitions to be seen; those of the "Caritas", those from the mission countries, those of religious art, and those of Byzantine art in particular. In addition several conventions, seminars and concerts were held in occasion of the Holy Year. Not by chance a book came out in Rome written by the well known English writer, G. K. Chesterton, entitled: *The Resurrection of Rome*, which tried to explain why Rome is eternal: because it has the ability, unique on earth, to rise up again and to bring the past to life.

In his Christmas message of 1950, Pius XII announced as the final triumph of this Holy Year, the rediscovery of St. Peter's grave, which excavations had just brought to light. It was found there, exactly where tradition had always maintained it to be, directly beneath the papal altar. On the 24th of December, the Pope sealed up the Holy Door in accordance with the age-old custom (fig. 145). First he went to venerate the relics of Christ's Passion in the chapel of the Blessed Sacrament, then, in a sign of humility, he simply walked to the Holy Door instead of being carried there, and was the last to walk through it, following the words of the prophet: "when he opens, no one will close, when he closes, no one will open" (Is 22:22). The choir sang *Tu es Petrus*, as the Pope blessed the mortar and the bricks which had been donated by the faithful. They bear the donors' names, so that after 24 years, when the door is opened up again, the bricks may be given back to them. The Pope then spread three applications of mor-

145. *Pius XII* sealing up the Holy Door at Christmas in 1950.

tar upon the threshold with a golden trowel and laid three gilded bricks there uttering the words: "We lay these first stones in order to close the Holy Door, which was opened exclusively for the Holy Year". The cardinals then each laid a silvered building stone, the father confessors of St. Peter's as well as some prelates laid normal bricks upon the threshold until the *sampietrini*, the building workers of St. Peter's, completed the closure of the door. All the while the choir was singing *Caelestis urbs Jerusalem*. This age old hymn belongs to the closing ceremony ritual; it lifts up our thoughts to the heavenly Jerusalem, to which all pilgrim wandering leads, and whose splendor is reflected by the earthly city of Rome. A bronze chest containing documents, certificates and commemorative medallions was also sealed up in the wall, and finally a metal cross affixed to the door once it was completely walled up.

We have described this ceremony of 1950 in such detail, because it was the last time that it would be performed in just this manner.

XVIII

The Holy Year of Paul VI 1975

Pilgrimages to Rome reached a new high point in the Holy Year of 1975. From the start great difficulties and complications had to be dealt with. It seemed as if everything had set itself against this new Holy Year, starting with the city administration, which had blocked all access roads to St. Peter's, leaving the Vatican isolated; free circulation of traffic was hindered and access to St. Peter's by tourist bus was made impossible. The civic administration suspended the completion of the pilgrims' village that had already been under construction. 10,000 pilgrims should have been housed in small pre-fabricated units there. The municipality also raised protests over the setting up of a tent city for young people instead only a simple campsite would be allowed. The press then set about with its inimical propaganda and prophesized that with the city's overcrowding there would be resultant breakdown of traffic circulation, a shortage of foodstuffs and water supply and the possibility of an outbreak of disease. None of these things ever happened, moreover, it can be said that in many parts of the city the Romans were not even aware that there was a Holy Year in progress. Still it seemed that everything was against it, even the heavens did their part. Unusually late snowfall and bad weather everywhere held up pilgrim transportation and often necessitated great detours.

Worse still were the prophets of gloom from within the ranks of the Church itself, asserting that Rome and modern man were no longer able to celebrate a Holy Year in a fitting and devout manner. Such ceremonies would be only outward show and therefore no longer valid. These false prophets lacked any understanding of the richness and beauty of tradition which, at least in Rome, has been preserved and embraces millenia of history. To the eyes of many critics of the Holy Year, it was nothing more than a "Reichsparteitag" of the Pope (a party convention of the regime). Furthermore, they asserted that the cult of the Pope was foreign to the very essence of Christianity, and by so saying overlooked the fact that the Pope is only the visible figurehead of the pre-existing inner unity of all the faithful. The same well-minded persons continued their reasoning saying that such feasts did not belong to a world and Church in crisis, especially in Italy with its difficult political situation.

Paul VI considered all these objections very carefully, but then in his general audience of the 9th of May 1973 declared: "After much prayer and thorough reflection we have decided, in accordance with the twenty-five year interval instituted by our predecessor, Paul II, in the papal bull *Ineffabilis Providentia* dated the 17th of April 1470, to celebrate a Holy Year in the coming year of 1975. We came to the conclusion that the celebration of the Holy Year might not only be inserted within the spiritual guidelines of the Council, whose faithful implementation is very close to our heart, but that it might also be able to support and relate in the best way to the untiring and loving efforts of the Church to burden itself with the moral hardships and with the profound longing of our era. To reach this multiplicity of goals, it becomes necessary to highlight the basic significance of the Holy Year, which lies in the continued renewal of man's inner self".[81]

Certainly all preceeding Holy Years had been aimed at the objective of reconciliation with God through confession, prayer and penance. This reconcilation would subsequently lead to a reconciliation with other peoples, those who one met as fellow travelers upon the long road to Rome, those who sang and prayed together in the different churches. Nevertheless, the pilgrims of early times were more concerned about their own salvation rather than that of others. At the present time however, in an era of greater social awareness and collectivity, more emphasis is placed upon the reconciliation of all men with each other, all peoples, all races and creeds. This reconciliation should be the fruit of the common experience of the Holy Year. The pilgrims in Rome ought to be and are the representatives of Christians everywhere in the world.

Certainly, every year should be holy for a Christian, but the "Holy Year" has a special significance. It is by its very name a visible represention of the invisible community of the faithful. Held in the geographical setting of Rome, the city of the apostles and of the Vicar of Christ, and recurring in pre-established intervals of twenty-five years it is called, therefore, a "Holy Year" or "Jubilee Year". What has come true here is that which we have so often repeated in the Apostles' Creed: " I believe in the communion of saints".

Following the old tradition, the bull of indiction was promulgated upon the feast of the Ascension, the 23rd of May 1974. Entitled *Apostolorum limina* after its opening words, it was written in Latin as usual, and upon parchment. Pope Paul VI signed it with the simple: "I, Paul, bishop of the Catholic Church". The ceremony of the presentation and signing of the bull, took place in the papal throne room in front of just a few witnesses. Afterwards, the deacon of the prothonotaries, Bishop Rossi, with great solemnity, carried the bull to the portico of St. Peter's where he was awaited by the basilica's chapter. The most important passages were read aloud, and then, to con-

146. The bronze chest containing documents from the previous Holy Year being extracted from the Holy Door.

clude, the master of ceremonies presented it to the archpriest of St. Peter's, Cardinal Marella, so that a copy of it could be posted upon the Holy Door. The ceremony would be repeated at each of the other three patriarchal basilicas, all of which are in possession of a Holy Door.

A few days before Christmas, yet another preliminary ceremony was held, without the presence of the public. This is the *recognitio portae*, the examining of the Holy Door. It is checked for damage, and the bronze chest which was sealed up at the last closing is extracted. It contains, as earlier mentioned, documents, commemorative medallions and a list of the names of the brick donors (fig. 146).

The opening ceremony took place in the portico and adhered to the rules of protocol established 475 years earlier by Master Burckard of Strasbourg, master of ceremonies at the court of Alexander VI (see p. 125 ff.). The only thing he did not foresee at that time, was the shower of plaster dust that hailed down upon the pontiff, which kept everyone in momentary suspence. Luckily no one was hurt. After it is thrice tapped with the hammer, the

147. The Holy Door of St. Peter's pivoting backwards after having been struck three times with the golden hammer by Pope Paul VI on Christmas Eve, 1974.

Holy Door is inclined and rolled backwards into the church, preventing the donors' bricks from suffering any damage (fig. 147) (one of the bricks is reproduced on the last page of this book to serve as a sort of keystone for the story of the Holy Years). Finally, the pope kneels reverently upon the threshhold and is the first to set foot in the basilica.

In concluding these ceremonies, Paul VI celebrated solemn midnight Christmas Mass (fig. 148). Papal masses were held almost every Sunday: on New Year's day a choir sang which was made up of 10,000 children from all over the world; for the feast of the Epiphany, there were 600 missionaries in attendance who received the mission cross from the Pope, among them were several lay-missionary couples. For Candlemas, 12,000 members of religious orders renewed their vows in front of the Pope. We do not, of course, intend to write a yearbook of the Holy Year, but only to touch upon a few of the important events: the Way of the Cross led by the Pope on Good Friday evening at the Colosseum, the solemn papal blessing at Easter in twelve different languages, the holy mass of Pentecost with 10,000 participants of the charismatic movement. They sang the Hallelujah in St. Peter's and danced with their arms lifted high in St. Peter's square, expressing their joy of life. The charismatic movement was also having its first international meeting here in Rome during the Holy Year. Cardinals Suenens and Willebrands conferred with them in the huge tents that had been pitched upon the grounds of the catacombs of St. Calixtus, and the Pope received them in a special audience. One was suddenly transported back to the first Holy Year in 1300 which was born of the same spontaneous fervor of the pilgrims. Just as Boniface VIII had known how to harness this free spirit and lead it along certain guidelines, so now Paul VI did the same in giving his blessing to the pentecostal movement.

272

148. Midnight Mass celebrated by Paul VI after the opening of the Holy Door on Christmas Eve, 1974.

149. Torchlight procession in St. Peter's Square by members of the organization for handicapped persons *Foi et Lumière*, 1975.

A truly moving sight was the pilgrim procession of *Foi et Lumière*, a Belgian organization for the mentally and physically handicapped. Counting both members and assistants, the group that came to Rome numbered 6,000. They conducted a torchlight procession in St. Peter's Square on the night of the 29th of October. It was touching to see, how many handicapped persons, with their deformed hands, held as best they could, their trembling torches, which the blind participants were not even able to see. The entire square was illumined with an ethereal light, that emanated from the faith of these less fortunate brethren (fig. 149).

Another unusual sight was the arrival of 13,000 uniformed soldiers who came from all corners of the world, unusual only for those who had never realized that the Holy Year had been a peace movement from its beginnings. It is precisely in the hands of soldiers that the peace

274

of the world lies. If these hands do not pray, how can there ever be peace?

The Central Organizing Committee for the Holy Year took especial care to address itself to youth. It had a mass held for young people which was celebrated in S. Cecilia in Trastevere, group prayer with the Little Sisters of Charles de Foucauld, at Tre Fontane, encounters at Boys Town of Rome, peace marches and torchlight processions. What made the biggest hit, if the expression may be used, was the event held in the big palace of sport and organized by GEN (Young Generation of the Focolarini Movement). There were, besides, encounters and debates amongst the young people themselves, that were held on the grounds of the catacombs of St. Calixtus, under the

150. Beatification on Mission Sunday, 1975. Among the guests of honor an Indian chief in feathered head-dress. Behind him and to the right can be seen the Empress Zita of Austria wearing a black veil. Next to her is her daughter-in-law, Regina of Hapsburg.

auspices of the GEN. The young people understood each other wonderfully notwithstanding the language barrier.

Ever since 1450, it has been customary for the Pope to canonize saints during a Holy Year. This particular year saw six canonizations and thirteen beatifications. On Mission Sunday two German missionares were beatified: Fr. Arnold Janssen (1837-1909), the founder of the Society of the Divine Word, and his close confrere, the missionary to China, Fr. Joseph Freinademetz (1854-1908) from South Tyrol. Natives from missionary countries were invited to attend this ceremony; one guest was an American Indian chief in full feather headdress (fig. 150). As we can see in the picture he is sitting in the front row and blocks the camera's view of Empress Zita, who is sitting behind him and next to her daughter-in-law, Princess Regina. The last empress of Austria had come to this ceremony from the seclusion of a Swiss religious home, since a relative of the house of Hapsburg was going to be beatified, the countess Maria Theresia Ledochowska (1863- 1922), founder of the Petrus-Claver Sodality. Times have changed since the early Holy Years, when the crowned heads were afford ed places of honor, high above evcryone else. Now the small darkly clad figure of the empress of Austria sat almost hidden behind an Indian chieftain. As far as crowned heads were concerned, only the king of Belgium and his consort, Fabiola, appeared for the Holy Mass of Pentecost.

Canonizations and beatifications were celebrated the entire year up until November. They were held in St. Peter's square whose 140 Baroque statues of saints standing upon the colonnade, seem to be rejoicing in receiving the newly proclaimed blesseds and saints among their heavenly number. The religious functions were held in marked simplicity. The sacred rites and the word of God were to speak for themselves. The only decoration were the portrait tapestries of the new saints or blesseds that were

151. Genoese *stevedores* carrying 3-meter high silver-filigree crosses into St. Peter's in occasion of the Holy Year of 1975.

hung from the balconies of St. Peter's façade. Scaffolding units made of iron tubing were erected above and to the sides of the papal altar. These were anything but decorative, and nothing was done to improve their appearance by the addition, say, of tapestries or garlands of flowers, but this spare and sober style was much in keeping with the tast of Paul VI. The stands built to the left and right sides of the papal altar were reserved for the ecclesiastical dignitaries and lay guests of honor respectively. The general public of the faithful sat below in admirable resistance to the elements, be it the broiling sun, the cold wind or the pouring rain.

Naturally, the Holy Year has always been linked to folk traditions, which enhance its beauty. One seemed to be transported back into the Baroque age when the confraternity of Good Death, who at one time used to accompany the condemned to the gallows, suddenly made their appearance. One could not help but shudder at the sight of these figures with their blood-red robes, hoods pulled down over their faces and their standards with a grim death's head upon it. The confraternity of stevedores from Genoa carried across the square and into the church thirty 3-meter high crosses that were entirely decorated with artistic silver filigree (fig. 151). It was evident that they were sweating and that they strained greatly under the weight of their heavy burden, but they would not have renounced the chance and the honor of carrying these hefty crosses. None of these folk traditions were sponsored by a tourist board or by business associations, no one had paid these confraternities for their pains, but instead they came for the sheer joy of being present and participating in the feast.

Gypsies had also come to the Holy Year in some thousands to honor the Pope with a gypsy serenade. The Abyssinians played their drums when Giustino de Jacobis, missionary-martyr of Abyssinia, was canonized. The Eucharistic Honor Guard from Essen, Germany, appeared wilth sabers and plumes. The Knights of the Holy Sepulchre in their white choir robes emblazoned with black crosses passed by in procession.

The Holy Year is not only a religious event, it is an educational one as well. Once again, various concerts and conferences were held, one on Christian archeology, another on Mariology, an extremely interesting exhibit of documents from the Vatican Archives that pertained to all Holy Years and a traveling exhibition of old copperplate engravings as well as a concert by the orchestra of the Bavarian Radio in *S. Maria in Trastevere*. Still within the framework of the "Holy Year" there was even a football match between a German team from Speyer and a team made up of Vatican City employees. A cavalcade of French horsemen who came all the way from Avignon, and two parachutists who landed in St. Peter's square, as the Pope watched, both added to the spectacle.

As far as the number of pilgrims who came to Rome, the temptation to exagerate always is quite strong. Estimates range between 8-9 million, however it is not possible to distinguish between the pilgrims and simply tourists. To be sure, the number of tourists in that year was most likely inferior to other years in that the tourists prefered to avoid the masses of pilgrims. Also, the number of pilgrims would certainly have been even higher had there been accomodations for all of them. Some reliable figures are the 400,000 pilgrims who availed themselves of finding lodgings through the Peregrinatio through and the German Pilgrims' Office which sold 70,000 prayer books to pilgrims.

In terms of participation the Holy Year can be registered as a "success story". This is not to infer that the Holy Year will change the face of the world, but everyone who took part in it can confirm that it was truly a great religious experience and a true spiritual joy. It was indeed a Holy Year of Prayer. Even the worst detractor was impressed by the pious sincerity that guided the pilgrims as they entered the Holy Door in song and prayer. Many knelt down there or kissed the doorposts, as much as the press of pilgrims would allow them to do. True, the door guards with their black robes no longer stood watch at the entry, nor were there alms chests to be seen as there used to. Wherever one looked or listened, one heard prayer or singing. Neither the space in the church nor that in the new audience hall provided enough room for the general audiences. Therefore, they had to be held in St. Peter's Square. The Pope rode in a jeep across the square so that he could be in full view of everyone. Every Sunday at noon he appeared at the window of his study to give his blessing (see fig. 95). Every Friday the Stations of the

Cross and on Saturdays the rosary was recited in St. Peter's Square.

During the Holy Year, all of the sacraments were given by the Pope. He baptized 21 adults (mostly Asians), he officiated at the nuptials of 13 couples who came from many different countries, he ordained 345 deacons to the priesthood. It was a truly stirring sight to see the many young men lying prostrate upon the steps of St. Peter's in an expression of complete dedication to God. The Pope for his part, knelt before the new priests while praying for them. A final event was the anointing of the sick and infirm who were brought there on stretchers and in wheelchairs. New liturgical celebrations where constantly being conceived always with a profound sense of symbolic ritual. These involved many lay persons from the world over who often came in national costume. They recited passages from Scripture and prayers of intercession, and brought offerings of palms, lambs, birds, wine and bread up to the papal throne. Each one of them felt personally addressed and involved in the ceremonial proceedings, not just as simple spectators but as active participants. These pilgrims acted as representatives for all the faithful, for all those who stayed at home. Therefore it can be said that the whole earthly communion of "saints" (in the biblical sense of the word) was assembled here. It was the Pope's intention that the Holy Year should correspond to the "spiritual guidelines set down by the Second Vatican Council", and so it did. It can even be said that it was the continuation of Vatican II. Just as the entire community of bishops had sat here ten years ago for the renewal of the Church, now their places were taken by the pilgrims who in turn confirmed their adherence to the universal Church and their desire for renewal.

* * *

It would be fitting at this point to dedicate an entire chapter to *women*, since the Pope's Holy Year occured

280

152. This picture of *St. Elizabeth Ann Seton* (1774-1821) was unveiled at her canonization on the 14th of September 1975 and hung from the loggia of St. Peter's. She was the first native-born U.S. citizen to be canonized. Having founded the teaching order of the Sisters of St. Joseph and many parrochial schools led to her being called "the mother of the Catholic Church in America".

simultaneously with the International Women's Year proclaimed by the United Nations. The question being then whether the Holy Year was indeed a Holy Year of women. As we already know, women have always played an active part in the Holy Years right back to the very beginning. This has always been a particular aspect of all Jubilee Years. No sacrifice had ever been too great for women, nor hardship or danger avoided by them in making the long journey to Rome with husband and family — or even alone. They had sometimes sold their dowries and possessions in order to make the pilgrimage, as was the case of a certain Dina of Florence who came for the first Holy Year of 1300. At times they were ambushed and raped as happened to a German princess in 1450. Later they came in splendor with magnificent retinues of knights and clerics as in the case of Queen Christina of Sweden or Queen

281

Casimira of Poland. In almost every Holy Year there had been women who were later canonized, such as St. Bridget of Sweden in 1350 and St. Francesca Romana in 1423. It is true that not all women who have taken part in the Holy Years were saintly, indeed, one needs only to think upon Lucrezia Borgia in 1500 or Donna Olimpia in 1650. The Holy Year of 1975 saw a presence of women that far out-numbered that of men. Among the nineteen new saints was *Elizabeth Ann Seton* (1774-1821), the first native born woman of the United States of American to be canonized (fig. 152). She was born into an affluent New York Episcopalian family, and was an active member of that church. She married a wealthy businessman and later as they were traveling in Italy his sudden death would leave her stranded and without means of support. She was taken in by a family from Livorno which she had known through business affairs and through them she first came into contact with the Catholic faith. When she eventually returned to New York, she and her five children converted to Catholicism which in the year 1805 in the United States was a solitary and courageous act. She was disowned by her family and knew poverty. She founded the religious community of the Sisters of Charity of Saint Joseph, who taught in Catholic parochial schools, and thanks to these schools the Catholic Church in the United States prospered. For this reason Elizabeth Ann Seton has been called "the mother of the Catholic Church in America". A delegation of the Episcopal Church in America was invited to attend her canonization. The head of the delegation, Bishop John C. Allin of New York explained to the press: "Our participation in this celebration shall serve as a reminder that Elizabeth Ann Seton's formative years had their roots in the Episcopalian Church. Our participation attests to the strong bond of baptism and belief in the body of Christ which ties us together, in spite of our separation. Perhaps the Lord may help us through this new saint to better recognize this truth".[82]

282

Her canonization on the 14th September took place in conjunction with a "Holy Year Celebration of Women". It was the first time that women had been honored in this way, that their contribution to the Holy Year had been given recognition and that a link to the International Women's Year was established. During the papal mass in St. Peter's Square, four women came up to the microphone to speak in four different languages reciting prayers of intercession for women of all social levels and of all vocations. The Vatican Post also commemorated the event by issuing its own series of stamps for the International Women's Year.

* * *

Let us also go into greater detail about another very special aspect of the Holy Year of 1975, which has not been touched upon anywhere else. Although the basic nature of the Holy Years stays the same, it has always been somewhat influenced by the trends of the times. What was new this time was the *ecumenical spirit* of the Holy Year.

As we know, the reconciliation of God and man had always been the main concern of the Holy Years. They are ecumenical by their very nature, even if this inherent quality has not always made itself manifest. Originally, the pilgrim's main motivation had been the salvation of his soul by gaining the Jubilee indulgences. Later it became the demonstration of his belonging to the Roman Church. An anti-Protestant stance had influenced the Holy Years from the time of the Counter-Reformantion right up until the present century. In the eyes of non-Catholics the Holy Year was, therefore, nothing more than a declaration of triumph on the part of the Roman pontiff.

The Holy Year of 1975 was, however, to have a strong ecumenical character from its very inception. The choice of the theme "Renewal and reconciliation" in itself had an ecumenical ring, bringing immediately to mind the similar theme: "Jesus Christ liberates and unites" of the general conference of the World Council of Churches in Nairobi which was held the same year. The two major blocks of Christians met simultaneously for the same theme but in two different parts of the world which gave proof of how close they were internally, though physically separated.

The Roman Central Organizing Committee for the Holy Year established a preparatory ecumenical commission in cooperation with the Vatican Secretariat for Christian Unity, with the objective of highlighting the ecumenical nature of the Holy Year. This commission came out with a brochure entitled "Ecumenical Holy Year" published in different languages, and distributed by the pilgrims' offices. It contained an ecumenical itinerary of the holy sites of Rome, recommendations for ecumenical prayer and meditation, a list of special events and useful addresses.

Non-Catholic observers from four different churches in Rome were invited to the meeting of the ecumenical commission. Briefly, it had even been hoped that the World Council of Churches in Geneva would also collaborate. The Reverend Lukas Vischer, executive-secretary of the Commission on Faith and Order, wrote a very favorable article dealing with the question: "Why not celebrate a joint Holy Year?" He stated: "The Holy Year could immediately become an extremely significant celebration if conceived along the lines of the Judaic Jubilee Year (Lv 25). As an opportunity for renewal of the community within the Church and between Churches, as a time for scrutinizing our lives". Similarily hopeful was the article: "Reflections of the Ecumenical Commission for the Holy Year". The report issued in May 1974 in Venice by the joint commission of the World Council of Churches and the Roman Catholic Church went so far as to speak of a "convergence of points of view".[83]

Whatever the expectations might have been, the ecumenical collaboration did not work out. The opening ceremony at Christmas 1974 took place in absence of representatives from non-Catholic Churches (with the exception of some Buddhists). For a good many Protestants, the Pope's speech did not go down well, due to his repeated demand: "Come all of you! We're saving the place of honor and love next to that of our and your Lord and Master. Come all! This is an ecumenical invitation". These words reminded them of the earlier exhortation of Pius XII, who on the occasion of the Holy Year 1950 spoke to the "great return". The Waldensian Church replied in its periodical *La Luce*: "From an ecumenical point of view, the Holy Year has started out badly. Paul VI's invitation is nothing more than a modern re-working of the old "return to the fold", which many believed to have been overcome forever...!"[84]

A month later on the 25th of January, a solemn papal mass was held in St. Paul's outside the Walls on the occasion of the week of prayer for Christian unity. This was the place prefered in Rome for ecumenical functions, as it was said that Paul, the apostle of the gentiles, brings Christians together, while they still stumble over Peter, the rock. Then Paul VI reiterated the admission of guilt that he had first pronounced before the Council. On the division between Christians he affirmed: "We Catholics are most certainly blameworthy for we have certainly our share of guilt in the present-day situation of devision. Should that not weigh sorrowfully upon our conscience?"[85]

The Holy Year's agenda also included weekly ecumenical group-prayer in four languages. It has to be admitted that participation in these ecumenical gatherings was scant. On the other hand there was not one general papal audience without non-Catholic groups who were welcomed most warmly by the Pope, to the point that it was jokingly said in Rome that in order to get good seats for a papal audience you had to be a Protestant. An especial group was that of 200 students from the Lutheran St. Olaf's College in Northfield, Minnesota. Their college choir sang during the audience and during an ecumenical service. The group's leader, Prof. Ansgar E. Sovik, prepared his students by having held a seminar on the Holy Year. The resultant work: "Insights for an evangelical understanding of the Holy Year", was distributed at their religious functions.

In March there was an ecumenical meeting with the Orthodox Church in the Focolarini-Movement's headquarters near Rome. During Holy Week, young Lutherans as well as young people from the Anglican Church joined a "March of Reconciliation" from Assisi to Rome. In April the Canon Heribert Abel of of Fulda, Germany, brought a group of 30 deacons of the regional Protestant Church of Hesse to Rome. A group of 40 Presbyterians from the United States came escorted by Reverend Howard C. Blake, brother of the former secretary-general of the World Council of Churches. Next came a group of 50 deans of American Episcopalian cathedrals. They requested to worship according to their own liturgy near St. Peter's tomb and obtained for the first time permission to hold an Episcopalian service in the Vatican. This was on the 27th of April, in the church of *St. Stefano degli Abissini* next to St. Peter's.

The delegation of the Russian Orthodox Church led by the Metropolitan Nikodim of Leningrad met with representatives of the Roman Catholic Church at a theological conference in Trent and immediately afterwards came to Rome and was recived in a private audience by the Pope. They were in attendance at the solemn ordination for the priesthood which the Pope held in St. Peter's square on the 4 th of July and celebrated a Russian Orthodox service at the tomb of St. Peter in the grottoes. In July, a "Holy Year Travel Seminar" was held by the Reformed Western Theological Seminary of Holland, Michigan. In August a National Egyptian pilgrimage came to Rome and representatives of all the Christian

Churches in Egypt took part in the papal mass which was said on the 15th of August in St. Peter's square.

A most singular personality was the former Protestant minister, Reverend Richard Baumann of Tübingen, Germany. He was a true lover of Rome who searched for the city with his soul. Already known for his book *Evangelische Romfahrt* (Protestant Pilgrimage to Rome), he now wrote a little book based on his own experiences entitled: *Das Heilige Jahr evangelisch* (An evangelical Holy Year). Mother Basilea Schlink distributed through her evangelical Sisters of Mary a booklet with "Some Words on the Holy Year 1975". The book was concerned with reconciliation amongst Christians and the spirit of martyrdom, "of which the sites of the Roman martyrs speak to us Christians as they never have before".

Of the 19 beatifications and canonizations two persons were converts, the formerly mentioned Elizabeth Ann Seton, and the German-born Carlo Steeb. A third was a martyr, the Irishman Oliver Plunkett (1625-81), archbishop of Armagh and primate of Ireland, who had had to live in hiding for many long years in order to carry out his mission in the face of persecutions. He was executed in London on charges of high treason. Notwithstanding the very tense atmosphere which prevailed in Ireland at this time, his canonization on the 12th of October did not set off any adverse reaction. The bishops of Ireland had written a pastoral letter asking for the reconciliation of men of all faiths, following the example set by Oliver Plunkett who, preached incessantly for comprehension and reconciliation, though he would pay for this with his life and fall victim to religious hatred.

There was no mention of gaining indulgences. At most one spoke about indulgences as a "gift of grace". This gift can only be obtained by prayer, in the belief that all Christians participate in the "Communion of Saints", as confessed in the Apostles' Creed, and thus share in their graces and merits.

The highlight of the Holy Year, from an ecumenical standpoint, was the papal Mass on the 14th of December in the Sistine Chapel on occasion of the tenth anniversary of the lifting of the reciprocal ban which had separated the Orthodox from the Catholic Church since 1054. The metropolitan *Meliton of Chalcedon* took part in this ceremony as representative of the patriarch of Constantinople. He announced that the Orthodox Church had unanimously decided to create a pan-orthodox commission preparatory to theological dialogue. In addition, the patriarch of Constantinople had set up his own special commission to further this dialogue with the Church of Rome. On the Roman Catholic side a similar *ad hoc* commission would be created as well, the Pope declaring that the "era of brotherhood" in which we find ourselves had entered into a new phase, and went on to say that the "dialogue of love", which had recently taken place would become a "dialogue of unity". Pope Paul optimistically expounded further in his discourse in the Sistine chapel: "We see now how the blessed and long awaited day appears on the horizon in which we can seal through the common celebration of the Eucharist, our refound and complete unity...If we respect the legitimate liturgical, spiritual, disciplinary and theological differences of our Churches, may God grant us the complete, unwavering and secure unity of our Churches".[86]

Towards the end of the ceremony something quite unexpected was to happen, completely beyond papal etiquette. The Pope moved towards the metropolitan Meliton and then suddenly knelt before him and kissed his feet. The metropolitan wanted to reciprocate but was impeded from doing so. This gesture, had never been made before in the entire history of the Church and was directed to Meliton as representative of the whole Orthodox Church. The patriarch of Constantinople, Demetrios, stated in a press release: "With this public gesture our most esteemed and deeply beloved brother, the Pope of Rome, Paul VI,

288

has outdone himself. He has shown to the Church and the world what a Christian bishop is and can be, above all the first bishop of Christianity; a moving force of reconciliation and unification for the Church and the world".

At the ceremony of the closing of the Holy Door, the representatives of the non-Catholic Churches were once again missing. Among the guests of honor were only three brothers of Taizé. The prior, *Roger Schutz*, explained to the press why for the first time, he was spending Christmas in Rome rather than in his monastic community: "The Holy Year is a year of reconciliation. For this reason, I wanted to meet Paul VI with a specific intention in mind. I have come to ask the forgiveness of the universal shepherd, Paul VI, for the fact that the reconciliation between Christians is proceeding so slowly... This midnight

153. Beams of light radiating from St. Peter's dome for the closing of the Holy Year of 1975.

mass in St. Peter's square has been, thanks to the deeply sincere prayers of the people of God assembled here, an anticipation of that community that is to come".[87] On this note of hope, the Holy Year came to a close. Although the cooperation on the part of the other Churches was still limited, the ecumenical spirit which pervaded this "year of grace" had been revealed.

The closing ceremony had to be shortened for the sake of television, which had been taken into the service of this Holy Year. Due to time limitations imposed by television programing, and perhaps to save the Pope the strain of bending over the threshold for a long while, he laid neither brick nor mortar upon the ground but simply closed the door (fig. 153). As he did this, he recited the words, "Christ yesterday and today, the beginning and the end, he opens and no one can close, he closes and no one can open. To him be the power and the glory for ever and ever, Amen".

Several days later the Holy Door was sealed up by the Sampietrini on its interior side so that today Vico Consorti's modern bronze doors can be admired on the church's exterior wall under the portico.

In bringing the Holy Year of 1975 to a close, the Pope celebrated midnight Mass in St. Peter's Square despite the ice-cold wind of this winter night. The dome of St. Peter's was illuminated with a magical glow. It seemed as if the light rays emanating from it in all directions would indicate the road to Rome to the coming generation.

XIX

Two Extraordinary
Jubilee Years
1983 - 1987

Now we all believed that the Holy Door would remain closed up until the time of the next regular Holy Year, which would have meant Christmas of 1999. But things took quite an unexpected course. Among the dramatic events of 1978 we twice saw a pope's humble coffin simply set upon the stark pavement of St. Peter's Square and then twice we awaited the white smoke-signal to rise from the chimney of the Sistine Chapel. Twice have we heard the Romans shouting out: "*Habemus Papam*"; (we have a new pope!). In the second instance, the Iron Curtain that had so long estranged Poland from Rome suddenly rose. Dressed in national folk costume, some Poles stood in the front row as "their" Pope John Paul II took possession of his office, and even the president of Poland was among the guests of honor. All governments and Churches sent their highest ranking representatives. St. Peter's colonnade embraced them all: it was as if the "O ye millions, I embrace ye", from Schiller's "Ode to Joy" was being acted out, right in front of our eyes.

This significant gesture of the colonnade is emblematic of the city's spirit, which has always welcomed anyone who ever came to Rome. This was something we would relive when John Paul II proclaimed an extraordinary Holy Year for 1983-84. He would entitle it "a Jubilee Year of Redemption" as our redemption began with God becoming man and by his sacrifice on the cross, this redemption had reached its fulfillment. It was for this reason that Pius XI in 1933 had proclaimed the first extraordinary Holy Year in commemoration of the anniversary of the death of Christ. John Paul II made use of this precedent by calculating 50 years from 1933 and 1950 years from the time of Christ's death which is usually taken as having been in 33 A.D. Since the Pope has never wanted to miss a chance of reminding man of the fundamental mystery of the Christian faith, he decided upon calling this second Holy Year of Redemption. Noteworthy too, was the use of the word "redemption", rather than the modern "liberation", as "redemption" is the theological term for salvation. It has become a key word for John Paul II. Indeed, his first encyclical was called *Redemptor hominis*, after the opening words: "The redeemer, Jesus Christ, is the center of the cosmos and of all history". For the Holy Year the bull of indiction began with the words *Aperite portas Redemptori*, "open the doors to the redeemer". These words recall his inaugural speech when he strongly encouraged mankind: "Have no fear! Open the doors to Christ, open them wide to him!"

In comparison with earlier times, the emphasis was less upon penance and indulgences as it was upon redemption and reconciliation, which does not exclude penance and indulgences, but rather includes them.

While the other Holy Years had been exclusively limited to Rome, this one was instead extended to the whole Catholic world. Every diocese, the Pope decreed, was to have its own Jubilee church, when possible the bishop's cathedral, which would enjoy the same rights and privileges that Rome did. However, for those who would come to or already were in Rome then simply going to one of the major basilicas (St. Peter's, St. Paul's, the Lateran or St. Mary Major) would be sufficient. In addition, instead of visiting the major basilicas it would now also do to visit the catacombs or the church of S. Croce in Gerusalemme. The reason for the choice of the latter is clear, as it possesses the most important relics of the true Cross which

154. John Paul II opens the Holy Door of the second "Extraordinary Holy Year of Redemption" (1983) with the same hammer used by Pius XI in 1933 for the first such Holy Year.

were said to have been found by the Empress Helen in Jerusalem and brought here to Rome, (see fig. 87).

On the cold and rainy afternoon of the feast of the Annunciation, the 25th of March 1983, the Holy Year had its beginning with a penitential procession which started at *S. Stefano degli Abissini* in the Vatican and moved across St. Peter's Square into the entry hall of St. Peter's. Here, John Paul II opened the Holy Door with the same hammer that Pius XI had used earlier in 1933, thus showing the link to the first Holy Year of Redemption (fig. 154).

Quite understandably, this year got off with a slower start; there had not been enough time to make the necessary preparations. Little by little, the habitual groups of pilgrimages arrived, organised by parishes and dioceses, by various religious orders, and Catholic associations. Of these groups, the ones that most stood out were the confraternities whose members paraded through the streets dressed with hoods upon their heads and wearing long black or red robes and carrying great banners and crucifixes.

There was a surprising turnout of young people as well. The Pope also opened an International Youth Center next to St. Peter's Square. Since that time young people from all over the world have been able to learn about each other, sit down for a chat, socialize, get help or obtain information. In addition they can come for meditation and to attend holy mass, held daily in the adjacent church of *S. Lorenzo in piscibus* (the last word refers to fish, as most likely a fish market once stood on this site). This Romanesque basilica holds special appeal for young people on account of its austere simplicity.

An international youth festival was scheduled from the 11th to the 15th of April, to which approximately 200,000 young people came from over 45 different countries. They paraded in endless lines with their colorful flags and white caps and succeeded in bringing the city traffic to a standstill. The Romans are well used to such upsets, but this time it was not caused by shouting demonstrators, but

155. Palm Sunday Procession in St. Peter's Square, 1983.

instead by singing Catholic youth. Especially impressive was the blessing of the palms and the procession that followed on Palm Sunday in St. Peter's Square, with over hundred thousand young people waving palm and olive branches high in the air (fig. 155). The whole square was transformed into a sea of surging green waves. It was easy to understand the fundamental mood of the Jubilee Years, and why they had been called in the past years of joy, the joy felt over God's love, that love that had been made manifest in the gift of our redemption.

This World Youth feast was followed by another Holy Year celebration, that of sports and athletics. Instead of being held in a church this was held in the Olympic stadium, where after a papal mass, the individual athletes (some of them international champions) showed their skills to the Pope and crowd. For its emblem the International Sports Jubilee used the dove of peace to signify that sports should serve communication between peoples and thus promote peace.

156. The Pope visiting his near-assassin in prison, 1983.

During the course of the year the Pope baptized 27 catachumens (mostly Asians) and officiated at the marriage of 38 couples. He beatified 99 martyrs of the French revolution and 2 martyrs of the Chinese revolution. He raised the small young Carmelite nun and mystic Baouardy (1846-78) from Palestine to the rank of blessed. He also proclaimed the painter-friar *Fra Angelico* (1400-55) blessed (or "beato" in Italian) which finally justified the appellation he had already unofficially enjoyed for the last 500 years in Italy, i.e. "Beato Angelico" which means "blessed angel-like". The Pope named him patron of artists, especially of painters, and together with them celebrated mass over the artist's tomb in S. Maria Sopra Minerva.

The year of reconciliation could not have been better exemplified and put into action than by the Pope's visit to his would-be assassin in the Roman prison Rebibbia (fig. 156).

Many of those who watched this scene on television remembered it as the most intense moment broadcast that year; how the pontiff leaned over as if confessing his failed killer. Alì Agcà asked the Pope, "Forgive me as a human being, as a brother". The Pope answered, "I have already sincerely forgiven". Alì Agcà later divulged this to the press and finished by saying, "We really spoke to each other as brothers".[88]

Three events which had nothing to do with each other took place at the same time: the Holy Year, the 500th anniversary of the birth of Martin Luther and the Pope's visit to the Lutheran Christ's Church in Rome. That they all happened at once was purely coincidental, and yet very meaningful. Prior to the Luther year and the Roman Jubilee a representative of the administrative committee of the German Evangelical Lutheran Church in Rome had quite spontaneously invited the Pope to visit their church, and the pontiff had just as spontaneously accepted, but it was thought to make the visit when a fitting occasion presents itself. This finally came about when the Pope was making one of his pastoral visits to a Roman parish in the vicinity of the Lutheran church. When the day arrived and he had paid a visit to the Catholic parish, he arrived at the Lutheran church unexpectedly early and caused an embarassed silence. As a true *Pontifex Maximus* (chief bridge-builder) he passed by each pew shaking the hand of whoever wished to do so. The Christ Church which has stood on this spot since 1921 and counts 500 members, had never seen as many people under its shimmering gold mosaic vaulting as for this "Advent service with the Bishop of Rome" (as was written upon the invitation cards). Not only did the Christ Church live an hour of glory, but the ecumenical spirit shared in it as well. As the Pope followed the minister up onto the pulpit, he stepped pensively as if wanting to measure this weighty moment (fig. 157). It seemed that history was moving along with him and that this 500 year period was drawing to a close. Wandering thoughts drifted into the minds of those present. They wondered what Martin Luther would have said if he were present, he who had been so convinced that the papacy

157. John Paul II preaching from the pulpit of the German Lutheran Church in Rome during an Advent Service in 1983.

had been defeated by him for ever and now would see the Pope standing upon his pulpit? Who was the winner? Both! Yet the word "win" does not fit in with the language of ecumenism. Morever, the Pope greeted the Protestant congregation as his "neighbors" who are united with the Catholic Christians by the "special bond of brotherhood". He thought that during the quincentenary of Luther's birth he saw the "daybreak of the advent of rebuilding of our unity and community. This unity is also the best preparation for the advent of God in our time... let us accept the invitation of reconciliation with God and each other!"[89] In conclusion, Catholics and Lutherans prayed the Apostles' Creed in unison. It was as if the daybreak, the Pope had spoken of, had truly arrived.

When John Paul II closed the Holy Door on Easter Sunday the 22nd of April 1984, we all believed, that he and his collaborators would take a well-deserved rest. But Vatican employees, from the Swiss guards up to the Secretary of State, are used to overtime. Half sighing, half smiling they where heard to say: "Per noi con Giovanni Paolo II è sempre Anno Santo", (For us, with John Paul II, it is always Holy Year).

* * *

This candid remark: "For us ...it is always Holy Year", had scarcely left their lips when the Pope proclaimed a Marian Year for 1987-88. A Marian Year had already been celebrated in 1954, but for a completely different reason. At that time it had been proclaimed to commemorate the promulgation of the dogma of the Immaculate Conception 100 years earlier. This time, however, the reason for its celebration was the approaching turn of the century. Just as advent prepares the way for Christmas, so too should all Christians properly prepare themselves for this major change of time. To this end the Pope on the 25th of March 1987 issued a special encyclical "On the Blessed Virgin Mary in the Life of the Peregrinating Church". The encyclical took, as is customary, its title from its opening words, *Redemptoris Mater*, Mother of the Redeemer. In the encyclical the Pope, using biblical texts and documents from the latest Council, described the Madonna's path of faith, upon which she had anticipated us here on earth. For this reason he placed the Marian Year within the context of the great story of salvation. Just as Mary had come before Christ "on the horizon the story of salvation" and her assent was the premise for God's incarnation, our meditation upon Mary should preceed the Jubilee Year of Christ's nativity. "If then we compare the years that are conducting us to the conclusion of the second millenium and into the third after Christ with the historical expectation of the Savior, then it becomes fully understandable that we, in this short period of time, wish to turn towards Mary who in the night awaiting that advent began to shine like a true morning star".[90] The morning star always appears before the sun, but the sun is Christ, he is the "sun of righteousness" (Ml 1:20).

The Marian Year began on the feast of Pentecost 1987. There is a strong sense of interrelation between the two events, since Mary had a special relationship to the Holy Spirit from the time of the Annunciation onwards, as the angel had said to her: "the Holy Spirit will come upon you, and the power of the Most High will cover you with its shadow" (Lk 1:35), this rapport lasted up until the day of Pentecost in Jerusalem. Mary brings together in herself, so explained the Pope, the two decisive moments of the story of salvation: the incarnation of Christ and the descent of the Holy Spirit, that is to say the birth of Christ and the birth of the Church. According to her son's will, Mary will always be maternally present in his Church, just as she was at the foot of the cross and in the room with the apostles at Pentecost. "We hold it, therefore, necessary to stress the particular presence of the mother of Christ throughout history, and especially now during these years preceeding the year 2000".

For the vigil of Pentecost, the Pope held a religious service meditating upon the rosary in St. Mary Major in a live world broadcast which was simultaneously transmitted with prayer services in various Marian sanctuaries. After the service, the image of the *Salus Populi Romani* (see fig. 48) was taken from St. Mary Major to St. Peter's Square where it was displayed, for the duration of the nocturnal vigil being held there. The venerable Greek hymn *Akatistos* was read in honor of the Blessed Virgin Mary: "Be thou greeted, seat of the eternal God; hail, spark of lightning which illumines man; hail, clap of thunder which beats the enemy to the ground...".

At the reciting of the Gloria, twelve young people ignited their torches from the light of the paschal candle and from these, twelve braziers in their turn were lit, the number twelve referring to the apostles. The flame was then passed on to the candles of the over 50,000 faithful present and they transformed the square into a sea of light. Then, the bells of St. Peter's started to chime and the Sampietrini (the workmen of St. Peter's) began lighting the grease-filled pan torches that in an instant linked together the façade, the dome and the colonnade in a single outline of flickering light (fig. 158). It left an overwelming impression. The small golden-yellow light looked like the many tongues of fire that the Holy Spirit had set upon the disciples at Pentecost. This kind of illumination had been the fashion in the Baroque period, but normally in our age of modern technology, spot lights have taken the place of torches. No one had imagined that the old-fashioned custom would be brought to life again. The Marian Year could not have had a better beginning.

On the morning of Pentecost Sunday, the Pope led a procession of pilgrims to the much loved sanctuary of the Madonna del Divino Amore, which lies on the outskirts of Rome. This event was followed, often simultaneously, by processions and religious functions in all churches of Marian pilgrimage shrines in all parts of the world. Exhibitions of Marian art as well as concerts were held, but the Holy Door remained shut awaiting its re-opening at Christmas 1999.

158. The *Marian Year 1987* began in St. Peter's Square with a night-time Pentecost liturgy. At the Gloria, to the accompaniment of the bells of Rome, the entire church and square was suddenly illuminated by small grease-pan lights.

Just as it had been meaningful to begin the Marian year at Pentecost, so was it also of great significance to end it with the feast of the Assumption on the 15th of August 1988. For the duration of the pontifical high mass, the famous image of the Blessed Virgin Mary, normally housed in St. Mary Major, was once again transported to St. Peter's. Next to it, in the fashion of the Orthodox Church, a

302

symbolic grave of Mary was set up to include the Orthodox Rite in this celebration. The Marian Year thus came to an auspicious conclusion, since the feast of the Assumption signifies the beginning and the anticipation of that final perfection that the mother of the Redeemer has already achieved and that for us is yet to come.

XX

A Look Forward to the Jubilee Year 2000

J ust as anniversaries are celebrated in everyday life, so are they celebrated in the Church, and what better and more important occasion could there be than the anniversary of the birth of Christ and especially when the number is the great round number of 2000! Let it be remembered, however, that the feast of the jubilee is independent from any chronological reference as no precise dating is possible.

Two thousand years - this is already but a small fragment of eternity. *Roma aeterna* has been a saying for the last two thousand years. Certainly, eternity can be sensed more in Rome than anywhere else. Continuity is perceived in the historical monuments despite their decay, constancy in the face of change. Through the great number of ancient temples and Christian churches one feels man's yearning for life everlasting, while the Romans' joy of life is reflected in the fanciful cascades of their numerous fountains.

Jubilee - the word has come to mean "jubilation" or "joy", and this it is. Every Holy Year is a grace from God, but the "Great Jubilee", as the Pope has named it, shall be a special song of praise and thanksgiving for the great mercy of God that was revealed through the Incarnation of His son. This joy shall not just be inner joy, but shall be externalized as well. It will be shared with everyone, as the birth of Christ is a historical event that is visible, tactile and audible in which everyone can and should take

159. The Pope leaving the Vatican in order to become a pilgrim himself.

part. In accordance with the Pope's wishes, the Second Vatican Council shall be realized and fulfilled with the Great Jubilee. The Marian Year 1987 had been a preliminary introduction (see p. 297 ff). In 1994 an apostolic Letter, *Tertio millenio adveniente,* followed in order to prepare for the celebration of the third millenium. In this letter, John Paul II establishes the stages of preparations and decides upon a theme for each of the three years that precede the Jubilee: for 1997 it is the person of Jesus Christ, for 1998 the Holy Spirit and for 1999 God the Father. These three streams will all come together in the year 2000 in the majesty of the Trinity, "from whence all things come and whither all things lead". The Jubilee will conclude with a look towards the end of all time and towards the second coming of Christ in the kingdom of God.

The Great Jubilee will be celebrated simultaneously in Rome, in the Holy Land and in the Eastern Churches. Rome is no longer only the destination but also the starting point for new pilgrimages. The pope will be himself a pilgrim (fig. 159) and plans a common pilgrimage following the path of the Chosen People of the Old Covenant from Egypt, over Sinai, to Jerusalem and on to Damascus, the city where Paul's conversion took place.

The Pope has asserted that in the twentieth century there has been a great return of martyrs. There exists, he says, an ecumenical communion of saints and martyrs from all faiths. It is, therefore, a particular matter of concern for the pontiff to acknowledge the guilt and remorse for the injustices that have been inflicted reciprocally since the time of the schism in the Church, and to do penance for the sins commited against the unity of God's Church. The Pope does not expect the Jubilee to overcome definitvely the separation of Christians, but he feels that many feasts can be celebrated in common, and in this way all sides can take a step closer each other. Encounters with Jews and Moslems are on the agenda. Apart from the standard conferences, conventions, synods and exhibitions a major International Eucharistic Congress is also planned to be held in Rome.

As in the past, numerous commissions and sub-commissions have been formed and this time one for pilgrims coming from the former Soviet republics, who will be able to take part in a Holy Year for the first time and must helped to make their journey as easy as possible. Social equality and solidarity have always been, as can be surmised in this book, a positive collateral aspect of the Holy Years.

Another positive side-benefit is that the city itself profits from the Jubilees in its being beautified. For the year 2000 the city fathers have drawn up ambitious plans to change the look of the city, starting quite literally, from the bottom up with underground passageways and transit systems. Also being planned are new streets, bridges, hotels and tented areas to meet the space requirements for the estimated 15 million pilgrims. Rome has always been maternally welcoming and this time wishes to be even more so.

Every Rome pilgrim knows the famous prophecy attributed to Venerable Bede. This English monk is supposed to have said sometime around the year 700 when the

Colosseum was beginning to show signs of decay: "As long as the Colosseum stands, so will Rome; when Rome falls, so will the world".[91] Until now Bede has been proved right. The Colosseum is still standing after 1900 years and the city of Rome with its over three million inhabitants is more than three times the size it was in antiquity. We want here to paraphrase the famous prophecy by saying: "Rome will stand as long as there are pilgrims. Pilgrims will come, so long as the world lasts". The history of the Holy Years has shown that pilgrimages are part of man's nature and of his sense of life.

With this in mind, the words of Paul VI from his encyclical *Gaudete in Domino* on occasion of the Holy Year 1975 are also pertinent to this upcoming Great Jubilee, and provide a fitting conclusion to this book:

> "We have invited you to make in actual deed or at least in spirit a pilgrimage to Rome, to the heart of the Catholic Church. Yet, it only too clear that Rome does not signify the goal of our pilgrimage here on earth. No wordly city, no matter how holy, can represent this goal. This is to be found beyond world, hidden from view in God's great mystery, it is invisible to us as we still wander in faith, not yet with clear vision, and that which we shall become has not yet been revealed. The New Jerusalem is that which will descend from God on high. We are, however, already its citizens, or at least are invited to become such. Every pilgrimage has in this its final destination".[92]

CHRONOLOGICAL TABLE

64	Most likely the year of death of the apostles Peter and Paul.
before 200	Bishop Aberkios, first pilgrim to Rome known by name.
258	First celebration of the feast of Peter and Paul.
313	Edict of Milan grants religious freedom. Immediately afterwards the first Christian basilicas were built in Rome.
about 600	First guide-books for pilgrims.
about 700	First pilgrimages of Irish and Anglosaxon penitents.
719	St. Boniface in Rome for the first time. Beginning of the bishops visits to Rome
774	Charlemagne comes to Rome for the first time. Beginning of the Emperors' march to Rome. Founding of the pilgrim-house for the Franks, now called Collegio Teutonico in Campo Santo.
after 1000	Petitioners come to the Roman Curia.
after 1100	The indulgences make up their appearance.
1300	Boniface VIII proclaims the first Year of Jubilee. Dante most likely in Rome.
1350	Second Jubilee. No Pope in Rome, but Petrarca and Bridget of Sweden.
1390	III Jubilee under Boniface IX. Visits to the four main basilicas are prescribed.
1400	IV Holy Year under Boniface IX. The term "Holy Year" comes up. "The passage of the White" reaches Rome.
1423	V Holy Year under Martin V.
1450	VI Holy Year under Nicholas V. Canonisations come in use during the Holy Years.
1475	VII Holy Year under Sisto IV. The Sistine Chapel, the Hospital of the Holy Spirit and the Sistine Bridge are being built.

1500	VIII Holy Year under Alexander VI.
	For the first time four Holy Doors are solemnly opened and closed.
1525	IX Holy Year under Clement VII.
1548	Filippo Neri founds the Confraternity and the Hospital of the Most Holy Trinity for the Pilgrims and Convalesces.
1550	X Holy Year under Julius III.
	Ignatius of Loyola and Filippo Neri take an active part.
1575	XI Holy Year under Gregory XIII.
	Highlight of the Jubilee Years.
	Cardinal Charles Borromeo sets a good example.
	The pilgrimages are organized by the confraternities.
	Visits to the seven churches become customary.
1600	XII Holy Year under Clemens VIII.
	Robert Bellarmin and Cardinal Baronius take part.
1625	XIII Holy Year under Urban VIII.
	He consacrates the new St. Peter's Church in 1626.
1650	XIV Holy Year under Innocent X.
	He rebuilds St. John the Lateran Church.
1675	XV Holy Year under Clemens X.
	Queen Christine of Sweden in Rome.
1700	XVI Holy Year under Innocent XII and Clement XI.
	Queen Casimira of Poland in Rome.
1725	XVII Holy Year under Benedict XIII.
1750	XVIII Holy Year under Benedict XIV.
	Fra Leonardo preaches the Via Crucis.
	The Colosseum is dedicated to the Passion of Christ and of the martyrs.
1775	XIX Holy Year under Pius VI.
1800	No Pope, no Jubilee Year.
1825	XX Holy Year under Leo XII.
1850	No Holy Year.
1875	XXI Holy Year under Pius IX, proclaimed but not celebrated.
1900	XXII Holy Year under Leo XIII.
1925	XXIII Holy Year under Pius XI.

1933	Extraordinary Holy Year under Pius XI to commemorate the year of death of Christ.
1950	XXIV Holy Year under Pius XII. New Holy Door in St. Peter's. Proclamation of the dogma of the Bodily Assumption of Mary into Heaven.
1975	XXV Holy Year under Paul VI.
1983-84	Extraordinary Holy Year of Redemption under John Paul II.
1987-88	Marian Year.
1999-2000	XXVI, the "Great Jubilee of the Year 2000".

BIBLIOGRAPHY

I. BIBLIOGRAFICAL NOTES

[1] HIERONYMUS, *Epistole*, 108, 14, in *PL* XX, 878 f.

[2] Cfr. *Pilgerreise der Etheria*, in H. DONNER, *Pilgerfahrt ins Heilige Land*, Stuttgart 1979, 69-137.

[3] EUSEBIO, *Storia ecclesiastica*, Milan 1979, XXV, 7.

[4] AMBROGIO, *Hymnus LXXI*, in *PL* XVII, 1253.

[5] B. KÖTTING, *Peregrinatio religiosa. Wallfahrt in der Antike und das Pilgerwesen in der alten Kirche*, Paderborn 1950, 236.

[6] *Guida ai Musei Vaticani*, Vatican City 1989, 133-134.

[7] IRENEO, *Adversus haereses*, III, 12, 5, in *PG* VII, 1142.

[8] B. KÖTTING, *cit.*, 225.

[9] MAXIMUS of Turin, *Homilia LXII*, in *PL* LVII, 405.

[10] H. JEDIN, *Die deutsche Romfahrt von Bonifatius bis Winckelmann*, Krefeld 1961, 9 f.

[11] TACITUS, *Annales*, XV, 44, 6-9.

[12] *Vita Hadriani*, in *Liber Pontificalis* I, 496-497.

[13] *Vita Leonis*, in *Liber Pontificalis* II, 7.

[14] N. PAULUS, *Geschichte des Ablasses im Mittelalter*, Paderborn 1922, I, 200.

[15] *Ibid.* II, 101.

[16] J. STEFANESCHI, *De centesimo seu Jubileo anno liber*, ed D. QUATTROCCHI, *L'Anno Santo del 1300*, Rome 1900, 300 ff.

[17] G. VENTURA, *Memoriale de gestis civium astensium*, cap. XXVI, in L. MURATORI, *Rerum italicarum scriptores*, Milan 1727, XI, 191.

[18] Cyprian of Carthage, *De unitate ecclesiae*, in *CSEL*, 3/1, 214.

[19] *Bullarum anni sancti*, ed. Hermann Schmidt, Rome 1949, 33-34.

[20] *Ibid.*

[21] A. MERCATI, *Una lettera dello scrittore pontificio Silvestro sul Giubileo del 1300*, Rome 1928, 7.

[22] J. STEFANESCHI, *cit.*, 302.

[23] G. VILLANI, *Cronica VIII*, XXXVI, Florence 1823, 51.

[24] G. MONACO, in A. FRUGONI, *Il Giubileo di Bonifacio VIII*, Rome 1950, 17.

[25] G. VENTURA, *cit.*, 31.

[26] G. VILLANI, *cit.*, 52.

[27] *Ibid.*, 52.

[28] *Ibid.*, 52.

[29] BUCCIO DI RANALLO, in P. BREZZI, *Storia degli Anni Santi*, Milan 1975, 45.

[30] *Acta et processus canonizationis beate Brigitte*, Uppsala 1924, 31.

[31] In G. JOERGENSEN, S. *Brigida di Svezia*, Brescia 1991, 286 and 289.

[32] F. PETRARCA, *Liber Epist. III*, Opera Omnia tom. III, Basilea 1554, 1372.

[33] F. PETRARCA, *Le Familiari*, IX, 13, Urbino 1974, 1024-26.

[34] S. R. WARLAND, *Das Brustbild Christi*, Freiburg 1986.

[35] F. MELIS, *Movimento di popoli e motivi economici nel giubileo del 1400*, in *Italia Sacra*, Padova 1970, 262 and 352.

[36] G. SERCAMBI, *Le Croniche*, Roma 1892, I, 371.

[37] ARCHIVIO SEGRETO VATICANO, *Mostra documentaria degli anni santi*, Vatican City 1975, 20.

[38] G. SERCAMBI, *cit.*, 405.

[39] Archivio Segreto Vaticano, *cit.*, 21-22.

[40] *Cronache romane*, in L. PASTOR, *Geschichte der Päpste*, Freiburg 1926, I, 457-459.

[41] N. PAULUS, *Geschichte des Ablasses am Ausgang des Mittelalters*, Paderborn 1923, 50.

[42] H. THURSTON, *The Holy Year of Jubilee*, London 1900, 257 f.

[43] F. MELIS, *cit.*, 343-367.

[44] NICOLA DELLA TUCCIA, *Cronaca di Viterbo*, ed. I. Campi, Florence 1872, 52.

[45] *Ibid.*, 177.

[46] G. RUCELLAI, *Lo Zibaldone*, ed. A. Perosa, London 1960, 67-78.

[47] N. MUFFEL, *Beschreibung der Stadt Rom*, ed. W. Vogt, Tübingen 1876, 19-20.

[48] N. PAULUS, *Zur Geschichte des Jubiläums vom Jahre 1500*, in *Zeitschrift für katholische Theologie*, XXIV, Innsbruck 1900, 175.

[49] JOHANNES BURCKARDI, *Liber Notarum*, ed. E. Celani, Città di Castello 1906, II, 179.

[50] *Ibid.*, 180.

[51] *Ibid.*, 190-191.

[52] N. PAULUS, *cit.*, 176-177.

[53] G. BERNI, *Le medaglie degli anni santi*, Barcelona 1950, 22.

[54] I. BURCKARD, *cit.*, II, 195.

[55] S. G. VASARI, *La Vita di Michelangelo*, Milan 1962, I, 89.

[56] M. LUTHER, *WA Tischreden*, II, 2488 a and b.

[57] H. THURSTON, *cit.*, 82.

[58] PONTIFICIO COLLEGIO ETIOPICO, *Giubileo d'oro*, Vatican City 1969, 14.

[59] More in my chapter, *Il Collegio Teutonico e il Collegio Etiopico*. in *Il Vaticano e Roma cristiana*, Vatican City 1976, 161 ff.

[60] J. BURCKARD, *cit.*, II, 190.

[61] D. MANNI, *Storia degli Anni Santi*, Florence 1750, 107.

[62] *Kunst und Kunsthandwerk, Meisterwerke im Bayerischen Nationalmuseum,* Munich 1955, 62.
[63] More in my study, *La Porta Santa,* in *Studi Romani,* Oct. 1975 and in M. GIUSTI, *Anno Santo e Porta Santa. Uno sguardo panoramico,* in *Divinitas,* XX (1976).
[64] S. PEDRO DE LETURIA, S. *Ignazio di Loyola e l'Anno Santo 1550,* in *Civiltà Cattolica,* Rome, December 1950.
[65] H. THURSTON, *cit.,* 261.
[66] L. PASTOR, *cit.,* IX, 144.
[67] G. MARTIN, *Roma Sacra,* ed. G. B. Parks, Rome, 1969.
[68] L. PASTOR, *cit.,* XIII, 591-2.
[69] Words of an eyewitness, Gaspar Schopp of Breslau, in *Sommario del processo di Giordano Bruno,* in *Doc. Rom,* XXX (1940).
[70] F. SCHILLER, *Horen- und Musenalmanach,* 1795-1799.
[71] C. GUALDI, *Vita di Donna Olimpia Maidalchini, che governò la Chiesa durante il pontificato d'Innocenzo X,* Ragusa 1667, pp. 247-249.
[72] A. BASSANI, *Viaggio a Roma della S. R. M. di Maria Casimira,* Rome 1700.
[73] L. GROTTANELLI, *Violante Beatrice di Baviera, Gran Principessa di Toscana,* Florence 1887, 37.
[74] L. MURATORI, *Annali d'Italia,* Milan, 1744-1749, XI, 327.
[75] *Narrazione dell'insigne miracolo operato da Dio per l'intercessione del glorioso S. Pietro,* Rome 1725, s.n.
[76] B. PICCARD, *Cérémonies et Coutumes Religieuses de tous les peuples du monde ... avec une Explication Historique & quelques Dissertations curieuses,* Amsterdam 1723, I, 173.
[77] G. G. BELLI, *L'Anno Santo,* in *Sonetti Romaneschi,* ed. P. Viga e G. Vergara Caffarelli, Rome 1944, I, 186.
[78] G. PASCOLI, in *L. Pietroboni, Commento a "La Porta",* in *Ecclesia,* 9, Rome 1950, 646-647.
[79] *Cronistoria dell'Anno Santo 1925,* Rome 1928, 3.
[80] Bolla *Quod nuper,* January 15, 1933, in *AAS* XXV, 1.
[81] *Bulletin des Heiligen Jahres 1975,* hg. vom Zentralkomitee, Nr. 1, 11-13.
[82] *National Catholic News Service,* Rome, September 14, 1975.
[83] The Secretariat for Promoting Christian Unity, *Information Service,* Vatican City, Nr. 24, 1974, II.
[84] *La Luce,* Casa Valdese, Torre Pellice 1975, 1.
[85] *L'Osservatore Romano,* January 27-28, 1975.
[86] *L'Osservatore Romano,* December 15-16, 1975.
[87] *La Documentation Catholique,* Paris 1976, Nr. 3.
[88] *Oggi,* Milan, January 9, 1984.
[89] *L'Osservatore Romano,* Dicember 16, 1983.
[90] Encyclica *Redemptoris Mater,* March 25, 1987, in *AAS* LXXIX, 4.

[91] Beda Venerabilis, in *PL*, XCIV, 543.

[92] Apostolic Letter, *Gaudete in Domino*, May 9, 1975, *AAS* LXVII, 5.

II. GENERAL MODERN BIBLIOGRAPHY

H. Thurston, *The Holy Year of Jubilee*, London 1890.

A. Frugoni: *Il Giubileo di Bonifacio VIII*, in: Archivio Muratoriano, 2, 1950.

P. Bargellini: *L'Anno Santo nella storia, nella letteratura e nell'arte*, Florence 1974.

P. Brezzi: *Storia degli Anni Santi*, Milan 1975.

P. Brezzi: *Roma e l'Anno Santo. Riflessioni degli Anni Santi sulla vita economica e sociale della città di Roma*, Rome 1975.

E. M. Jung-Inglessis: *Das Heilige Jahr in der Geschichte*, Bozen 1975

R. Morghen: *Bonifacio VIII e il Giubileo del 1300 nella storiografia moderna*, Rome 1975.

A. Stickler: *Il Giubileo di Bonifacio VIII Aspetti giuridico-pastorali*, Rome 1975.

N. Ohler: *Pilgerleben im Mittelalter zwischen Andacht und Abenteuer*, Freiburg 1994.

Il Giubileo, Storia e pratiche dell'anno santo, di G. Bof, P. Cannata, P. Golinelli, R. Stoppani, Florence 1995.

Tertio Millennio adveniente. Text and commentary by the Council of the Great Jubilee of the year 2000. Cinisiello Balsamo (Milan) 1996.

III. EXHIBITION CATALOGUES

In the Vatican Archives:

Mostra documentaria degli Anni Santi, Vatican City, 1975.

In Palazzo Braschi in Rome:

Immagini di Giubilei nei secoli XV-XVIII. Mostra iconografico-documentaria, Rome 1975.

In Palazzo Venezia in Rome:

L'Arte degli Anni Santi. Roma 1300-1875, ed. M. Fagiolo e M. Madonna, Milan 1984.

Roma, la città degli Anni Santi 1300-1875. Atlante, ed. M. Fagiolo M. Madonna, Milan 1985.

In the Bayerisches Nationalmuseum, Munich:

Wallfahrt kennt keine Grenzen, Munich 1984.

INDEX OF PLACES

INDEX OF NAMES

319

Ferrari Ettore: 176
Ferri Ciro: 263
Filarete: 186
Filippo Neri: 149ff, 168
Fontana Carlo: 215f.
Fontana Domenico: 181, 183
Fra Angelico: 106f, 223, 296
Francesca Romana: 103
Frederick III: 22
Fuga Ferdinando: 232f.

Gaius Presbyter: 10
Galla Placidia: 76
Gallilei Alessandro: 210f.
Gaspare del Bufalo: 243
Gioachino da Fiore: 30
Giordano Bruno: 175ff.
Giotto: 23, 34, 41f, 185
Giovanni Eudes: 254
Giovanni Monaco: 39
Goethe: 236
Goretti Maria: 262f.
Gregory V: 200
Gregory XI: 98
Gregory XIII: 157ff.
Gregorini Domenico: 232f.
Gualdi Cesare: 204

Hadrian VI: 138
Holstenius Lukas: 214, 216
Honorius III: 78f.
Hosius Stanislaus: 156
Humbert of Romans: 29

Ine of Wessex: 15f.
Innocent III: 23, 33
Innocent X: 203ff, 212
Ippolito d'Este: 133
Irenaeus of Lyon: 12
Isabella d'Este: 142

James Apostle: 24, 52
Janssen Arnold: 275
Jerome St.: 9
John XXIII: 200

John Paul I: 200
John Paul II: 291ff, 299
Julius II: 158
Julius III: 145f.

Kaas Ludwig: 260

Lafréry: 83, 169
Ledòchowska M. Th.: 276
Leo III: 19
Leo X: 142, 183
Leo XII: 241
Leo XIII: 249ff.
Leonardo da Porto Maurizio: 227f.
Liberius: 90
Louis of Hungary: 55
Luther Martin: 131, 141, 171, 176, 183, 210f, 297ff.

Macchiavelli: 142
Maderno Carlo: 180f, 186
Maderno Stefano: 54
Maggi Giovanni: 72, 91, 166, 174f, 178
Mameli Goffredo: 152
Marchionni Carlo: 223
Maria Clementina Stuart: 120, 220f.
Maria Cristina of Savoy: 243
Martin V: 102ff.
Martin Gregory: 160, 237
Masini Girolamo: 46
Matilda of Canossa: 120
Maximilian I: 22
Maximus of Turin: 12
Meli Giuseppe: 103
Meliton Metropolit: 287f.
Melozzo da Forlì: 113
Meyer Conrad F.: 143, 183
Michelangelo: 114ff, 133ff, 143, 180, 194f, 223
Mochi Francesco: 70
Muffel Nikolaus: 124

A brick from
the Holy Door

VATICAN PRESS